RELIGIOUS SECTS OF THE HINDUS

RELIGIOUS SECTS OF THE HINDUS

BY

H. H. WILSON

Edited by Ernst R. Rost

GYAN

Published by

GYAN

Gyan Publishing House
5, Ansari Road
Daryaganj, New Delhi-110002
Phone: 011-47034999, 9811692060
E-mail: books@gyanbooks.com

Distribution Network
gyanbooks.com
India, USA, Canada, UK, Australia, France

ISBN : 978-81-212-2498-7 (HB)
First Published, 1958

2nd Impression 2021

Printed at: Gyan Press, Delhi.

Religious Sects of the Hindus
Author: H. H. Wilson

RELIGIOUS SECTS OF THE HINDUS

By

H. H. WILSON

Edited by Ernst R. Rost

SUSIL GUPTA (INDIA) PRIVATE LIMITED
CALCUTTA 12
1958

INDEX.

Part I.

Part II.

A SKETCH

OF THE

RELIGIOUS SECTS OF THE HINDUS.

Introductory Observations.

The Hindu religion is a term, that has been hitherto employed in a collective sense, to designate a faith and worship of an almost endlessly diversified description: to trace some of its varieties is the object of the present enquiry.

An early division of the Hindu system, and one conformable to the genius of all Polytheism, separated the practical and popular belief, from the speculative or philosophical doctrines. Whilst the common people addressed their hopes and fears to stocks and stones, and multiplied by their credulity and superstition the grotesque objects of their veneration, some few, of deeper thought and wider contemplation, plunged into the mysteries of man and nature, and endeavoured assiduously, if not successfully, to obtain just notions of the cause, the character and consequence of existence. This distinction prevails even in the *Védas*, which have their *Karma Kánda* and *Jnyána Kánda*, or Ritual and Theology.

The worship of the populace being addressed to different divinities, the followers of the several gods, naturally separated into different associations, and the adorers of Brahma', Vishnu, and Siva, or other phantoms of their faith, became distinct and insulated bodies, in the general aggregate: the conflict of opinion on subjects, on which human reason has never yet agreed, led to similar differences in the philosophical class, and resolved itself into the several *Dersanas*, or schools of philosophy.

It may be supposed, that some time elapsed before the practical worship of any deity was more than a simple preference, or involved the assertion of the supremacy of the object of its adoration, to the degradation or exclusion of the other gods :* in like manner also, the conflicting opinions were matters rather of curiosity than faith, and were neither regarded as subversive of each other, nor as incompatible with the public worship: and hence, notwithstanding the sources of difference that existed in the parts, the unity of the whole remained undisturbed : in this condition, indeed, the apparent mass of the Brahmanical order at least, still continues : professing alike to recognise implicitly the authority of the *Védas,* the worshippers of Siva, or of Vishnu, and the maintainers of the *Sánk'hya* or *Nyáya* doctrines, consider themselves, and even each other, as orthodox members of the Hindu community.

To the internal incongruities of the system, which did not affect its integral existence, others were, in time, superadded, that threatened to dissolve or destroy the whole : of this nature was the exclusive adoration of the old deities, or of new forms of them ; and even it may be presumed, the introduction of new divinities. In all these respects, the *Puránas* and *Tantras* were especially instrumental, and they not only taught their followers to assert the unapproachable superiority of the gods they worshipped, but inspired them with feelings† of animosity towards those

* One division of some antiquity, is the preferential appropriation of the four chief divinities to the four original castes; thus Siva is the *Adideva* of the *Brahmans,* Vishnu of the *Kshettriyas,* Brahma' of the *Vaisyas,* and Ganesa of the *Súdras.*

विप्राणांदैवतंशम्भुः क्षत्रियानां तु माधवः ।
वैश्यानांतु भवेद्ब्रह्मा शूद्राणां गणनायकः । । इति मनु ॥

† Thus in the Bhágavat :

भवव्रतधरायेच येच तान्समनुव्रताः ।
पाषण्डिनस्ते भवन्तु सच्छास्त्रपरिपन्थिनः ॥

Those who profess the worship of Bhava, (Siva,) and those who follow their doctrines, are heretics and enemies of the sacred *Sástras.*—Again,

मुमुक्षवो घोररूपान् हित्वा भूतपतीनथ ।
नारायणकलाः शान्ताभजन्तिह्यनसूयवः ।

who presumed to dispute that supremacy: in this conflict the worship of BRAHMA' has disappeared,* as well as, indeed, that of the whole pantheon, except VISHNU, SIVA, and SAKTI, or their modifications; with respect to the two former, in fact, the representatives have borne away the palm from the prototypes, and KRISHNA, RA'MA, or the *Linga*, are almost the only forms under which VISHNU and SIVA are now adored in most parts of India.†

Those desirous of final emancipation, abandoning the hideous gods of the devils, pursue their devotions, calm, blameless, and being parts of NA'RA'YANA. The *Padma Purána* is more personal towards VISHNU.

विष्णुदर्शनमात्रेण शिवद्रोहः प्रजायते ॥
शिवद्रोहान्नसन्देहो नरकं याति दारुणं ।
तस्मान्नविष्णुनामापि नवक्तव्यं कदाचन ॥

From even looking at VISHNU, the wrath of SIVA is kindled, and from his wrath, we fall assuredly into a horrible hell; let not, therefore, the name of VISHNU ever be pronounced. The same work is, however, cited by the VAISHNAVAS, for a very opposite doctrine.

वासुदेवं परित्यज्य योऽन्यदेवमुपासते ।
तृषितो जाह्नवीतीरेकूपं खनति दुर्मतिः ॥

He who abandons VA'SUDEVA and worships any other god, is like the fool, who being thirsty, sinks a well in the bank of the Ganges—The principle goes still further, and those who are inimical to the followers of a deity, are stigmatised as his personal foes—thus in the *Adi Purána*, VISHNU says:

मद्भक्तो वल्लभो यस्य स एव मम वल्लभः ।
तत्परो वल्लभो नास्ति सत्यं सत्यं धनञ्जय ॥

He to whom my votary is a friend, is my friend—he who is opposed to him, is no friend of mine—be assured, *Dhananjaya*, of this:

* SIVA himself, in the form of KA'LA BHAIRAVA, tore off BRAHMA''s fifth head, for presuming to say, that he was BRAHME, the eternal and omnipotent cause of the world, and even the creator of SIVA, notwithstanding the four VEDAS and the personified *Omkára*, had all given evidence, that this great, true and indescribable deity was SIVA himself. The whole story occurs in the *Kási K'hand* of the *Skánda Purána*, and its real signification is sufficiently obvious.

† The great text-book of the *Vaishnavas* is the *Bhágavat*, with which it may be supposed the present worship, in a great measure, originated, although, the Mahábhárat and other older works had previously introduced this divinity. The worship of the *Lingam* is, no doubt, very ancient, although it has received, within a few centuries, its present degree of popularity: the *Kási K'hand* was evidently written to enforce it, and at Benares, its worship entirely overshadows every other ritual.

The varieties of opinion kept pace with those of practice, and six heretical schools of philosophy disputed the pre-eminence with their orthodox brethren: we have little or no knowledge of these systems, and even their names are not satisfactorily stated: they seem, however, to be the *Saugata* or *Bauddha*, *Arhata*, or *Jain*, and *Várhaspatya*, or Atheistical, with their several sub-divisions.*

Had the difference of doctrine taught in the heretical schools been confined to tenets of a merely speculative nature, they would, probably, have encountered little opposition, and excited little enmity among the Brahmanical class, of which, latitude of opinion is a very commen characteristic. The founder of the Atheistical school, however, VRIHASPATI, attacks both the *Védas* and the *Brahmans*, and asserts that the whole of the Hindu system is a contrivance of the Priesthood, to secure a means of livelihood for themselves,† whilst the *Bauddhas* and *Jainas*, equally disregarding the *Védas* and the *Brahmans*, the practice and opinions of the Hindus, invented a set of gods for themselves, and deposed the ancient pantheon: these aggressions provoked resentment: the writings of these sects are alluded to with every epithet of anger and contempt, and they are all anathematised as heretical and atheistical: more active measures than anathemas, it may be presumed, were had recourse to: the followers of VRIHASPATI, having no worship at all, easily eluded the storm, but the *Bauddhas* of Hindustan were annihilated by its fury, and the *Jainas* apparently evaded it with difficulty, although they have undoubtedly survived its terrors, and may now defy its force.

* In a work written by the celebrated *Mádhava*, describing the different sects as they existed in his day, entitled the *Sarva Darsana;* the *Várhaspatyas*, *Lokáyatas*, and *Chárvákas* are identified, and are really advocates of an atheistical doctrine, denying the existence of a god, or a future state, and referring creation to the aggregation of but four elements. The *Bauddhas*, according to the same authority, admit of four sub-divisions, the *Madhyámikas*, *Yogáchdras*, *Sautrdntikas*, and *Vaibháshicas*. The Jains or Arhats, as still one of the popular divisions, we shall have occasion to notice in the text.

† Vrihaspati has the following texts to this effect:

अग्निहोत्रं त्रयोवेदा त्रिदण्डंभस्मगुंठनं ।
वुद्धिपौरुषहीनानाञ्जीविकेतिवृहस्पति ॥

The varieties thus arising from innovations in practice and belief, have differed, it may be concluded, at different eras of the Hindu worship. To trace the character of those which have latterly disappeared, or to investigate the remote history of some which still remain and are apparently of ancient date, are tasks for which we are far from being yet prepared: the enquiry is in itself so vast, and so little progress has been made in the studies necessary to its elucidation, that it must yet remain in the obscurity in which it has hitherto been enveloped; so ambitious a project as that of piercing the impenetrable gloom has not instigated the present attempt, nor has it been proposed to undertake so arduous a labour, as the investigation and comparison of the abstruse notions of the philosophical sects.* The humbler aim of these researches has been that of ascertaining the actual condition of the popular religion of the inhabitants of some of the provinces subject to the Bengal Government; and as a very great variety prevails in that religion, the subject may be considered as not devoid of curiosity and interest, especially as it has been left little better than a blank, in the voluminous compositions or compilations, professing to give an account of the native country of the Hindus.

The description of the different sects of the Hindus, which I propose to offer, is necessarily superficial: it would, indeed, have been impossible to have adopted the only unexceptionable method of acquiring an accurate

"The Agnihotra, the three Vedas, the Tridanda, the smearing of ashes, are only the livelihood of those who have neither intellect nor spirit." After ridiculing the Sráddha, shrewdly enough, he says:

ततस्वजीवनोपायोब्राह्मणैर्विहितस्त्विह ।
मृतानांप्रेतकार्य्याणि नत्वन्यद्विद्यतेकचित् ॥

Hence it is evident, that it was a mere contrivance of the Brahmans to gain a livelihood, to ordain such ceremonies for the dead, and no other reason can be given for them. Of the *Vedas*, he says:

त्रयो वेदस्य कर्तारो भण्डधूर्त्तनिशाचराः ॥

The three Authors of the *Vedas* were Buffoons, Rogues, and Fiends—and cites texts in proof of this assertion.

* Something of this has been very well done by *Mr. Ward*, in his account of the Hindus: and since this Essay was read before the Society, the account given by H. T. Colebrooke, Esq. in the first part of the Transactions of the Royal Asiatic Society, of the Sánkhya and Nyáya Systems, has left little more necessary on this subject.

knowledge of their tenets and observances, or of studying the numerous works in Sanscrit, Persian, or the provincial dialects of Hindi, on which they are founded. I have been obliged to content myself, therefore, with a cursory inspection of a few of those compositions, and to depend for much of my information on oral report, filling up or correcting from these two sources, the errors and omissions of two works, on this subject professedly, from which I have derived the groundwork of the whole account.

The works alluded to are in the Persian language, though both were written by Hindu authors: the first was compiled by SI'TAL SINH, Munshi to the *Raja* of Benares; the second by MATHURA' NA'TH, late librarian of the Hindu College, at the same city, a man of great personal respectability and eminent acquirements: these works contain a short history of the origin of the various sects, and descriptions of the appearance, and observances, and present condition of their followers: they comprise all the known varieties, with one or two exceptions, and, indeed, at no one place in India could the enquiry be so well prosecuted as at Benares.* The work of MATHURA' NA'TH is the fullest and most satisfactory, though it leaves much to be desired, and much more than I have been able to supply. In addition to these sources of information, I have had frequent recourse to a work of great popularity and extensive circulation, which embodies the legendary history of all the most celebrated *Bhaktas* or devotees of the Vaishnava order. This work is entitled the *Bhakta Málá*. The original, in a difficult dialect of Hindi, was composed by NA'BHA'JI, about 250 years ago, and is little more than a catalogue, with brief and obscure references to some leading circumstances connected with the life of each individual, and from the inexplicit nature of its allusions, as well as the difficulty of its style, is far from intelligible to the generality even of the natives. The work, in its present form, has received some modifi-

* The acknowledged resort of all the vagabonds of India, and all who have no where else to repair to: so, the *Kási K'hand*,

श्रुतिस्मृतिविहीनानां येशौचाचारविवर्जिताः ।
येषाम् क्वापिगतिर्नास्ति तेषांवाराणसीगतिः ॥

"To those who are strangers to the *Sruti* and *Smriti*, (Religion and Law); to those who have never known the observance of pure and indispensable rites; to those who have no other place to repair to; to those, is Benares an asylum."

cations, and obvious additions from a later teacher, NA'RA'YAN DA's. whose share in the composition is, no doubt, considerable, but cannot be discriminated from NA'BHA'JI's own, beyond the evidence furnished by the specification of persons unquestionably subsequent to his time.—NA'RA'YAN DA's probably wrote in the reign of SHA'H JEHA'N. The brevity and obscurity of the original work pervade the additional matter, and to remedy these defects, the original text, or *Múla*, has been taken as a guide for an amplified notice of its subjects, or the *Tíká* of KRISHNA DA's; and the work, as usually met with, always consists of these two divisions. The *Tíká* is dated *Samvat*, 1769 or A. D. 1713. Besides these, a translation of the *Tíká*, or a version of it in the more ordinary dialect of Hindustan, has been made by an anonymous author, and a copy of this work, as well as of the original, has furnished me with materials for the following account. The character of the *Bhakta Málá*, will best appear from the extracts of translations from it to be hereafter introduced: it may be sufficient here to observe, that it is much less of a historical than legendary description, and that the legends are generally insipid and extravagant: such as it is, however, it exercises a powerful influence in Upper India, on popular belief, and holds a similar place in the superstitions of this country, as that which was occupied in the darkest ages of the Roman Catholic faith, by the Golden Legend and Acts of the Saints.*

* In further illustration of our text, with regard to the instrumentality of the *Puránas* in generating religious distinctions amongst the Hindus, and as affording a view of the *Vaishnava* feelings on this subject, we may appeal to the *Padma Purána*. In the *Uttara Khanda*, or last portion of this work, towards the end of it, several sections are occupied with a dialogue between SIVA and PA'RVATI', in which the former teaches the latter the leading principles of the *Vaishnava* faith. Two short sections are devoted to the explanation of who are heretics, and which are the heretical works. All are *Páshandas*, SIVA says, who adore other gods than VISHNU, or who hold, that other deities are his equals, and all Brahmans who are not *Vaishnavas*, are not to be looked at, touched, nor spoken to:—

ये अन्यं देवं परत्वेन वदन्त्यज्ञानमोहिताः ।
नारायणाज्जगन्नाथात्तेवै पाषण्डिनःस्मृताः ॥
यस्तु नारायणं देवं ब्रह्मरुद्रादि देवतैः ।
सममन्यै र्निरीक्षेत सपाषण्डी भवेत्सदा ॥

SECTION II.

State of the Hindu Religion, anterior to its present condition.

Although I have neither the purpose nor the power to enter into any detail of the remote condition of the Hindu faith, yet as its present state is of comparatively very recent origin, it may form a not unnecessary, nor uninteresting preliminary branch of the enquiry, to endeavour to determine its existing modifications, at the period immediately preceding the few centuries, which have sufficed to bestow upon it its actual form: it happens, also, that some controversial works exist, which throw considerable light upon the subject, and of which the proximity of their date, to the matters of which they treat, may be conjectured with probability or positively ascertained. Of these, the two principal works, and from which I shall derive such scanty information as is

किमत्रबहुनोक्तेन ब्राह्मणा येप्यवैष्णवाः ।
न स्पृष्टव्या न वक्तव्या न द्रष्टव्या कदाचन ॥

SIVA, in acknowledging that the distinguishing marks of his votaries, the skull, tiger's skin, and ashes, are reprobated by the Vedas (Srutigerhitam) states, that he was directed by VISHNU to inculcate their adoption, purposely to lead those who assumed them into error.—NAMUCHI and other *Daityas* had become so powerful by the purity of their devotions, that INDRA and the other gods were unable to oppose them. The gods had recourse to VISHNU, who, in consequence, ordered SIVA to introduce the *Saiva* tenets and practices, by which the *Daityas* were beguiled, and rendered "wicked, and thence weak."

In order to assist SIVA in this work, ten great Sages were imbued with the *Támasa* property, or property of darkness and ignorance, and by them such writings were put forth as were calculated to disseminate unrighteous and heretical doctrines, these were KANA'DA, GAUTAMA, SAKTI, UPAMANYU, JAIMINI, KAPILA, DURVA'SAS, MRIKANDA', VRIHASPATI, and BHA'RGAVA.

By SIVA himself, the *Pásupata* writings were composed; KANA'DA is the author of the *Vaisheshika* Philosophy. The *Nyáya* originates with GAUTAMA. KAPILA, is the founder of the *Sánkhya* school, and VRIHASPATI of the *Chárváka*. JAIMINI, by SIVA's orders, composed the *Mimánsa*, which is heretical, in as far as it inculcates works in preference to faith, and SIVA himself, in the disguise of a Brahman, or as VYA'SA, promulgated the Vedánta, which is heterodox in *Vaishnava* estimation, by denying attainable, are the *Sankara Digvijaya* of ANANDA GIRI, and the *Sarva Dersana Sangraha* of MA'DHAVA'CHA'RYA, the former a reputed disciple of SANKARA himself, and the latter a well known and able writer, who lived in the commencement of the fourteenth century.

the sensible attributes of the deity. VISHNU, as BUDDHA, taught the *Bauddha Sástra*, and the practices of going naked, or wearing blue garments, meaning, consequently, not the *Bauddhas*, but the *Jainas*, (बौद्धशास्त्रमसत्प्रोक्तं नग्ननीलपटादिकं ।) The *Puránas* were partly instrumental in this business of blinding mankind, and they are thus distinguished by our authority and all the *Vaishnava* works.

The *Mátsya*, *Kaurma*, *Lainga*, *Saiva*, *Skánda* and *Agneya*, are *Támasa*, or the works of darkness, having more or less of a *Saiva* bias.

The *Vishnu*, *Náradiya*, *Bhágavat*, *Garura*, *Pádma* and *Váráha*, are *Sátwika*, pure and true; being, in fact, *Vaishnava* text-books.

The *Brahmánda*, *Brahma Vaivertta*, *Márkandeya*, *Bhavishya*, *Vámana* and *Bráhma*, are of the *Rájasa* caste, emanating from the quality of passion. As far as I am acquainted with them, they lean to the *Sákta* division of the Hindus, or the worship of the female principle. The *Márkandeya* does so notoriously, containing the famous *Chandi Páth*, or *Durgá Máhátmya*, which is read at the *Durga Pujá*; the *Brahma Vaivertta*, is especially dedicated to KRISHNA as GOVINDA, and is principally occupied by him and his mistress RA'DHA'. It is also full on the subject of *Prakriti* or personified nature.

A similar distinction is made even with the *Smritis*, or works on law. The codes of VASISHTHA HA'RI'TA, VYA'SA, PARA'SARA, BHARADWAJA and KASYAPA, are of the pure order. Those of YAJNAWALKYA, ATRI, TITTIRI, DAKSHA, KA'TYA'YANA and VISHNU of the *Rájasa* class, and those of GAUTAMA, VRIHASPATI, SAMVARTTA, YAMA, SANKHA and USANAS, are of the *Támasa* order.

The study of the Puránas and Smritis of the *Sátwika* class, secures *Mukti*, or final emancipation, that of those of the *Rájasa* obtains *Swerga*, or Paradise; whilst that of the *Támasa* condemns a person to hell, and a wise man will avoid them.

किमत्र बहुनोक्तेन पुराणेषु स्मृतिष्वपि ।

तामसा नरकायैव वर्ज्जयेत्तान् विचक्षणः ॥

The Vaishnava writers endeavour to enlist the *Védas* in their cause, and the following texts are quoted by the Tátparya Nirnaya:

एको नारायण आसीन्न ब्रह्मा न शंकरः ।

NA'RA'YANA alone was, not BRAHMA' nor SANKARA.

वासुदेवो वा इदमग्र आसीन्न ब्रह्मा न च शङ्करः ।

Or VASUDEVA was before this (universe), not BRAHMA' nor SANKARA.

The Saivas cite the Védas too, as

सर्व्वव्यापी स भगवान् स्तस्मात्सर्व्वगतः शिवः ॥

The authenticity of the latter of these two works, there is no room to question; and there is but little reason to attach any doubt to the former. Some of the marvels it records of SANKARA, which the author professes to have seen, may be thought to affect its credibility, if not its authenticity, and either ANANDA GIRI must be an unblushing liar, or the book is not his own: it is, however, of little consequence, as even, if the work be not that of ANANDA GIRI himself, it bears internal and indisputable evidence of being the composition of a period, not far removed from that at which he may be supposed to have flourished, and we may, therefore, follow it as a very safe guide, in our enquiries into the actual state of the Hindu Religion about eight or nine centuries ago.

The various sectaries of the Hindu Religion then existing, are all introduced to be combated, and, of course, conquered, by SANKARA: the list is rather a long one, but it will be necessary to go through the whole, to ascertain the character of the national faith of those days, and its present modifications, noticing, as we proceed, some of the points of difference or resemblance between the forms of worship which then prevailed, and which now exist. The two great divisions of *Vaishnavas* and *Saivas* were both in a flourishing condition, and each embraced six principal subdivisions: we shall begin with the former, who are termed; *Bháktas, Bhágavatas, Vaishnavas, Chakrinas*, or *Pancharátrakas, Vaik'hánasas* and *Karmahínas*.

But as each of these was subdivided into a practical and speculative, or *Kerma* and *Jnyána* portion, they formed, in fact, twelve classes of the followers of VISHNU, as the sole and supreme deity.

The *Bháktas* worshipped VISHNU as VA'SUDEVA, and wore no characteristic marks. The *Bhágavatas* worshipped the same deity as BHAGAVAT, and impressed upon their persons the usual *Vaishnava* insignia, representing the discus, club, &c. of that divinity; they likewise reverenced the *Sálagrám* stone, and *Tulasí* plant, and in several of their doctrinal

The Lord who pervades all things, is thence termed the omnipresent Siva.
Rudra is but one, and has no second—

एकोपिरुद्रो न द्वितीयः ॥

These citations would scarcely have been made, if not authentic; they probably do occur in the Védas, but the terms *Nárάyana* and *Vásudeva*, or *Siva* and *Rudra*, are not to be taken in the restricted sense, probably, which their respective followers would assign them.

notions, as well as in these respects, approach to the present followers of RA'MA'NUJA, although they three be regarded as exactly the same. The authorities of these three sects were the *Upanishads* and *Bhagavad Gitá.* The names of both the sects still remain, but they are scarcely applicable to any particular class of *Vaishnavas :* the term *Bhakta*, or *Bhagat*, usually indicates any individual who pretends to a more rigid devotion than his neighbours, and who especially occupies his mind with spiritual considerations: the *Bhágavat* is one who follows particularly the authority of the *Sri Bhágavat Purána.*

The *Vaishnavas* adored VISHNU as NA'RA'YANA, they wore the usual marks, and promised themselves a sort of sensual paradise after death, in *Vaikunt'ha*, or VISHNU'S heaven ; their tenets are still current, but they can scarcely be considered to belong to any separate sect.

The *Chakrinas, or Pancharátrakas* were, in fact, *Sáktas* of the *Vaishnava* class, worshipping the female personifications of VISHNU, and observing the ritual of the *Pancharátra Tantra :* they still remain, but scarcely individualised, being confounded with the worshippers of KRISHNA and RA'MA on the one hand, and those of *Sakti* or *Deví* on the other.

The *Vaik'hánasas* appear to have been but little different from the *Vaishnavas* especially so called; at least ANANDA GIRI has not particularised the difference ; they worshipped NA'RA'YANA as supreme god, and wore his marks. The *Karmahínas* abstained, as the name implies, from all ritual observances, and professed to know *Vishnu* as the sole source and sum of the universe, सर्व्वं विष्णुमयं जगत्। they can scarcely be considered as an existent sect, though a few individuals of the *Rámánujíya* and *Rámánandi Vaishnavas* may profess the leading doctrines.

The *Vaishnava* forms of the Hindu faith, are still, as we shall hereafter see, sufficiently numerous; but we can scarcely identify any one of them with those which seem to have prevailed when the *Sankara Vijaya* of ANANDA GIRI was composed. The great divisions, of RA'MA'NUJA and RA'MA'NAND—the former of which originated, we know, in the course of the eleventh century, are unnoticed, and it is also worth while to observe, that neither in this, nor in any other portion of the *Sankara Vijaya*, is any allusion made to the separate worship of KRISHNA, either in his own person, or that of the infantine forms in which he is now so pre-eminently venerated in many parts of India, nor are the names of R'AMA and SITA', of LAKSHMANA or HANUMA'N, once particularised, as enjoying any portion of distinct and specific adoration.

The *Saiva* sects are the *Saivas*, *Raudras*, *Ugras*, *Bhâktas*, *Jangamas*, and *Pásupatas*. Their tenets are so blended in the discussion, that it is not possible to separate them, beyond the conjectural discrimination which may be derived from their appellations: the text specifies merely their characteristic marks: thus the *Saivas* wore the impression of the *Linga* on both arms; the *Raudras* had a *Trisula*, or trident, stamped on the forehead; the *Ugras* had the *Damaru*, or drum of *Siva* on their arms, and the *Bhâktas* an impression of the *Linga* on the forehead—the *Jangamas* carried a figure of the *Linga* on the head, and the *Pásupatas* imprinted the same object on the forehead, breast, navel, and arms. Of these sects, the *Saivas* are not now any one particular class—nor are the *Raudras*, *Ugras*, or *Bhâktas*, any longer distinct societies: the *Jangamas* remain, but they are chiefly confined to the south of India, and although a *Pásupata*, or worshipper of SIVA as PASUPATI, may be occasionally encountered, yet this has merged into other sects, and particularly into that of the *Kanp'hata Jogis*: the authorities cited by these sects, according to ANANDA GIRI, were the *Siva Gítá*, *Siva Sanhitá*, *Siva Rahasya*, and *Rudra Yámala Tantra*: the various classes of *Jogis* are never alluded to and the work asserts, what is generally admitted as a fact, that the *Dandis*, and *Dasnámi Gosains* originated with SANKARA ACHA'RYA.

Worshippers of BRAHMA, or HIRANYAGARBHA, are also introduced by ANANDA GIRI, whom now it might be difficult to meet with: exclusive adorers of this deity, and temples dedicated to him, do not now occur perhaps in any part of India; at the same time it is an error to suppose that public homage is never paid to him. BRAHMA is particularly reverenced at *Pokher*, in Ajmer, also at *Bithúr*, in the *Doab*, where, at the principal Ghat, denominated *Brahmavertta Ghat*, he is said to have offered an *Aswamedha* on completing the act of creation: the pin of his slipper left behind him on the occasion, and now fixed in one of the steps of the Ghat, is still worshipped there, and on the full moon of Agraháyana (Nov.-Dec.) a very numerously attended *Mela*, or meeting, that mixes piety with profit, is annually held at that place.

The worshippers of AGNI no longer form a distinct class: a few *Agnihotra Brahmans*, who preserve the family fire, may be met with, but in all other respects they conform to some mode of popular devotion.

The next opponents of SANKARA ACHARYA were the *Sauras*, or worshippers of the sun, as the creator and cause of the world: a few *Sauras*, chiefly *Brahmans*, still exist as a sect, as will be hereafter noticed; but the divisions enumerated by ANANDA GIRI, are now, it is believed, unknown: he distinguishes them into the following six classes.

Those who adored the rising sun, regarding it as especially the type of BRAHMA' or the creative power. Those who worshipped the meridian sun as ISWARA, the destructive and regenerative faculty; and those who reverenced the setting sun, as the prototype of VISHNU, or the attribute of preservation.

The fourth class comprehended the advocates of the *Trimurti*, who addressed their devotions to the sun in all the preceding states, as the comprehensive type of these three divine attributes.

The object of the fifth form is not quite clearly stated, but it appears to have been the adoration of the sun as a positive and material body, and the marks on his surface, as his hair, beard, &c. The members of this class so far correspond with the *Sauras* of the present day, as to refrain from food until they had seen the sun.

The sixth class of *Sauras*, in opposition to the preceding, deemed it unnecessary to address their devotions to the visible and material sun: they provided a mental luminary, on which they meditated, and to which their adoration was offered: they stamped circular orbs on their foreheads, arms, and breasts with hot irons; a practice uniformly condemned by SANKARA, as contrary to the laws of the *Védas*, and the respect due to Brahmanical flesh and blood.

GANESA, as well as SURYA, had formerly six classes of adorers; in the present day he cannot boast of any exclusive worship, although he shares a sort of homage with almost all the other divinities: his followers were the worshippers of MAHA' GANAPATI, of HARIDRA GANAPATI, or DHUNDI RAJ, who is still a popular form of GANESA, of UCH'CHISHTHA G, of NAVANI'TA G, of SWERNA G, and of SANTA'NA G. The left hand subdivision of the UCH'CHISHTHA GANAPATI' sect, also called *Hairamba*, abrogated all obligatory ritual and distinction of caste.

The adorers of the female personifications of divine power, appear to have been fully as numerous as at present, and to have worshipped the same objects, or BHAVA'NI', MAHA' LAKSHMI', and SARASWATI' : even as personifications of these divinities, however, the worship of SITA' and RA'DHA', either singly, or in conjunction with RA'MA and KRISHNA, never makes its appearance. The worshippers of *Sakti* were then, as now, divided into two classes, a right and left hand order, and three subdivisions of the latter are enumerated, who are still well known—the *Purnábhishiktas, Akritárthas*, and *Kritákrityasamas*.

There can be little doubt, that the course of time and the presence of foreign rulers, have very much ameliorated the character of much of the Hindu worship : if the licentious practices of the SA'KTAS are still as prevalent as ever, which may well be questioned, they are, at least, carefully concealed from observation, and if they are not exploded, there are other observances of a more ferocious description, which seem to have disappeared. The worship of BHAIRAVA, still prevails amongst the *Sáktas* and the *Jogis ;* but in Upper India, at least, the naked mendicant, smeared with funeral ashes, armed with a trident or a sword, carrying a hollow skull in his hand, and half intoxicated with the spirits which he has quaffed from that disgusting wine-cup, prepared, in short, to perpetrate any act of violence and crime, the *Kápálika* of former days, is now rarely, if ever, encountered. In the work of ANANDA GIRI, we have two of these sectaries introduced, one a Brahman by birth, is the genuine *Kápálika :* he drinks wine, eats flesh, and abandons all rites and observances in the spirit of his faith, his eminence in which has armed him with supernatural powers, and rendered BHAIRAVA himself, the reluctant, but helpless minister of his will. The other *Kápálika* is an impostor, the son of a harlot, by a gatherer of *Tari*, or Palm juice, and who has adopted the character as an excuse for throwing off all social and moral restraint. The *Kápálikas* are often alluded to in controversial works, that appear to be the compositions of a period at least preceding the tenth century.*

The next classes of sectaries, confuted by SANKARA, were various infidel sects, some of whom avowedly, and perhaps all covertly, are still in being : the list is also interesting, as discriminating their opinions which, in the ignorance subsequent to their disappearance from Hindustan, have very commonly been, and, indeed, still are frequently confounded.

* See the Prabodha Chandriká, translated by Dr. Taylor.

These are the *Chárvákas*, or *Súnya Vádis*, the *Saugatas*, the *Kshapanakas*, the *Jainas*, and the *Bauddhas*.

The *Chárvákas* were so named from one of their teachers, the MUNI CHA'RVA'KA. From VRIHASPATI—some of whose dogmas have been quoted from the work of MA'DHAVA, they are termed also *Várhaspatyas*. The appellation *Súnya Vádí*, implies the asserter of the unreality and emptiness of the universe, and another designation, *Lokáyata*, expresses their adoption of the tenet, that this being is the *Be-all* of existence: they were, in short, the advocates of materialism and atheism, and have existed from a very remote period, and still exist, as we shall hereafter see.

The *Saugatas* are identified even by MA'DHAVA with the *Bauddhas*, but there seems to have been some, although probably not any very essential difference: the chief tenet of this class, according to ANANDA GIRI, was their adopting the doctrine taught by SUGATA MUNI, that tenderness towards animated nature comprehends all moral and devotional duty, a tenet which is, in a great measure, common to both the *Bauddha* and *Jaina* schisms: it is to be feared, that the personal description of the *Saugata*, as a man of a fat body and small head, although possibly intended to characterise the genus, will not direct us to the discovery of its origin or history. The *Kshapanaka* again has always been described by *Hindu* writers as a *Bauddha*, or sometimes even a *Jaina* naked mendicant: in the work before us he appears as the professor of a sort of astrological religion, in which* time is the principal divinity, and he is described as carrying, in either hand, the implements of his science, or a *Gola Yantra*, and *Turya Yantra*, the former of which is an armillary sphere, and the latter a kind of quadrant, apparently for ascertaining time;† from the geographical controversy

* Time is the Supreme Deity. ISWARA cannot urge on the present. He who knows time knows BRAHME. Space and time are not distinct from God.

किञ्च कालः परमदेवता। प्रत्यक्षञ्च लयितुं ईश्वरानसमर्थः।
कालविद्ब्रह्मविदिति दिक्कालौ नेश्वरादतिरिच्येते।

† तूर्य्ययन्त्रं मण्डलं चतुर्भागमित्यर्थः।
The Turya Yantra, is the fourth part of an orb.

that occurs between him and SANKARA, it appears that he entertains the doctrine regarding the descent of earth in space, which is attributed by the old astronomers to the *Bauddhas*, and controverted by the author of the *Surya Siddhánta*,* and subsequently by BHA'SKARA: the former is quoted by SANKARA, according to our author. These doctrines, the commentators on BHA'SKARA's work, and even he, himself, commenting on his own text, say, belong to the *Jainas*, not to the *Bauddhas*; but, possibly, the correction is itself an error, it does not appear that the *Kshapanaka* of ANANDA GIRI argues the existence of a double set of planetary bodies, which is, undoubtedly, a *Jainu* doctrine,† and the descent of the earth in space may have been common to all these sects.

The *Jainas* that existed in the time of ANANDA GIRI, appear as *Digambaras* only; he does not notice their division into *Digambaras* and *Swetámbaras*, as they at present are found, and existed indeed prior to the age of MA'DHAVA. The *Bauddhas* are introduced personally, although it may be questioned whether they were very numerous in India in so comparatively modern a period: according to ANANDA GIRI, a persecution of this sect, and of the *Jainas*, took place in one part of the peninsula, the state of *Rudrapur*, during SANKARA's life time, but he, as well as MA'DHAVA,‡ excludes SANKARA from being at all concerned in it. He ascribes its occurrence to the same source, the instigation of a *Bhatta*, from the north, or, in fact, of CUMA'RIL BHATTA, a *Bengali*, or *Maithilí Brahman*.

A long series of sectaries then ensues, of a more orthodex description, and who only err in claiming primeval and pre-eminent honors for the objects of their adoration—none of these are to be found; and, although, to a certain extent, the places of some of them may be supplied by the local deities of the villagers, and by the admission of others to a participatiom in the worship paid to the presiding deities of each sect,

तत्रयन्त्रोपरिकीलद्वयमखिलं ज्ञात्वा ।
तन्मध्ये दृष्ट्वाचविज्ञानेन कालज्ञानं जायते ॥

Fixing above it two pins, and looking between them, the time is ascertained by science.

* A. R. XII. 229.

† A. R. IX. 321.

‡ Preface to Wilson's Sanscrit and English Dictionary.

yet there can be little doubt, that a large portion of the Hindu Pantheon formerly enjoyed honours, which have for some centuries past been withheld. In this predicament are INDRA, KUVERA, YAMA, VARUNA, GARU'DA, SESHA, and SOMA, all of whom, in the golden age of Hindu idolatry, had, no doubt, temples and adorers: the light and attractive service of the god of love, indeed, appears to have been formerly very popular, as his temples and groves make a distinguished figure in the* tales, poems, and dramas of antiquity: it is a feature that singularly characterises the present state of the Hindu religion, that if in some instances it is less ferocious, in others, it has ceased to address itself to the amiable propensities of the human character, or the spontaneous and comparatively innocent feelings of youthful natures. The buffoonery of the *Holi*, and barbarity of the *Cherak Puja*, but ill express the sympathies which man, in all countries, feels with the vernal season, and which formerly gave rise to the festive *Vasanotsava* of the Hindus, and the licentious homage paid to *Sakti* and BHAIRAVA, has little, in common with the worship, that might be supposed acceptable to KA'MA and his lovely bride, and which it would appear they formerly enjoyed.

Besides the adorers of the secondary divinities, we have a variety of sects who direct their devotions to beings of a still lower rank, and of whom none, at present, exist as distinct bodies, although individuals may be found, either detached or comprehended in other classes, who, more or less, reverence similar objects. Thus, the worship of *Akás*,† or *Ether*, as the supreme deity, is still occasionally met with: all classes pay daily homage to the *Pitris* or Manes, and a few of the *Tántrikas* worship the *Siddhas*, or Genii, in the hope of acquiring super-human powers: the same class furnishes occasional votaries of the *Vasus*, *Yakshas*, and *Gandharbas*, and even of the *Vetálas* and *Bhútas*, or goblins and ghosts, and the latter also receive still, from the fears of the villagers, propitiatory adoration. It does not appear, that in any form, the worship of the moon and stars, of the elements, and divisions of the universe, is still practised, although that of the *Tirthas*, or holy places and rivers, is as popular as ever.

* In the *Vrihat Kathá—Dasa Kumára*, *Málati Mádhava*, *Mrichch'hakati*, &c.

† I have encountered but one Professor, however, of this faith, a miserable mendicant, who taught the worship of Ether, under the strange name of *Baghela*.

We have thus completed the enumeration of the sects as described by the author of the *Sankara Vijaya*, and have had an opportunity of observing, that, although the outlines of the system remain the same, the details have undergone very important alterations, since the time at which this work was composed : the rise of most of the existing modifications, we can trace satisfactorily enough, as will hereafter appear, and it is not improbable, that the disappearance of many of those, which no longer take a part in the idolatry of the Hindus, may be attributed to the exertions of SANKARA and his disciples : his object, as appears from the work we have hitherto followed, was by no means the suppression of acts of outward devotion, nor of the preferential worship of any acknowledged and pre-eminent deity : his leading tenet is the recognition of *Brahme Para Brahme,** as the sole cause and supreme ruler of the universe, and as distinct from SIVA, VISHNU, BRAHMA', or any individual member of the pantheon : with this admission, and in regard to the weakness of those human faculties, which cannot elevate themselves to the conception of the inscrutable first cause, the observance of such rites, and the worship of such deities, as are either prescribed by the *Védas*, or the works not incompatible with their authority, were left undisturbed by this teacher ;† they even received, to a certain extent, his particular sanction, and the following divisions of the Hindu faith were, by his express permission, taught by some of his disciples, and are, consequently, regarded by the learned Brahmans in general, as the only orthodox and allowable forms in the present day.‡ The *Saiva* faith was instituted by PARAMATA

* As in these texts of the Védas सदेव सौम्येदमग्र आसीत्। and आत्मा वा इदमेक एवाग्रआसीत्।

† आगमेतिहासपुराणोक्ताचारस्तु वेदानुकूलवृत्त्याग्राह्यः। अग्राह्य एवतत्प्रतिकूले।

Ordinances founded on the *Tantras*, the *Puráns*, or historical record, are admissible if accordant with the *Vedás ;* they must be rejected if repugnant.

‡ कलावस्मिन्युगे नाना पापध्वस्तज्ञानाङ्कुरेषु मर्त्येषु शुद्धाद्वैतविद्यायामनधिकारिषु तेषां वृत्तिः पुनरपियथेप्सिता भवतीति विचार्य्यं

KA'LA'NALA, who is described as teaching at Benares, and assuming the insignia that characterise the *Dandis* of modern times. The *Vaishnava* worship was taught at *Kánchi*, or *Conjeveram*, by LAKSHMANA A̤CHA'RYA and HASTA'MALAKA ; and the latter seems to have introduced a modified adoration of VISHNU, in the character of KRISHNA. The *Saura* sect was continued under the auspices of DIVA'KARA, *Brahmáchári*, and the *Sákta*, under those of the *Sanyasi*, TRIPURAKUMA'RA : the *Gánapatya* were allowed to remain under the presidence of GIRIJAPUTRA, and from such persons as had not adopted either of the preceding systems, B̤ATUKANATH, the professor of the *Kápálika*, or *Bhairava* worship, was permitted to attract followers : all these teachers were converts and disciples of SANKARA, and returned to his superintending guidance, when they had effected the objects of their missions.

The notice that occurs in the *Serva Dersana* of any of the sects which have yet been mentioned, has been already incidentally adverted to : this work is less of a popular form than the preceding, and controverts the speculative rather than the practical doctrines of other schools : besides the atheistical *Bauddha* and *Jaina* sects, the work is occupied chiefly with the refutation of the followers of *Jaimini*, *Gautama*, and *Patanjala*, and we have no classes of worshippers introduced but those of the *Vaishnavas* who follow RA'MA'NUJA, and *Madhwáchárya*, of the *Saivas*, the *Pásupatas*, the followers of ABHINAVA GUPTA, who taught the *Mantra* worship of *Siva* ; and the alchemical school, or worshippers of SIVA's type in quicksilver, and the *Rasendra Linga :* most of these seem to have sprung into being in the interval between the tenth and thirteenth centuries, and have now either disappeared, or are rapidly on the decline : those which actually exist, we shall recur to in the view we are now prepared to take of the actual condition of the Hindu faith.

लोकरक्षार्थं वर्णाश्रम परिपालनार्थं च परमतत्वकल्पनां जीवेशभे
दास्पदां च रचयितुमुपक्रम्य निजशिष्यमाह।

In the present impure age, the bud of wisdom being blighted by iniquity, men are inadequate to the apprehension of pure unity ; they will be apt, therefore, again to follow the dictates of their own fancies, and it is necessary for the preservation of the world, and the maintenance of civil and religious distinctions, to acknowledge those modifications of the divine spirit which are the work of the SUPREME. These reflexions having occurred to SANKARA, he addressed his disciples, &c.

SECTION III.

Present divisions of the Hindus, and of the Vaishnavas in particular.

The classification adopted by the works, I especially follow, if not unexceptionable, is allowable and convenient, and may, therefore, regulate the following details : it divides all the Hindus into three great classes or *Vaishnavas, Saivas,* and *Śáktas,* and refers to a fourth or miscellaneous class, all not comprised in the three others.

The worshippers of Vishnu, Siva, and Sakti, who are the objects of the following description, are not to be confounded with the orthodox adorers of those divinities : few Brahmans of learning, if they have any religion at all, will acknowledge themselves to belong to any of the popular divisions of the Hindu faith, although, as a matter of simple preference, they more especially worship some individual deity, as their chosen, or *Ishta Devata :* they refer also to the *Védas,* the books of law, the Puránas, and Tantras, as the only ritual they recognise, and regard all practices not derived from those sources as irregular and profane : on the other hand, many of the sects seem to have originated, in a great measure, out of opposition to the Brahmanical order : teachers and disciples are chosen from any class, and the distinction of castes is, in a great measure, sunk in the new one, of similarity of schism : the ascetics and mendicants, also, in many instances, affect to treat the Brahmans with particular contempt, and this is generally repaid with interest by the Brahmans. A portion, though not a large one, of the populace is still attached to the *Smárta* Brahmans, as their spiritual guides, and are so far distinct from any of the sects we shall have to specify, whilst most of the followers, even of the sects, pay the ordinary deference to the Brahminical order, and especially evince towards the Brahmans of their own fellowship, of whom there is generally abundance, the devotedness and submission which the original Hindu Code so perpetually inculcates.

Excluding, therefore, those who may be regarded as the regular worshippers of regular gods, we have the following enumeration of the several species of each class :

Vaishnavas.

1 Rámánujas, or Sri Sampradáyis, or Sri Vaishnavas.
2 Rámánandis, or Rámáwats.
3 Kabir Panthis.
4 K'hákis.
5 Maluk Dásis.
6 Dádu Pant'his.
7 Ráya Dásis.
8 Senais.
9 Vallabhácháris, or Rudra Sampradáyis.
10 Mira Bais.
11 Madhwácháris, or Brahma Sampradáyis.
12 Nimáwat, or Sanakádi Sampradáyis.
13 The Vaishnavas of Bengal.
14 Rádhá Vallabhis.
15 The Sak'hi Bhávas.
16 Charan Dásis.
17 Harischandis.
18 Sadhna Panthis.
19 Madhavis.
20 Sanyásis, Vairágis and Nágas.

Saivas.

1 Dandis and Dasnámis.
2 Jogis.
3 Jangamas.
4 Paramahansas.
5 Urdhabá'hus, Akas Muk'his, and Nak'his.
6 Gúdaras.
7 Rúk'haras, Súk'haras and Uk'haras.
8 Kara Lingis.
9 Sanyásis, &c.

Sa'ktas.

1 Dakshinis.
2 Vámis.

3 Káncheliyas.

4 Karáris.

Miscellaneous Sects.

1 Gánapatyas.

2 Saurapatas.

3 Nának Sháhis of seven classes.

- 1 Udásis.
- 2 Ganjbakhshis.
- 3 Rámráyis.
- 4 Suthra Sháhis.
- 5 Govind Sinhis.
- 6 Nirmalas.
- 7 Nágas.

4 Jainas of two principal orders.

- 1 Digambaras.
- 2 Swetámbaras.

5 Bába Lális.

6 Prán Náthis.

7 Sádhs.

8 Satnámis.

9 Siva Náráyinis.

10 Súnyabádis.

These will be regarded as varieties enough, it may be presumed, especially when it is considered, that most of them comprise a number of sub-divisions, and that besides these acknowledged classifications, many individual mendicants are to be found all over India, who can scarcely be included within the limits of any of them, exercising a sort of independence both in thought and act, and attached very loosely, if at all, to any of the popular schismatical sects.*

* Some of the popular works adopt a different classification, and allude to 96 *Páshandas*, or heresies, which are thus arranged:—

Amongst the Brahmans,	24
Sanyásis,	12
Vairágis,	12
Sauras,	18
Jangamas,	18
Jogis,	12

VAISHNAVAS.

1 *Sri Sampradáyis*, or *Rámánujas*.

Amongst other divisions of less importance, the *Vaishnavas* are usually distinguished into four principal *Sampradáyas*, or *sects*;* of these, the most ancient and respectable is the *Sri Sampradáya*, founded by the

* Thus the *Bhakta Málá*, चाावीस प्रथम हरि वपु धस्यौ त्यौं चतुर व्युंह कलियुग प्रगट। श्रीरामानुज उद्दार सुधानिधि अवनि कल्पतरु। विष्णुस्वामी वोच्हितसिंधु संसार पारकरु। मध्वाचारज मेघभक्ति श्ररज सर भरिया। निम्वादित्य आदित्य कुहर अज्ञान जुहरिया। जन्मकर्म्म भागौत धर्म्मसम्प्रदायथापी अघट। चौवीस प्रथम हरिइत्यादि। "HARI, in preceding ages, assumed twenty-four principal shapes, but four were manifest in the *Kali Yug*: the magnanimous *Rámánuja*, a treasure of Ambrosia and terrestrial tree of plenty: the ocean of kindness and transporter across the sea of the universe, *Vishnu Swami*: *Madhu Achárj*, a rich cloud in the autumnal season of piety: and *Nimbáditya*, a sun that illumined the cave of ignorance; by them acts of piety and obligation were divided, and each sect was severally established." There are also Sanscrit texts authorising the different institution, and characteristic term of each *Sampradáya*, one of these is from the *Padma Purána*.

सम्प्रदाय विहीना ये मन्त्रास्तेनिष्फलामताः। अतः कलोभविष्यन्ति चत्वारःसम्प्रदायिनः॥ श्रीमाध्वीरुद्रसनकावैष्णवाः च्छितिपावनाः। चत्वारस्ते कलौदेवि सम्प्रदायप्रवर्त्तकाः॥

"Those *Mantras*, which belong to no system, are of no virtue; and, therefore, in the *Kali* age, there shall be followers of four sects. *Sri*, *Mádhwi*, *Rudra* and *Sanaka*, shall be the *Vaishnavas*, purifying the world, and these four, *Dévi*, (*Siva* speaks,) shall be the institutors of the *Sampradáyas* in the *Kali* period." We may here observe in passing, that if this text is genuine, the *Padma Purána* must be very modern: another similar text is the following:

रामानुजं श्रीस्स्वीचक्रे मध्वाचार्य्यंच्चतुर्मुखः। श्रीविष्णुस्वामिनं रुद्रो निम्वादित्यच्चतुस्मनः॥

"LAKSHMI' selected *Rámánuja*; BRAHMA *Madhwáchárya*; *Rudra* gave the preference to *Vishnu Swámi*, and the four *Sanakas* to *Nimbáditya*." The cause of the election is not very evident, as the creeds taught by those teachers, have little connexion with the deity who lends the appellation to the sects.

Vaishnava reformer *Rámánuja Achárya*, about the middle of the twelfth century.*

The history of RA'MA'NUJA, and his first followers, is well known in the south of India, of which he was a native, and is recorded in various legendary tracts and traditional narratives.

According to the *Bhárgava Upapurána*, RA'MA'NUJA is said to have been an incarnation of the serpent *Sesha*, whilst his chief companions and disciples were the embodied *Discus*, *Mace*, *Lotus*, and other insignia of *Vishnu*. In a *Kanara* account of his life, called the *Divya Charitra*, he is said to have been the son of *Sri Kesava Achárya* and *Bhúmi Deví*; and, as before, an incarnation of *Sesha*. He was born at *Perumbur*, and studied at *Kánchi*, or *Conjeveram*, where also he taught his system of the *Vaishnava* faith. He afterwards resided at *Sri Ranga*, worshipping *Vishnu* as *Sri Ranga Nát'ha*, and there composed his principal works : he then visited various parts of India, disputing with the professors of different creeds, overcoming them of course, and reclaiming various shrines, then in possession of the *Saivas*, for the worshippers of *Vishnu*, particularly the celebrated temple of *Tripeti*.

On his return to *Sri Ranga*, the disputes between the *Vaishnava* and *Saiva* religions, became exceedingly violent, and the *Chola* monarch, who, according to some accounts, was at that time KERIKA'LA CHOLA, subsequently named KRIMI KONDA CHOLA, being a devout worshipper of *Siva*, commanded all the *Brahmans* in his dominions to sign an acknowledgement of the supremacy of that divinity, bribing some of the most refractory, and terrifying others into acquiescence. RA'MA'NUJA, however, was impracticable, and the king sent armed men to seize him. With the assistance of his disciples, he effected his escape, and ascending the Ghats, found refuge with the *Jain*

* The *Smriti Kála Taranga* places the date of RA'MA'NUJA's appearance in *Saka*—1049 or A.D. 1127. A note by Colonel Mackenzie on an inscription, given in the Asiatic Researches 9, 270, places the birth of RA'MA'NUJA in A.D. 1008 : various accounts, collected by Dr. Buchanan, make it 1010 and 1025 (Buchanan's Mysore, 2, 80) and 1019 (Ibid, 3, 413,) Inscriptions make him alive in 1128, (Ibid) which would give him a life of more than a century : according to Col. Wilks, indeed, (History of Mysore, 1,41, note and appendix), he was alive in 1133. The weight of authority seems to be in favour of the more recent date, and we may conclude that he was born about the end of the eleventh century, and that the first half of the twelfth century was the period at which his fame, as a teacher, was established.

sovereign of Mysore, VITALA DEVA, *Velála Ráya.* In consequence of rendering medical service to the daughter of this prince, or in the terms of the legend, expelling an evil spirit, a *Brahma Rákshasa*, by whom she was possessed, he obtained the monarch's grateful regard, and finally converted him to the *Vaishnava* faith. The *Rája* assumed the title of *Vishnu Verddhana.* RA'MA'NUJA remained several years in Mysore, at a temple founded by the *Rája* on *Yádava Giri*, now known as *Mail Cotay*, for the reception of an image called *Chavala Ráya*, a form of *Ranachhor*, or *Krishna*, which the local traditions very ridiculously pretend he obtained from the *Mohammedan* sovereign of Delhi. RA'MA'NUJA resided here twelve years, but on the death of his persecutor, the *Chola* king, he returned to *Sri Ranga*, on the *Káverí*, and there spent the remainder of his life in devout exercises and religious seclusion.

The establishments of the Rámánujiyas are numerous in the Dekhin still, and the same country comprehends the site of the *Gaddi*, the pillow or seat of the primitive teacher; his spiritual throne, in fact, to which his disciples are successively elevated.* This circumstance gives a superiority to the *Achâryas* of the *Dekshina*, or South, over those of the *Uttara*, or North, into which they are at present divided.

The worship of the followers of RA'MA'NUJA, is addressed to VISHNU and to LAKSHMI, and their respective incarnations, either singly or conjointly; and the *Sri Vaishnavas*, by which general name the sect is known, consist of corresponding subdivisions, as NA'RA'YANA', or LAKSHMI, or LAKSHMI NA'RA'YAN, or RA'MA or SITA, or SITA RA'MA, or KRISHNA, or RUKMINI, or any other modifications of *Vishnu*, or his consort, is the preferential object of the veneration of the votary.† The

* According to information obtained by Dr. Buchanan, RA'MA'NUJA founded 700 *Matts*, of which four only remain; one of the principal of these is at *Mail Cotay*, or *Dakshina Badarikásrama*, the *Badari* station of the South. RA'MA'NUJA also established 74 hereditary *Guruships* amongst his followers, the representatives of which still remain and dispute the supremacy with the *Sanyási* members of the order; these last, however, are generally considered of the highest rank, (Buch. Mysore, 2, 75). In another place (1, 144), he says that 89 *Guruships* were established, 5 in the *Sanyasi* class, and 84 in the secular order: the *Matams* of the five former are *Ahobalem*, *Totádri*, *Raméswara*, *Sri Rangam*, and *Kánji*.

† Mr. Colebrooke, A. R. 7, says the *Rámánujas* are of three classes, those who worship RA'MA alone, SITA alone, and SITA and RA'MA conjointly. One of my authorities, *Mathura Náth*, says, they worship *Mahá Lakshmi*, and other information agrees with

Sri Vaishnava worship in the north of India, is not very popular, and the sect is rather of a speculative than practical nature, although it does not require, in its teachers, secession from the world : the teachers are usually of the Brahmanical order, but the disciples may be of any caste.*

Besides the temples appropriated to VISHNU and his consort, and their several forms, including those of KRISHNA and RA'MA, and those which are celebrated as objects of pilgrimage, as *Lakshmi-Balaji*, *Rámnáth*, and *Ranganáth*, in the south ; *Badarinat'h*, in the *Himálaya*, *Jagannát'h*, in *Orissa*, and *Dwáraká*, on the Malabar Coast, images of metal or stone are usually set up in the houses of the private members of this sect, which are daily worshipped, and the temples and dwellings are all decorated with the *Sálagráma* stone and *Tulasi* plant.

The most striking peculiarities in the practices of this sect, are the individual preparation, and scrupulous privacy of their meals : they must not eat in cotton garments, but having bathed, must put on woollen or silk : the teachers allow their select pupils to assist them, but, in general, all the *Rámánujas* cook for themselves, and should the meal during this process, or whilst they are eating, attract even the looks of a stranger, the operation is instantly stopped, and the viands buried in the ground : a similar delicacy, in this respect, prevails amongst some other classes of Hindus, especially of the *Rajaput* families, but it is not carried to so preposterous an extent.†

his; from the texts quoted in the *Sarva Dersana Sangraha*, VISHNU as VA'SUDEVA, is the deity to be worshipped, but no doubt all the varieties exist : without, however, affecting the identity of the sect, the real object of whose devotion is VISHNU, as the cause and creator of the world, and any of his, or his *Sakti's* more especial manifestations, are consequently entitled to reverence. The term *Sri Vaishnavas*, most commonly applied to them, denotes an original preference of the female deity or *Mahá Lakshmi* : the worship of RA'MA is more properly that of the *Rámánandis*, and they may be the persons intended by Mr. Colebrooke's informants, as those of the *Rámánujiyas* who worship RA'MA only, (A. R. 7, 281). It may also be observed, that the *Rámánujiyas* unite with KRISHNA, *Rukmini*, not *Rádhá*, the latter being his mistress only, not his wife, and being never named in the *Bhágavat*, except in one ambiguous passage.

* The *Mantra*, and mark, are never bestowed on any person of impure birth.—Buch Mysore, 1, 146.

† It is said, however, that there are two divisions of the sect, one called *Avarani* from *Avarana*, screening, or surrounding, and the other *Anávarini*, from the member not observing such punctilious privacy.

The chief ceremony of initiation in all Hindu sects, is the communication by the teacher to the disciple of the *Mantra*, which generally consists of the name of some deity, or a short address to him; it is communicated in a whisper, and never lightly made known by the adept to profane ears. The *Mantra* of the RA'MA'NUJA sect is said to be the six syllable *Mantra*—or *Om Rámàya namah;* or Om, salutation to RA'MA.*

Another distinction amongst sects, but merely of a civil character, is the term or terms with which the religious members salute each other when they meet, or in which they are addressed by the lay members. This amongst the *Rámánujas* is the phrase, *Dásosmi*, or *Dásóham;* I am your slave; accompanied with the *Pranám*, or slight inclination of the head, and the application of the joined hands to the forehead. To the *Achàryas*, or supreme teachers of this sect, the rest perform the *Ashtánga Dandawat* or prostration of the body, with the application of eight parts—the forehead, breast, hands, knees, and insteps of the feet, to the ground.

The Hindu sects are usually discriminated by various fantastical streaks on their faces, breasts, and arms: for this purpose, all the *Vaishnavas* employ especially, a white earth called *Gopichandana*, which, to be of the purest description, should be brought from *Dwárakà*, being said to be the soil of a pool at that place, in which the GOPI's drowned themselves when they heard of *Krishna's* death. The common *Gopichandana*, however, is nothing but a *magnesian* or *calcareous clay*.

The marks of the *Rámánujas* are two perpendicular white lines, drawn from the root of the hair to the commencement of each eye-brow, and a transverse streak connecting them across the root of the nose: in the centre is a perpendicular streak of red, made with red Sanders, or *Roli*, a preparation of turmeric and lime; they have also patches of *Gopichandana*, with a central red streak on the breast, and each upper arm: the marks are supposed to represent the *Sank'h, Chakra, Gadá,*

* In giving the *Mantras*, as they have been communicated to me, it may be necessary to suggest a doubt of their accuracy: a Hindu evades what he dislikes to answer, and will not scruple a falsehood to stop enquiry; men above prejudice, in other respects, find it so difficult to get over that of communicating the *Mantra*, that when they profess to impart it, even their sincerity can scarcely be admitted without a doubt.

and *Padma*,* or Shell, Discus, Club, and Lotus, which Vishnu bears in his four hands, whilst the central streak is Sri, or Lakshmi.† Some have these objects carved on wooden stamps, with which they impress the emblems on their bodies, and others carry their devotion so far as to have the parts cicatrized with heated metallic models of the objects they propose to represent, but this is not regarded as a creditable practice :‡ besides these marks, they wear a necklace of the wood of the *Tulasi*, and carry a rosary of the seeds of the same plant, or of the Lotus.

* The *Vaishnava* is thus described in the *Bhakta Málá*, the text is probably that of the *Bhágavat*—

ये कण्ठलग्नतुलसीनलिनाक्षमाला: ये बाहुमूलपरिचिह्नितशङ्ख-चक्रा: । येवाललाटपटलेलसदूर्द्ध्वपुण्ड्रास्ते वैष्णवाभुवनमासुपवित्त्रयन्ति ।

" They who bear the *Tulasi* round the neck, the rosary of Lotus seeds, have the shell and discus impressed upon their upper arm, and the upright streak along the centre of the forehead, they are *Vaishnavas*, and sanctify the world."

† The efficacy of these marks is very great: we are told in the *Kási Khand*, that Yama directs his ministers to avoid such as bear them, and the same work observes, that no sin can exist in the individuals who make use of them, be they of whatever caste.

ब्राह्मण: क्षत्त्रियो वैश्य: शूद्रो वा यदि वेतर: । विष्णुभक्तिसमायुक्तो ज्ञेय: सर्व्वोत्तमश्च स: ॥ शङ्खचक्राङ्कित तनु: शिरसामंजरीधर: । गोपीचन्दन लिप्ताङ्गो दृष्टश्चेत्तदघं कुत: ॥

‡ The *Vrihat Náradiya Purána* sentences every Brahman adopting the practice to endless degradation, and even to the infernal regions.

तथाहि सन्तप्त शङ्खादि लिङ्गचिह्नतनुर्नर: । स सर्व्वपातकाभोगी चाण्डालो जन्मकोटिभि: ॥ तं द्विजं तप्तशङ्खादि लिङ्गाङ्किततनुं हर: । संभाष्यरौरवं याति यावदिन्द्राश्चतुर्दश: ।

The reason also occurs—ब्राह्मणस्य तनुर्ज्ञेया सर्व्वदेवानामाश्रिता । सा चेत्संतापिता राजन किमुवत्स्यामहे वयम् ॥ The body of a Brahman is the abode of all the gods; if that is consumed, where shall we abide? It appears, however, that stamping the mark with a hot iron, is commonly in use in the *Dekhin*. A similar practice seems to have been known to some of the early Christians, and baptizing with fire, was stamping the cross on the forehead with a hot iron.

The principal authorities of this sect, are the comments of the founder on the *Sútras* of VYA'SA, and other Vaidika works: they are written in Sanscrit, and are the *Sri Bháshya*, the *Gítá Bháshya*, the *Védártha Sangraha*, *Védanta Pradípa*, and *Vedántá Súra:* besides these, the works of *Venkáta Achárya*, are of great repute amongst them, as the *Stotra Bháshya*, and *Satadushini*, and others: the *Chanda Máruta Vaidika*, and *Trinsatadhyánam*, are also works of authority, as is the *Pancharátra* of NAREDA: of the *Puránas* they acknowledge only six as authorities, the *Vishnu*, *Náredíya*, *Garura*, *Padma*, *Varáha* and the *Bhágavat:* the other twelve are regarded as *Támasi*, or originating in the principles of darkness and passion, as we have already observed. Besides these, the *Rámánujas* have a variety of popular works in the dialects of the South, one of which, the *Guru Para*, containing an account of the life of RA'MA'NUJA, was procured by Dr. Buchanan, in the course of his statistical researches in *Mysore*.

The chief religious tenet of the *Rámánujas*, is the assertion that *Vishnu* is BRAHME; that he was before all worlds, and was the cause and the creator of all. Although they maintain that *Vishnu* and the universe are one, yet, in opposition to the *Védanta* doctrines, they deny that the deity is void of form or quality, and regard him as endowed with all good qualities, and with a two-fold form: the supreme spirit, *Paramátmá*, or cause, and the gross one, the effect, the universe or matter. The doctrine is hence called the *Visishthádwaita*, or doctrine of unity with attributes. In these assertions they are followed by most of the *Vaishnava* sects. Creation originated in the wish of VISHNU, who was alone, without a second, to multiply himself: he said, I will become many; and he was individually embodied as visible and etherial light. After that, as a ball of clay may be moulded into various forms, so the grosser substance of the deity became manifest in the elements, and their combinations: the forms into which the divine matter is thus divided, are pervaded by a portion of the same vitality which belongs to the great cause of all, but which is distinct from his spiritual or etherial essence; here, therefore, the *Rámánujas* again oppose the *Védántikas*, who identify the *Paramátmá* and *Jiválmá*, or etherial and vital spirit: this vitality, though endlessly diffusible, is imperishable and eternal, and the matter of the universe, as being the same in substance with the Supreme Being, is alike without beginning or end; PURUSHOTTAMA, or

Na'ra'yan, after having created man and animals, through the instrumentality of those subordinate agents whom he willed into existence for that purpose, still retained the supreme authority of the universe : so that the *Rámánujas* assert three predicates of the universe, comprehending the deity : it consists of *Chit*, or spirit, *Achit*, or matter, and *Iswara*, or god, or the enjoyer, the thing enjoyed, and the ruler and controuler of both. Besides his primary and secondary form as the creator, and creation, the deity has assumed, at different times, particular forms and appearances, for the benefit of his creatures : he is, or has been, visibly present amongst men, in five modifications : in his Archa', objects of worship, as images, &c. ; in the *Vibhávas*, or *Avatáras*, as the fish, the boar, &c. ; in certain forms called *Vyúhas*, of which four are enumerated, Va'sudeva, or Krishna, Balara'ma, Pradyumna, and Aniruddha ; fourthly, in the *Sukshma* form, which, when perfect, comprises six qualities : *Viraja*, absence of human passion ; *Vimrityu*, immortality ; *Visoka*, exemption from care or pain ; *Vijighatsá*, absence of natural wants ; *Satya kama*, and *Satya sankalpa*, the love and practice of truth ; and sixthly, as the *Antarátma*, or *Antaryámi*, the human soul, or individualised spirit : these are to be worshipped seriatim, as the ministrant ascends in the scale of perfection, and adoration therefore is five-fold ; *Abhigamanam*, cleaning and purifying the temples, images, &c. *Upádánam*, providing flowers and perfumes for religious rites ; *Ijyá*, the presentation of such offerings, blood offerings being uniformly prohibited, it may be observed, by all the *Vaishnavas ; Swádhyáya*, counting the rosary and repeating the names of the divinity, or any of his forms ; and *Yoga*, the effort to unite with the deity : the reward of these acts is elevation to the seat of Vishnu, and enjoyment of like state with his own, interpreted to be perpetual residence in *Vaikunt'ha*, or *Vishnu's* heaven, in a condition of pure ecstasy and eternal rapture.

The *Rámánujas* are not very numerous in the North of India, where they are better known as *Sri Vaishnavas ;* they are decidedly hostile to the *Saiva* sect, and are not on very friendly terms with the modern votaries of Krishna, although they recognise that deity as an incarnation of Vishnu.*

* Dubois, in his 8th Chapter, has some details of the *Vaishnava* mendicants, as met with in the Dekhin: his account, however, does not apply to the *Rámánuja*, or

RAMANANDIS, OR RAMAWATS.

The followers of RA'MA'NAND are much better known than those of RA'MA'NUJA in Upper Hindustan: they are usually considered as a branch of the RA'MA'NUJA sect, and address their devotions peculiarly to RA'MACHANDRA, and the divine manifestations connected with VISHNU in that incarnation, as SITA, LAKSHMANA, and HANUMA'N.

RA'MA'NAND is sometimes considered to have been the immediate disciple of RA'MA'NUJA, but this appears to be an error: a more particular account makes him the fifth in descent from that teacher, as follows—The pupil and successor of RA'MA'NUJA was DEVA'NANDA; of DEVA'NANDA, HARINANDA; of HARINANDA, RA'GHAVA'NAND, and of this last, RA'MA'NAND, an enumeration which, if correct, would place RA'MA'NAND about the end of the thirteenth century:* there is great reason, however, to doubt his being entitled to so remote a date, and consequently to question the accuracy of his descent from RA'MA'NUJA: we shall have occasion to infer, hereafter, from the accounts given of the dates of other teachers, that RA'MA'NAND was not earlier than the end of the fourteenth, or beginning of the fifteenth, century.

According to common tradition, the schism of RA'MA'NAND originated in resentment of an affront offered him by his fellow disciples, and sanctioned by his teacher. It is said, that he had spent some time in travelling through various parts of India, after which he returned to

any other Vaishnava sect, as known in these provinces although a few of the particulars may be true, if confined to the Vaishnava Vairagis—the *Dekhini Vaishnavas* must be, therefore, a very different class from those that are met with in any other part of India, or the *Abbé* must have mixed, as is not unusual with him, a small quantum of truth, with a very large portion of error: it is, indeed, impossible to think him correct, when he states, that "the sectaries of *Vishnu* eat publicly of all sorts of meat, except beef, and drink spirituous liquors without shame or restraint, and that they are reproached with being the chief promoters of that abominable sacrifice, the *Sakti Puja*:" now, it is not true of any sect in Upper India, that the practices the *Abbé* mentions occur at all, except in the utmost privacy and secrecy, and if even in that way they do occur, it is certainly not amongst the *Vaishnava Vairágis*, but with very different sects, as we shall hereafter see.

* The enumeration in the *Bhakta Málá* is different: it there occurs 1 RA'MA'NUJA, 2 DEVA'CHA'RJ, 3 RA'GHA'VANAND, 4 RA'MA'NAND; making him the fourth.

the *Mat'h*, or residence of his superior. his brethren objected to him that in the course of his peregrinations, it was impossible he could have observed that privacy in his meals, which is a vital observance of the *Rámánuja* sect, and as RA'GHAVA'NAND admitted the validity of the objection, RA'MA'NAND was condemned to feed in a place apart from the rest of the disciples · he was highly incensed at the order, and retired from the society altogether, establishing a schism of his own

The residence of RA'MA'NAND was at Benares, at the *Pancha Ganga Ghát*, where a *Mat'h*, or monastery of his followers is said to have existed, but to have been destroyed by some of the Musselman princes at present there is merely a stone plat-form in the vicinity, bearing the supposed impression of his feet, but there are many *Mat'hs* of his followers, of celebrity, at *Benares*, whose *Panchait*, or council, is the chief authority amongst the *Rámáwats* in Upper India · we shall have frequent occasion to mention these *Mat'hs*, or convents, and a short account of them may, therefore, here be acceptable.

Most of the religious sects of which we have to give an account, comprise various classes of individuals, resolvable, however, especially into two, whom (for want of more appropriate terms) we must call, perhaps, *Clerical* and *Lay:* the bulk of the votaries are generally, but not always, of the latter order, whilst the rest, or the *Clerical* class, are sometimes monastic, and sometimes secular : most of the sects, especially the *Vaishnavas*, leave this distinction a matter of choice : the *Vallabhácháris*, indeed, give the preference to married teachers, and all their *Gosains* are men of business and family : the preference, however, is usually assigned to teachers of an ascetic or cœnobitic life, whose pious meditations are not distracted by the affections of kindred, or the cares of the world : the doctrine that introduced similar unsocial institutions into the Christian Church, in the fourth century, being still most triumphantly prevalent in the east, the land of its nativity, the establishments of which we are treating, and the still existing practices of solitary mortification, originating in the " specious appearance and pompous sound of that maxim of the ancient philosophy, that in order to the attainment of true felicity and communion with God, it was necessary that the soul should be separated from the body even here below, and that the body was to be macerated and mortified for that purpose." (*Mosheim* i 378.)

Of the cœnobitic members of the different communities, most pursue an erratic and mendicant life: all of them, indeed, at some period have led such a life, and have travelled over various parts of India singly or in bodies, subsisting by alms, by merchandise, and sometimes, perhaps, by less unexceptionable means, like the *Sarabaites* of the east, or the mendicant friars of the Latin Church they have, however, their fixed rallying points, and are sure of finding, in various parts of their progress, establishments of their own, or some friendly fraternity where they are for a reasonably moderate period lodged and fed. When old or infirm, they sit down in some previously existing *Mat'h*, or establish one of their own.

The *Mat'hs*, *Asthals*, or *Akáras*, the residences of the monastic communities of the Hindus, are scattered over the whole country. they vary in structure and extent, according to the property of which the proprietors are possessed; but they generally comprehend a set of huts or chambers for the *Mahant*,* or Superior, and his permanent pupils, a temple, sacred to the deity whom they worship, or the *Samádh*, or shrine of the founder of the sect, or some eminent teacher, and a *Dharma Sálá*, one or more sheds, or buildings for the accommodation of the mendicants or travellers, who are constantly visiting the *Mat'h* ingress and egress is free to all; and, indeed, a restraint upon personal liberty seems never to have entered into the conception of any of the religious legislators of the Hindus

The *Mat'h* is under the entire controul of a *Mahant*, or Superior, with a certain number of resident *Chélas*, or disciples; their number

* The following description of the residence of MANDANA MISRA, from the *Sankara Vijaya* of ANANDA GIRI, is very applicable to a modern *Mat'h*.

"At the distance of four Yojanas, west from Hastinapur, was a square plot of ground, extending a cos on each side; in the centre of it stood a large mansion, constructed of the timber of the Tal, and exactly facing it another a hundred cubits in length; upon the top of this last, were many cages full of parrots, and within it resided five hundred pupils, occupied in the study of various Sástras. the first was the dwelling of the Teacher, like Brahma with four heads, like the Serpent King, with a thousand faces, and Rudra, with a five-fold head, amongst his disciples like the waves of the ocean, and enabling them to overcome the universe in unparalleled profundity and extent of knowledge he was attended by numerous slaves of both sexes attached to his dwelling, were wells and reservoirs, and gardens and orchards, and his person was pampered with the choicest viands procured daily by his disciples. In his court-yard were two Temples, on a circular mound, for the worship of the *Viswadévas* and the *Sálagrám*, in the form of *Lakshmí Náráyana* varies from three or four to thirty or forty, but in both cases there are always a number of vagrant or out-members : the resident *Chélas* are usually the elders of the body, with a few of the younger as their attendants and scholars ; and it is from the senior and more proficient of these ascetics, that the *Mahant* is usually elected.

In some instances, however, where the *Mahant* has a family, the situation descends in the line of his posterity : where an election is to be effected, it is conducted with much solemnity, and presents a curious picture of a regularly organised system of church policy, amongst these apparently unimportant and straggling communities.

The *Mat'hs* of various districts look up to some one of their own order as chief, and they all refer to that connected with their founder, as the common head : under the presidence, therefore, of the *Mahant* of that establishment, wherever practicable, and in his absence, of some other of acknowledged pre-eminence, the *Mahants* of the different *Mat'hs* assemble, upon the decease of one of their brethren, to elect a successor. For this purpose they regularly examine the *Chélas*, or disciples of the deceased, the ablest of whom is raised to the vacant situation : should none of them be qualified, they choose a *Mahant* from the pupils of some other teacher, but this is rarely necessary, and unless necessary, is never had recourse to. The new *Mahant* is then regularly installed, and is formally invested with the cap, the rosary, the frontal mark, or *Tiká*, or any other monastic insignia, by the president of the assembly. Under the native Government, whether Mohammedan or Hindu—the election of the superior of one of these establishments was considered as a matter of sufficient moment, to demand the attention of the Governor of the province, who, accordingly, in person, or by his deputy, presided at the election : at present, no interference is exercised by the ruling authorities, and rarely by any lay character, although occasionally, a *Raja* or a *Zemindar*, to whose liberality the *Mat'h* is indebted, or in whose lands it is situated, assumes the right of assisting and presiding at the election.

The *Mahants* of the sect, in which the election takes place, are generally assisted by those of the sects connected with them : each is attended by a train of disciples, and individuals of various mendicant tribes repair to the meeting; so that an assemblage of many hundreds, and sometimes of thousands, occurs : as far as the resources of the *Mat'h*, where they are assembled, extend, they are maintained at its expense; when those fail, they must shift for themselves; the election is usually a business of ten or twelve days, and during the period of its continuance, various points of polity or doctrine are discussed in the assembly.

Most of the *Mat'hs* have some endowments of land, but with the exception of a few established in large cities, and especially at Benares, the individual amount of these endowments is, in general, of little value. There are few *Mat'hs* in any district that possess five hundred bigahs of land, or about one hundred and seventy acres, and the most usual quantity is about thirty or forty bigahs only: this is sometimes let out for a fixed rent; at other times, it is cultivated by the *Mat'h* on its own account; the highest rental met with, in any of the returns procured, is six hundred and thirty rupees per annum. Although, however, the individual portions are trifling, the great number of these petty establishments renders the aggregate amount considerable, and as the endowed lands have been granted *Mafi*, or free of land tax, they form, altogether, a serious deduction from the revenue of each district.

Besides the lands they may hold, the *Mat'hs* have other sources of support: the attachment of lay votaries frequently contributes very liberally to their wants: the community is also sometimes concerned, though, in general, covertly, in traffic, and besides those means of supply, the individual members of most of them sally forth daily, to collect alms from the vicinity, the aggregate of which, generally in the shape of rice or other grains, furnishes forth the common table: it only remains to observe, that the tenants of these *Mat'hs*, particularly the *Vaishnavas*, are most commonly of a quiet inoffensive character, and the *Mahants* especially are men of talents and respectability, although they possess, occasionally, a little of that self-importance, which the conceit of superior sanctity is apt to inspire: there are, it is true, exceptions to this innocuous character, and robberies and murders have been traced to these religious establishments.

The especial object of the worship of RA'MA'NANDA's followers is VISHNU, as RA'MA'CHANDRA: they, of course, reverence all the other incarnations of VISHNU, but they maintain the superiority of RA'MA, in the present or *Kali Yug*; hence they are known collectively as *Rámáwats*, although the same variety prevails amongst them, as amongst the *Rámánujas*, as to the exclusive or collective worship of the male and female members of this incarnation, or of *Ráma* and *Sitá*, singly, or jointly, or *Sitá Ráma* :* individuals of them also pay particular veneration to some of the other forms of VISHNU, and they hold in like estimation, as the *Rámánujas*, and every *Vaishnava* sect, the *Sálagrám* stone and *Tulasi* plant : their forms of worship correspond with those of the Hindus generally, but some of the mendicant members of the sect, who are very numerous, and are usually known as *Vairágis*, or *Viraktas*, consider all form of adoration superfluous, beyond the incessant invocation of the name of KRISHNA and RA'MA.

The practices of this sect are of a less precise nature than those of the RA'MA'NUJAS, it being the avowed object of the founder to release his disciples from those fetters which he had found so inconvenient : in allusion to this, indeed, he gave, it is said, the appellation *Avadhuta*, or *Liberated*, to his scholars, and they admit no particular observances with respect to eating or bathing,† but follow their own inclination, or comply with the common practice in these respects. The initiatory *Mantra* is said to be *Sri Ráma*—the salutation is *Jaya Sri Ráma*, *Jaya Rám*, or *Sitá Rám* : their marks are the same as those of the preceding, except that the red perpendicular streak on the forehead is varied, in shape and extent, at the pleasure of the individual, and is generally narrower than that of the RA'MA'NUJAS.

Various sects are considered to be but branches of the *Rámánandì Vaishnavas*, and their founders are asserted to have been amongst his disciples : of these disciples, twelve are particularised as the most eminent, some of whom have given origin to religious distinctions of great celebrity, and, although their doctrines are often very different from those of RA'MA'NAND, yet the popular tradition is so far corroborated, that they maintain an amicable intercourse with the followers of R'AMA'NAND, and with each other.

The twelve chief disciples of RA'MA'NAND, are named, as follows—ASA'NAND, KABIR, the weaver, RAEDA'S, the *Chamár*, or currier, PI'PA, the *Rajaput*, SURSURA'NAND, SUKHA'NAND, BHA'VANAND, DHANNA, the *Ját*, SENA, the barber—MAHA'NAND, PARAMA'NAND, and SRIA'NAND,‡ a

* Amongst the temples of this sect at Benares, are two dedicated to *Rádhá Krishna*, although attached to *Mat'hs* belonging to the *Rámávat* order, and not at all connected with the followers of VALLABHA, or of CHAITANYA and NITYA'NAND.

† The *Vairágis* of this sect, and some others, eat and drink together, without regard to tribe or caste, and are thence called *Kulatut*, or *Vernatut*.

‡ The *Bhakta Málá* has a rather different list : 1 RAGHUNA'TH, 2 ANANTA'NAND,

list which shews, that the school of RA'MA'NAND admitted disciples of every caste: it is, in fact, asserted in the *Bhakta Málá*, that the distinction of caste is inadmissible according to the tenets of the *Rámánandis*: there is no difference, they say, between the BHAGAVA'N and the *Bhakt*, or the deity and his worshipper; but BHAGAVA'N appeared in inferior forms, as a *Fish*, a *Boar*, a *Tortoise*, &c., so therefore the *Bhakt* may be born as a *Chama*, a *Kori*, a *Ch'hipi*, or any other degraded caste.

The various character of the reputed disciples of RA'MA'NAND, and a consideration of the tenets of those sects which they have founded, lead to a conclusion, that this individual, if he did not invent, gave fresh force to a very important encroachment upon the orthodox system: he, in fact, abrogated the distinction of caste amongst the religious orders, and taught, that the holy character who quitted the ties of nature and society, shook off, at the same time, all personal distinction—this seems to be the proper import of the term *Avad'huta*, which RA'MA'NAND is said to have affixed to his followers, and they were liberated from more important restraints than those of regimen and ablution: the popular character of the works of this school, corroborates this view of RA'MA'NANDA's innovation; SANKARA and RA'MA'NUJA, writing to and for the Brahmanical order alone, composed chiefly, if not solely, Sanscrit commentaries on the text of the *Védas*, or Sanscrit expositions of their peculiar doctrines, and the teachers of these opinions, whether monastic or secular, are indispensably of the Brahmanical caste— it does not appear that any works exist which are attributed to RA'MA'NAND himself, but those of his followers are written in the provincial dialects, and addressed to the capacity, as well as placed within the reach, of every class of readers, and every one of those may become a *Vairági*, and rise, in time, to be a *Guru* or *Mahant*.

We shall have occasion to speak again particularly of such of the above mentioned disciples of RA'M'ANAND, as instituted separate sects, but there are several who did not aspire to that distinction, and whose celebrity is, nevertheless, still very widely spread throughout Hindustan:

3 KABIR, 4 SUK'HA'SUR, 5 JIVA, 6 PADMA'VAT, 7 PI'PA, 8 BHAVA'NAND, 9 RAIDA'S, 10 DHANNA, 11 SEVA, 12 SURSURA. His successors, again, were somewhat different, or 1 RAGHUNA'TH, 2 ANANTA'NAND, JOGA'NAND, RA'MDA'S, SRI RANJA, and NARAHARI.

there are also several personages belonging to the sect of particular note, and we may, therefore, here pause, to extract a few of the anecdotes which the *Bhakta Málá* relates of those individuals, and which, if they do not afford much satisfactory information regarding their objects, will at least furnish some notion of the character of this popular work.

Pi'pa, the *Rajaput*, is called the Raja of *Gangaraon:* he was originally a worshipper of Devi', but abandoned her service for that of Vishnu, and repaired to Benares to put himself under the tuition of Ra'ma'nand. Having disturbed the sage at an inconvenient season, Ra'ma'nand angrily wished that he might fall into the well of his court-yard, on which Pi'pa, in the fervour of his obedience, attempted to cast himslf into it to accomplish the desire of the saint. This act was with difficulty prevented by the by-standers, and the attempt so pleased Ra'ma'nand that he immediately admitted the *Raja* amongst his disciples.

Pi'pa, after some time abandoned his earthly possessions, and accompanied by only one of his wives, named Sita', as ardent a devotee as himself, adopting a life of mendicity, accompanied Ra'ma'nand and his disciples to *Dwáraká.* Here he plunged into the sea to visit the submarine shrine of Krishna, and was affectionately received by that deity: after spending some days with him, Pi'pa returned, when the fame of the occurrence spread, and attracted great crowds to see him. Finding them incompatible with his devotions, Pi'pa left *Dwáraká* privately: on the road some Patans carried off his wife, but Ra'ma himself rescued her, and slew the ravishers. The life of this vagrant *Raja* is narrated at considerable length in the *Bhakta Málá*, and is made up of the most absurd and silly legends. On one occasion the *Raja* encounters a furious lion in a forest; he hangs a rosary round his neck, whispers the Mantra of *Ráma*, and makes him tranquil in a moment; he then lectures the lion on the impropriety of devouring men and kine, and sends him away penitent, and with a pious purpose to do so no more.

Of Sursura'nand we have a silly enough story of some cakes that were given to him by a *Mlechch'ha* being changed when in his mouth into a *Tulasi* leaf. Of Dhana, it is related that a Brahman, by way of a frolic, gave him a piece of stone, and desired him to offer to it first, whatever he was about to eat. Dhana obeyed, looking upon the stone as the representative of Vishnu, who being pleased with his devotion, appeared, and constantly tended the cattle of the simple *Ját:* at last he recommended his becoming the disciple of RA'MA'NAND, for which purpose he went to Benares, and having received the Mantra, returned to his farm. RAGHUNA'TH, or in the text ASA'NAND, succeeded RA'MA'NAND in the *Gaddi*, or the pillow of the *Mahant*. NARAHARI or HARYA'NAND was also a pupil of RA'MA'NAND, whom it is difficult to identify with any one in the list above given: we have a characteristic legend of him.

Being one day in want of fuel to dress his meat, he directed one of his pupils to proceed to a neighbouring temple of DEVI', and bring away from it any portion of the timber he could conveniently remove: this was done, to the great alarm, but utter helplessness, of the goddess, who could not dispute the authority of a mortal of HARYA'NAND's sanctity. A neighbour who had observed this transaction laboured under a like want of wood: at the instigation of his wife, he repaired also to the temple, and attempted to remove one of the beams, when the goddess, indignant at his presumption, hurled him down and broke his neck: the widow hearing of her husband's fate, immediately hastened to the temple, and liberally abused the vindictive deity. DEVI' took advantage of the business to make a bargain for her temple, and restored the man to life, on condition that he would ever afterwards buy fuel for HARYA'NAND.

The legends of such other disciples of RA'MA'NAND as occur in the *Bhakta Málá* will be given in their proper places, and it will be sufficient here to confine our further extracts from that authority to NA'BHA'JI, the author, SUR DA's, and TULASI DA's, to whose poetical talents the late version of it is largely indebted, and JAYADEVA, whose songs have been translated by Sir William Jones.

NA'BHA'JI, the author of the *Bhakta Málá*, was by birth a *Dom*, a caste whose employ is making baskets and various sort of wicker work. The early commentators say he was of the *Hanumán Bans*, or Monkey tribe, because, observes the modern interpreter, *Báner*, a monkey, signifies in the *Marwar* language, a *Dom*, and it is not proper to mention the caste of a *Vaishnava* by name: he was born blind, and when but five years old, was exposed by his parents, during a time of scarcity, to perish in the woods: in this situation he was found by AGRADA's and KI'L, two *Vaishnava* teachers: they had compassion upon his helplessness, and KI'L, sprinkled his eyes with the water of his *Kamandalu*, or water-pot, and the child saw: they carried NA'BHA'JI to their *Mat'h*, where he was brought up, and received the initiatory Mantra from AGRADAS: when arrived at maturity, he wrote the *Bhakta Málá* by desire of his *Guru*. The age of NA'BHA'JI must be about two centuries, or two and a half, as he is made cotemporary with MA'N SINH, the Raja of *Jaynagar*, and with AKBER. He should date much earlier, if one account of his spiritual descent which makes him the fourth from RA'MA'NAND* be admitted, but in the *Bhakta Málá*, KRISHNA DA's, the second in that account, does not descend in a direct line from RA'MA'NAND, but derives his qualifications as teacher from the immediate instructions of VISHNU himself: there is no necessity, therefore, to connect NA'BHA'JI with RA'MA'NAND. The same authority places him also something later, as it states that TULASI DA's, who was cotemporary with SHAH JEHAN, visited NA'BHA'JI at *Vrindavan*. It is probable, therefore, that this writer flourished at the end of AKBER's reign, and in the commencement of that of his successor.

The notices we have of SUR DA's are very brief: he was blind, a great poet, and a devout worshipper of VISHNU, in whose honour all his poems are written: they are songs and hymns of various lengths, but usually short, and the greater number are *Padas*, or simply stanzas of four lines, the first line forming a subject, which is repeated as the last and the burthen of the song, *Padas* being very generally sung, both at public entertainments, and the devotional exercises of the *Vaishnava* ascetics. SUR DA's is said to have composed 125,000 of these *Padas*: he is almost entitled to be considered as the founder of a sect, as blind beggars carrying about some musical instruments, to which they chaunt stanzas in honour of VISHNU, are generally termed *Súr Dásis*. The tomb of SUR DA's, a simple mound of earth, is considered to be situated in a tope near *Sivpur*, a village about two miles to the North of Benares. There is also an account of a saint of the same name in the *Bhakta Málá*, who is possibly a different person from the blind bard. This was a Brahman, *Amin*, or collector of the Pergunnah of *Sandíla*, in the reign of AKBER, and who with more zeal than honesty made over his collections to the shrine of MADANA MOHANA, a form of KRISHNA, at *Vrindavan*, and sent to the treasury chests filled

* 1 RA'MA'NAND, 2 ASA'NAND, 3 KRISHNA DA's, 4 KI'L and AGRADA's, 5 NA'BHA'JI. See the next division of this section.

with stones :* the minister TODER MULL, however, although a Hindu, was not disposed to confirm this transfer, and he had the defaulter arrested and thrown into prison. SUR DA'S then applied to AKBER, and the good-natured monarch, who probably thought his collector more fool than knave, set him at liberty. He retired to *Vrindaban*, and there continued to lead a religious and ascetic life.

The account of TULASI DA'S in the *Bhakta Málá*, represents him as having been incited to the peculiar adoration of RA'MA by the remonstrances of his wife, to whom he was passionately attached: he adopted a vagrant life, visited Benares, and afterwards went to *Chitrakuta*, where he had a personal interview with *Hanumán*, from whom he received his poetical inspiration, and the power of working miracles: his fame reached *Dehli*, where SHAH JEHA'N was emperor: the monarch sent for him, and desired him to produce the person of RA'MA, which TULASI DA'S refusing to do, the king threw him into confinement; the people of the vicinity, however, speedily petitioned for his liberation, as they were alarmed for their own security: myriads of monkies having collected about the prison, and begun to demolish it, and the adjacent buildings. SHAH JEHA'N set the poet at liberty, and desired him to solicit some favour as a reparation for the indignity he had suffered: TULASI DA'S, accordingly requested him to quit ancient *Dehli*, which was the abode of RA'MA, and in compliance with this request the emperor left it, and founded the new city, thence named *Sháh Jehánábád*. After this, TULASI DA'S went to *Bindraban*, where he had an interview with NA'BHA'JI: he settled there; and strenuously advocated the worship of *Sitá Ráma*, in preference to that of *Rádhá Krishna*.

Besides these legendary tales of this celebrated writer, whose works exercise more influence upon the great body of Hindu population, than the whole voluminous series of Sanscrit composition, we have other notices of him collected from his own works, or preserved by tradition, that

* He accompanied them also with the following rhyme: तेरह लाख संडीले उपजे सब सन्तन मिले गटके । सूरदास मदनमोहन आधी रात हि सटके ॥ which may be thus rendered:

The Saints have shared Sandilàs taxes,
Of which the total thirteen lacks is,
A fee for midnight service owen,
By me *Sur Dás* to *Madan Mohen*.

differ in some respects from the above. From these it appears, that TULASI DA's was a Brahman of the *Serwariah* branch, and a native of *Hájapur*, near *Chitrakuta;* when arrived at maturity, he settled at *Benares*, and held the office of *Dewan* to the *Raja* of that city: his spiritual preceptor was JAGANNA'TH DA's, a pupil, as well as NA'BHA'JI of AGRADA's: he followed this teacher to *Goverdhan*, near *Bindraban*, but afterwards returned to Benares, and there commenced his Hindi version of the *Rámáyana*, in the year of Samvat 1631, when he was thirty-one years of age—besides this work, which is highly popular, TULASI DA's is the author of a *Sat Sai*, or collection of one hundred stanzas on various subjects: of the *Rám Gunávalí*, a series of verses in praise of RA'MA, of a *Gítávali*, and *Vinaya Patriká*, poetical compositions of a devotional or moral tendency, and of a great variety of *Hymns*—as *Rágas*, *Kavits*, and *Padas*, in honour of his tutelary deity and his consort, or RA'MA and SITA'. TULASI DA's continued to reside at Benares, where he built a temple to *Sitá Ráma*, and founded a *Mat'h* adjoining, both which are still in existence: he died in the year of the *Samvat* era, 1680, or A. D. 1624, in the reign of JEHA'NGIR,* and the legendary story therefore, of his intercourse with SHAH JEHA'N, is consequently an anachronism.

JAYADEVA was an inhabitant of a village called *Kinduvilwa*, where he led an ascetic life, and was distinguished for his poetical powers, and the fervour of his devotion to VISHNU. He at first adopted a life of continence, but was subsequently induced to marry. A Brahman had dedicated his daughter to JAGANNA'TH, but on his way to the shrine of that deity was addressed by him, and desired to give the maiden to JAYADEVA, who was one with himself. The saint, who it should appear had no other shelter than the shade of a tree, was very unwilling to burthen himself with a bride; but her father disregarded his refusal, and leaving his daughter with him, departed. JAYADEVA then addressed the damsel, and asked her what she proposed to do, to which she replied; "Whilst I was in my father's house, I was obedient to his will; he has now presented me to you, and I am subject to your pleasure; if you reject me, what remains for me but to die." The saint finding there was no help,

* According to this memorial verse—

संवत सोलह सय. असी गंगाके तीर। सावण शुक्ला सत्तम तुलसी तज्यौ शरीर ॥

turned householder, and removed the image he had worshipped in the air into his dwelling, by desire, it is said, of the object of his adoration. In his new condition he composed the *Gítá Govinda*, in which KRISHNA himself assisted, for on one occasion, JAYADEVA being puzzled how to describe the charms of RA'DHA', laid down the paper for a happier moment, and went to bathe. KRISHNA, assuming his person, entered his house, and wrote the requisite description, much to the poet's astonishment on his return home.

Of the *Gítá Govinda* it is said, that the *Raja of Niláchala* (Orissa) composed a poem similarly named, but when the two works were placed before JAGANNA'TH, he took the work of JAYADEVA to his bosom, and threw that of the *Raja* out of his temple. It is also said, that the *Gítá Govinda* was sung in the court of VIKRAMA, thus assigning to it an antiquity which there is no reason to suspect it can justly claim.

JAYADEVA being desirous of performing a particular rite for his idol, resumed his erratic habits, and succeeded in collecting a considerable sum of money for this purpose : on the road, he was attacked by *Thegs*, or thieves, who robbed him, and cut off his hands and feet. In this state he was found by a *Raja*, who took him home, and had his wounds healed. Shortly afterwards the thieves, disguised as religious mendicants, came to the court of the Raja. JAYADEVA recognized them, and overwhelmed them with benefits. On their departure, two of the Raja's people were sent to attend them to the confines of the *Raj*, who on their way asked them how they had merited the saint's particular regard. To this they replied, that they had been his fellows in the service of a Raja, who had ordered them to put him to death : they however only mutilated him, and his gratitude for their sparing his life was the reason he had treated them so kindly. They had no sooner uttered these words, than the earth opened and swallowed them. The servants of the Raja returned, and reported the occurrence, when a fresh miracle took place—the hands and feet of JAYADEVA sprouted forth again. The *Raja* being filled with astonishment, requested the saint to explain these events, which he did by narrating what had befallen him.

After remaining some time with the *Raja*, where he restored to life his own wife PADMA'VATI, who had voluntarily put an end to herself, he returned to *Kinduvilwa*. Here the Ganges, which was then eighteen cos distant, and to which he went daily to bathe, requested him not to undergo so much fatigue, as she would rather come to him. The proposal was accepted by the saint, and, according to our guide, the river now runs close to the village.

The ascetic and mendicant followers of RA'MA'NAND, known indiscriminately as *Rámánandis* or *Rámáwats*, are by far the most numerous class of sectaries in Gangetic India : in Bengal they are comparatively few : beyond this province, as far as to *Allahabad*,* although perhaps the most numerous, they yield in influence and wealth to the *Saiva* branches, especially to the *Atits:* hence, however, they predominate, and either by themselves, or their kindred divisions, almost engross the whole of the country along the *Ganges* and *Jumna :* in the district of *Agra*, they alone constitute seven-tenths of the ascetic population. The *Rámánandis* have very numerous votaries, but they are chiefly from the poorer and inferior classes, with the exception of the *Rájaputs* and military *Brahmans*, amongst whom the poetical works of SUR DA's and TULASI DA's, maintain the pre-eminence of *Ráma* and his *Bhakts*.

KABIR PANT'HIS.

Amongst the twelve disciples of RA'MA'NAND, the most celebrated of all, and one who seems to have produced directly or indirectly, a greater effect on the state of popular belief than any other, was KABIR : with an unprecedented boldness he assailed the whole system of idolatrous worship, and ridiculed the learning of the *Pandits*, and doctrines of the Sastras, in a style peculiarly well suited to the genius of his countrymen to whom he addressed himself, whilst he also directed his compositions to the Musselman, as well as to the Hindu faith, and with equal severity attacked the *Mulla* and *Koran*. The effect of his lessons,

* Some of the principal Mat'hs at Benares are the following : RAMJIT, *Mahant*, a temple of RA'MA. MA'YA RAM, *Mahant*, a temple of RA'MA. RA'MA'NUJA, *Khâki*, *Mahant*, a temple of SITA' RA'M. PURUSHOTTAMA DA's, *Khâki*, *Mahant*, a temple of RA'MA. PITA'MBARA DA's, *Mahant*, *Sitá Rám ;* this is the *Mandir* of *Tulasi Dás*. GOVIND DA's, *Mahant*, *Rádhá Krishna*. RA'MACHARAN, ditto ditto.

At a late meeting (1820) to elect a *Mahant* of one of the Vaishnava *Mat'hs*, in the vicinity of Benares, about 5000 mendicants of the various branches of the sect attended ; of these, at least 3000 were *Rámáwats*, the rest were *Sri Vaishnavas*, *Kabir Pant'his*, and others.

as confined to his own immediate followers, will be shewn to have been considerable, but their indirect effect has been still greater; several of the popular sects being little more than ramifications from his stock, whilst *Nának Sháh*, the only Hindu reformer who has established a national faith, appears to have been chiefly indebted for his religious notions to his predecessor KABIR.* This sect therefore claims particular attention.

The origin of the founder of this sect is variously narrated, although in the main points, the traditions are agreed: the story told in the *Bhakta Málá*, is, that he was the son of the virgin widow of a Brahman, whose father was a follower of RA'MA'NAND: at his daughter's repeated request, he took her to see RA'MA'NAND, and that teacher, without adverting to her situation, saluted her with the benediction he thought acceptable to all women, and wished her the conception of a son: his words could not be re-called, and the young widow, in order to conceal the disgrace thus inflicted on her, contrived to be privately delivered, and exposed the child: it was found by a weaver and his wife, and brought up as their own.

The followers of KABIR do not admit more than the conclusion of this legend: according to them, the child, who was no other than the incarnate deity, was found floating on a Lotus in *Lahartaláb*, a lake, or pond near Benares, by the wife of a weaver, named NIMA', who, with her husband NURI, was attending a wedding procession; she took the

* Malcolm says, that NANAK constantly referred to the writings of the celebrated Mohammedan CABIR, (A. R. XI. 267,) and the *Kabir Pant'his* asserts, that he has incorporated several thousand passages from *Kabir's* writings. As to *Kabir's* being a Mohammedan, I shall allude to the improbability of this, I may say impossibility, in the text, nor is Col. Malcolm more accurate when he calls him a celebrated *Sufi*, for his doctrines have nothing in common apparently with that sect; indeed I think it not at all improbable that no such person as KABIR ever existed, and that his name is a mere cover to the innovations of some free-thinker amongst the Hindus: perhaps some one of those considered as his principal disciples: his names are very suspicious, and *Jnyáni*, the sage, or *Kabir*, the greatest, are generic rather than individual denominations: at any rate, even if the individual were distinct, we must suppose that the name which occurs in his writings is nothing more than the *Tak'hallus* or assumed name, under which both *Musselman* and *Hindu* poets have been accustomed to send their compositions into the world. To return, however, to the obligations which the popular religions owe to the real or supposed KABIR, I find him avowedly or unavowedly cited by *Bába Lál*, and in the writings of the *Sádhs*, the *Satnámis*, the *Sri Naráinis* and *Sunyábádis*, and I am told that the *Dádu Pant'his*, and *Derya Dásis* are equally indebted to him.

child up, and shewed it to her husband, who being addressed by the child, and desired to take him to *Kasi*, fled with terror, thinking they had got hold of some incarnate demon : after having run to the distance of about a mile, he was surprised to find the child before him, by whom his fear was tranquillised, and he was persuaded to return to his wife, and bring up, without anxiety or alarm, the infant they had so marvellously discovered.

All traditions concur in making KABIR the disciple of RA'MA'NAND, although various stories are narrated of the method by which he obtained that distinction, and overcame the objections started to him as a man of low caste, or, according to very general belief, of the Mohammedan persuasion : he succeeded at last by surprise, having put himself in the way of that teacher on the steps of the *ghát* down which he went at daybreak to bathe, so as to be struck with his foot, on which RA'MA'NAND exclaimed *Rám, Rám,* words that KABIR assumed, and RA'MA'NAND acknowledged to be the initiatory Mantra, which forms the bond of union between a *Guru* and his disciple.

The story of KABIR's being a disciple of RA'MA'NAND, however told, and, although perhaps not literally true in any fashion, may be so far correct, that KABIR was roused by the innovations of that sectary to adopt and extend the schism, and seems to place at contiguous periods the eras at which they flourished : according to the *Kabir Pant'his,* their founder was present in the world three hundred years, or from 1149 to 1449,* but of these dates we cannot admit the accuracy of more than one at most, and as the latter is the more recent, it is the more probable : agreeable to this, is the connexion of KABIR's writings with the faith of NA'NAK SHAH, who began to teach about 1490, and it also confirms a particular account, current amongst his followers, of

* सम्वत् वारहसये औ पांच मों ज्ञानी कियौ विचार। काशी मांहि प्रगट भयौ शब्द कह्यौ टकसार॥ सम्वत् पंदरहसये औ पांच मों मगरकियौ गवन। अगहन् सुदि येकादसी मिले पवन सों पवन॥ In the Sambat 1205 JNYA'NI meditated, was manifest at *Kási*, and declared the text called *Taksár* : in the Sambat 1505 he journeyed to *Magar*, and on the 11th of the light fortnight of *Aghan*, air mixed with air.

his openly vindicating his doctrines before SEKANDER SHAH,* in whose time FERISHTA has noticed, that some religious disputes, possibly connected with the history of KABIR, or that of some of his disciples, did occur.

These circumstances, connected with the acknowledged date of his death, render it exceedingly probable that *Kabir* flourished about the beginning of the 15th century; and as it is also not unlikely that his innovations were connected with the previous exertions of RA'MA'NAND, consequently that teacher must have lived about the end of the 14th.

According to one account, KABIR was originally named *Jnyáni*, the knowing or wise. The Musselmans, it is said, claim him as one of their persuasion, but his conversancy with the *Hindu Sástras*, and evidently limited knowledge of the Mohammedan authorities in matters of religion, render such a supposition perfectly unwarrantable: at any rate tradition represents it to have occasioned a contest between them and the Hindus respecting the disposal of his corpse, the latter insisting on burning, the Musselmans, on burying it; in the midst of the

* There is a *Ramaini* to that effect, and the following story is told, with the usual marvellous embellishments, in the *Bhakta Málá*; in that work it is said, his mother complained to SEKANDER *Padshah* of her son's having deserted the true faith, on which the king sent for him: he appeared with the *Tika* and *Málá*, and when told to make the customary *Salám*, he replied, "I know none but *Rám*, what use is there in prostrating myself to a monarch." Enraged at his behaviour, the king ordered him to be chained hand and foot, and thrown into the river. The water bore him to shore. He then commanded him to be cast into fire, but the flames played harmless round him. He then directed him to be trodden to death by an elephant, but as soon as the animal saw the sage, he turned tail and ran away. The king mounted his own elephant, resolved to execute his commands in person; but when he approached, KABIR transformed himself into a lion. The monarch then convinced of his divine character alighted, and falling at his feet, offered him any lands and villages he might chuse: these offers he declined, saying, "RA'M is my wealth: of what avail are worldly possessions, but to set father, and son, and brother, at deadly variance." He returned to his abode, and remained unmolested.

Colonel Malcolm in the note before cited, places him in the reign of SHIR SHAH; this is, however, at variance with his own statements; NA'NAK was in the height of his career in 1527, (A. R. XI. 206,) then imparting to BABER, tenets which he had partly borrowed from the writings of KABIR, and which must consequently have been some time *previously* promulgated: but SHIR SHAH did not commence his reign till 1542, and it was therefore impossible for KABIR to have lived in his reign, and at the same time to have instigated by his own innovations, the more successful ones of NA'NAK. KABIR's being contemporary with SEKANDER, is also mentioned in PRIYA DASA's expansion of the *Bhakta Málá*: it is likewise stated in the *Kholasset al tawárikh*, and is finally establisheded by ABULFAZL, who says that KABIR the Unitarian lived in the reign of *Sultan* SECANDER LODI, (*Ay. Ac.* 2. 38.)

dispute, KABIR himself appeared amongst them, and desiring them to look under the cloth supposed to cover his mortal remains, immediately vanished: on obeying his instructions, they found nothing under the cloth, but a heap of flowers : one half of these BAN'AR *Raja* or BIRSINHA *Raja*, then Raja of Benares, removed to that city, where they were burnt, and where he appropriated the spot now called the *Kabir Chaura*, to the reception of their ashes, whilst BIJILI KHAN *Patan*, the head of the Mohammedan party, erected a tomb over the other portion at *Magar* near *Gorakhpur*, where KABIR had died. This latter place was endowed by MANSUR ALI KHAN with several villages, and it divides with the *Chaura* the pilgrimage of the followers of this sect.

The *Kabir Pant'his* in consequence of their master having been the reputed disciple of RA'MA'NAND, and of their paying more respect to VISHNU, than the other members of the Hindu triad, are always included amongst the *Vaishnava* sects, and maintain with most of them, the *Rámáwats* especially, a friendly intercourse and political alliance : it is no part of their faith, however, to worship any Hindu deity, or to observe any of the rites or ceremonials of the Hindus, whether orthodox or schismatical; such of their members as are living in the world conform outwardly to all the usages of their tribe and caste, and some of them even pretend to worship the usual divinities, although this is considered as going rather farther than is justifiable. Those however who have abandoned the fetters of society, abstain from all the ordinary practices and address their homage, chiefly in chanting hymns, exclusively to the invisible KABIR : they use no *Mantra* nor fixed form of salutation ; they have no peculiar mode of dress, and some of them go nearly naked without objecting however to clothe themselves in order to appear dressed, where clothing is considered decent or respectful—the *Mahants* wear a small scull cap: the frontal marks, if worn, are usually those of the *Vaishnava* sects, or they make a streak with sandal, or *Gopichandan* along the ridge of the nose, a necklace and rosary of *Tulasi* are also worn by them, but all these outward signs are considered of no importance, and the inward man is the only essential point to be attended to.*

* To avoid unnecessary contention, and its probable concomitant in other days, persecution, was the object probably of the following prudent maxim, one of the

The doctrines of Kabir are taught in a great variety of works in different dialects of Hindi; they are the acknowledged compositions of his disciples and successors, but they are mostly in the form of dialogues, and profess to be of his utterance, either in his own words, with the phrase, *Kaháhi Kabir*, 'Kabir verily says,' or to the same substance, which is marked by the qualification, *Kahai Kabir*, '*Kabir* has said,' or they are given in the language of his followers, when the expression *Dás Kabir*, the slave of *Kabir*, is made use of. The style of all their works is very peculiar, they are written in the usual forms of *Hindi* verse, the *Doha*, *Choupai* and *Samai*; and are very voluminous as may be inferred from the following collection, preserved as the *Khás Grantha*, or *The Book* at the *Chaura*.

1. *Suk'h Nidhán.*
2. *Goraknát'hki Goshthí.*
3. *Kabir Pánji.*
4. *Balak'hki Ramaini.*
5. *Rámánandki Goshthí.*
6. *Anand Rám Ságara.*
7. *Sabdávalí*, containing 1000 *Sabdas*, or short doctrinal expositions.
8. *Mangala*, 100 short poems, amongst which is the account of Kabir's discovery as given above.
9. *Vasant*, 100 hymns in that *Rága*.
10. *Holi*, 200 of the songs, called *Holi*.
11. *Rék'htas*, 100 odes.
12. *Jhulanas*, 500 odes, in a different style.
13. *Kaháras*, 500 odes, in a different style.

Sák'his of their founder: सवसे छिलिये सव से मिलिये सव का लिजिये नाउं । हां जी हां जी सवसे किजिये वसे आपने गाउं ॥ "Associate and mix with all, and take the names of all; say to every one, Yes sir, yes sir. Abide in your own abode."—They do not admit that taking the names of all, implies the invocation of the illusory deities of the Hindu Pantheon, but means that they should reply as they are addressed, whether the phrase be *Bandagi*, *Dandáwat*, or *Rám Rám*: the proper salutation of an inferior to a superior amongst them, if any be particularly proper, is *Bandagi Sahib*, Service Sir; to which the latter replies, *Guru ki Dayá*, the mercy of the Lord be upon you.

14. *Hindolas*, 12 odes, in a different style. The subject of all these odes, or hymns, is always moral or religious.

15. *Bárah Mása*, the 12 months in a religious view, agreeably to KABIR's system.

16. *Chancharas* 22.

17. *Chautisas* 2 : the 34 letters of the *Nagari* alphabet, with their religious signification.

18. *Alefnámah*, the Persian alphabet, in the same manner.

19. *Ramainis*, short doctrinal or argumentative poems.

Sák'his 5000 ; these may be considered as texts, consisting of one stanza each.

20. The *Víjek*, in 654 Sections.*

There are also a variety of stanzas, called *Agams, Bánis, &c.* composing a very formidable course of study to those who wish to go deep into the doctrine of this school, and one in which the greatest proficients amongst the *Kabir Pant'his* are but imperfectly versed. A few *Sák'his*, *Sabdas* and *Rékh'tas*, with the greater portion of the *Víjek*, constituting their acquirements : these, however, they commit to memory, and quote in argument with singular readiness and happiness of application ; the *Gosht'his*, or disputations of KABIR with those opposed to him, as GORAKHNATH, RA'MA'NAND and even in spite of chronology with *Mohammed* himself, are not read till more advanced, whilst the *Suk'h Nidhán*, which is the key to the whole, and which has the singularity

* There are two *Bijeks*, however, only differing in the occasional omission of some passages and introduction of others; the longer of the two, they say, was communicated by KABIR himself to the *Raja* of Benares. I rather suspect, however, that the varieties are only those common to most Hindu Manuscripts, and that many more than two varieties are to be found. A curious Italian work on the *Kabir Pant'his*, entitled, but not accurately, *Mulapanci*, intending no doubt *Mulapant'hi*, or Radical disciple, not as rendered, *Della Radice*, is published in the third volume of the *Mines of the East* : it was found amongst the papers of the Propaganda, and is communicated by Monsignore Munter, Bishop of Zealand, in Denmark; an eminent scholar, the author of a valuable work on the Sahidic Version of the N. T. &c. It is to be presumed that it is intended to be a translation of some KABIRI work, but how correctly it deserves this character, may be questioned ; much of the phraseology of the sect is indeed closely followed, but the minute and ridiculous details of its cosmogony are, with very few exceptions, exceedingly different from those notions entertained by the followers of *Kabir*, as explained in the *Bijeks*, or *Suk'h Nidhán*. The extract published in the *Mines*, appears to be a portion, the second book, of some work, thus described " Il libro primario dei Cabiristi (Specie di riforma della gentilita,) si chiama *Satnam Kabir :* questo libro e fra le carte di Propaganda."

of being quite clear and intelligible, is only imported to those pupils whose studies are considered to approach perfection.

The author or compiler of the *Bijek* or *Vijck*, was *Bhagodas*,* one of KABIR's immediate disciples : it is the great authority amongst the *Kabir Pant'his* in general ; it is written in very harmonious verse, and with great ingenuity of illustration : its style, however, is more dogmatical than argumentative, and it rather inveighs against other systems than explains its own : in the latter respect it is, indeed, so inexplicit and obscure, that it is perhaps impossible to derive from it any satisfactory conclusion as to the real doctrines of KABIR. The followers of the *Sect* admit this obscurity, and much difference of opinion prevails amongst them in the interpretation of many passages : some of the teachers have a short work professedly written as a key to the most difficult parts, but this is in the hands of a chosen few : it is of no great value, however, as it is little less puzzling than the original, of a few passages of which the following translations will best exemplify the description thus given :

RAMAINI THE 1ST.—God, light, sound, and one woman ; from these have sprung HARI, BRAHMA', and TRIPURA'RI. Innumerable are the emblems of SIVA and BHAVA'NÍ, which they have established, but they know not their own beginning nor end : a dwelling has been prepared for them : HARI, BRAHMA', and SIVA, are the three headmen, and each has his own village : they have formed the *Khandas* and the egg of *Brahmá*, and have invented the six *Dersanas*, and ninety-six *Páshandas* : no one has ever read the *Védas* in the womb, nor has any infant been born a member of *Islam*. 'The woman,' relieved from the burthen of the embryo, adorned her person with every grace. I and you are of one blood, and one life animates us both ; from one mother is the world born : what knowledge is this that makes us separate, no one knows the varieties of this descent, and how shall one tongue declare them ; nay, should the mouth have a million of tongues, it would be incompetent to the task. *Kabir* has said, I have cried aloud from friendship to mankind ; from not knowing the name of RA'MA, the world has been swallowed up in death.

In this *Ramaini*, the first passage contains an allusion to the notions of the sect regarding the history of creation. God is called ANTER,

* Of the shorter work : it is undoubtedly the one most generally current.

Inner, that which was in all, and in which all was, meaning the first self-existent and all comprehensive being. *Jyotish* is the luminous element, in which he manifested himself, and *Sabda,* the primitive *sound* or *word* that expressed his essence—the woman, is *Máyá,* or the principle of error and delusion: the next passage relates to the impotence of the secondary gods, and the unnatural character of religious distinctions: "the *woman,*" is MA'YA' the self-born daughter of the first deity, and at once the mother and wife of BRAHMA', VISHNU, and SIVA. "*I and you, &c.*" is addressed by her to them, "*no one knows, &c.*" is an allusion to the blindness of all worldly wisdom, and the passage winds up with a word of advice, recommending the worship of RA'MA, implying the true god, agreeably to the system of KABIR.

The style of the whole *Bíjek* is of this kind: straggling allusions to the deceits of *Máyá,* to the errors of other sects, and the superiority of their own, being strung together with very little method: it will not, however, be necessary to analyse any more of the passages, and they will become clear by reference to the general view of the system, with which we shall be furnished from the *Suk'h Nidhán:* it may be sufficient here to observe, that the doctrines of *Kabir,* are said to be conveyed in four-fold language, or that of *Máyá, Atmá, Man* or intellect; and the *Védas*.

RAMAINI THE 6TH.—(*Maya's* account of the first being, and of herself.) What is his colour, form, and shape; what other person has beheld him: the *Omkára* did not witness his beginning, how then can I explain it; can you say from what root he sprang: he is neither the stars, nor sun, nor moon; he has neither father nor mother; he is neither water nor earth, nor fire, nor air: what name or description can I give of him: to him is neither day nor night, nor family nor caste; he resides on the summit of space; a spark of his substance was once manifest, of which emanation I was the bride; the bride of that being who needs no other.

SABDA THE 56TH.—To ALI and RA'MA we owe our existence, and should, therefore, shew similar tenderness to all that live: of what avail is it to shave your head, prostrate yourself on the ground, or immerse your body in the stream; whilst you shed blood you call yourself pure, and boast of virtues that you never display: of what benefit is cleaning your mouth, counting your beads, performing ablution, and bowing yourself in temples, when, whilst you mutter your prayers, or journey to *Mecca* and *Medina*, deceitfulness is in your heart. The Hindu fasts every eleventh day, the Musselman during the *Ramazan*. Who formed the remaining months and days, that you should venerate but one? If the Creator dwell in tabernacles, whose residence is the universe? Who has beheld *Ráma* seated amongst images, or found him at the shrine to which the pilgrim has directed his steps? The city of Hara is to the east, that of Ali to the west; but explore your own heart, for there are both *Ráma* and *Karím*. Who talks of the lies of the *Véds* and *Tebs*; those who understand not their essence. Behold but one in all things, it is the second that leads you astray. Every man and woman that has ever been born is of the same nature with yourself. *He*, whose is the world, and whose are the children of *Ali* and *Rám*, he is my *Guru*, he is my *Pír*.

The following *Sabda*, is peculiarly illustrative of the mystical and unintelligible style of parts of the *Bíjek*; the explanation of the terms is taken from the key above referred to, but the interpreter is, perhaps, the most unintelligible of the two.

Sabda the 69th.—Who is the (1) magistrate of this city, (2) the meat (3) is exposed, and the (4) vulture sits guarding it; the (5) rat is converted into a (6) boat, and the (7) cat is in charge of the helm; the (8) frog is asleep, and the (9) snake stands sentinel; the (10) ox bears, the (11) cow is barren, and the (12) heifer is milked thrice a day; the (13) rhinoceros is attacked by the (14) jackal: very few know the (15) station of *Kabir*. (16)

Key. 1. *Man* the pride of intellect. 2. The body. 3. The *Védas*, or scriptural writings of any sect, which teach the true nature of God. 4. The *Pandit*, or worldly expounder of divine truths. 5. *Man* or intellect. 6. A mere vehicle for the diffusion of 7. *Maya*, illusion and falsehood. 8. The *Siddha* or saint. 9. *Paraméswara*, the supreme being. 10. *Vishnu*. 11. *Máyá* or *Deví*. 12. *Paraméswara*, the supreme. 13. A holy man. 14. Intellectual or doctrinal pride. 15. The divine nature. 16. God identified with man and nature.

The *Sák'his* of *Kabir* deserve, perhaps, a more copious exemplification: they are very gradually current even amongst those not his followers, they contain much curious matter, and they have often been referred to without their character being duly understood; there are some thousands of them, of which the *Bíjek* comprehends between three and four hundred:

one hundred will be sufficient, as a specimen of the whole: they are taken with one or two exceptions, from the *Bíjek* of the *Kabir Chaura,* in the order in which they occur.

Sák'hais.

1. When man springs from the womb, he is void of every care: pass but the sixth day, and he feels the pains of separation.

2. My word is of the word: hear it, go not astray; if man wishes to know the truth, let him investigate the word.

3. My word is from the first: the word has been deposited in life; a basket has been provided for the flowers; the horse has eaten up the *ghee.*

4. My word is from the first: meditate on it every moment; you will flourish in the end like the *Joar* plant, which shews externally but beards and leaves.

5. Without hearing the word, it is utter darkness: say, whither shall any one go; without finding the gateway of the word, man will ever be astray.

6. There are many words, but take the pith of them: he who takes not the essence, saith Kabir, will live a profitless life.

7. For the sake of the word, some have died, and some have resigned dominion: he who has investigated the word, has done his work.

8. Lay in your provender, and provide your carriage; for if your food fail, and feet be weary, your life is in the hands of another.

9. Lay in provender sufficient for the road, whilst time yet serves: evening comes on; the day is flown, and nothing will be provided.

10. Now is the time to prepare, henceforth the path is difficult: the travellers all hasten to purchase where there is neither trade nor market.

11. He who knows what life is, will take the essence of his own; such as it is now, he will not possess it a second time.

12. If you know how mankind pass their lives, you will live according to your knowledge: fetch water for your own drinking, nor demand it from others and drink.

13. Why go about to offer water; there is abundance in every house: when man is really thirsty, he needs no solicitation, but will drink by force.

14. The goose (the world or life) sells pearls; a gold vessel is full of them; but with him, who knows not their value, what can be done.

15. The goose abandons the lake; the body is withered and dry: *Kabir* has called aloud, here is a path, there is a resting place!

16. The goose abandons the lake, and lodges in a water jar: *Kabir* calls aloud, repair to your village, nor demolish your habitation.

17. The goose and the paddy bird are of one colour, and frolic in the same pool; the goose extracts the milk from the water, and the paddy bird drinks the mire.

18. Why comes the feeble doe to the green pool; numerous foes lie in wait for her: how should she escape.

19. The three worlds form a cage; vice and virtue spread a net: life is the prey, and time the fowler.

20. The half of a *Sák'hi* is sufficiently arduous, if duly investigated; of what avail are the books of the *Pandit*, or incessant study.

21. Having combined the five elements, I found one offspring; now I ask the *Pandit*, whether life or the word be the greater.

22. Of the five elements, the body was formed: when the body was formed what was done: subservient to action, it is called life; but by action, life is destroyed.

23. The offspring of the five elements is called *Man*; if one element be withdrawn, the whole compound is destroyed.

24. With the five elements is the abode of a great mystery; when the body is decomposed, has any one found it; the word of the teacher is the guide.

25. Colour proceeds from colour, yet behold all are but one: of what colour then is life: think well of this.

26. Life is wakefulness: the word is like *borax*, white: who has seen the yellow drop, saith *Kabir*, that has turned the water of that colour.

27. There is a mirror in the heart; but the face is not visible in it: then only will the face be reflected there, when doubleness of heart shall disappear.

28. The dwelling of *Kabir* is on the peak of a mountain, and narrow path leads to it; an ant cannot put its foot upon it, but the pious man may drive up an ox.

29. The blind man talks of a district, which he has not seen; they are possessed of a salt pit, and offer camphor for sale.

30. The road that Sanaka and his brethren, that Brahma', Vishnu,

and Mahesa have travelled, is still traversed by mankind : what advice can I bestow.

31. The plough ascends the hill ; the horse stops in the village : the bee seeks for honey, where there are no flowers : declare the name of the plant.

32. Sandal ! restrain thy fragrance : on thy account, the wood is cut down ; the living slay the living, and regard only the dead.

33. The sandal (the soul,) is guarded by serpents, (passion ;) what can it effect ? Every hair is impregnated with venom ; where shall ambrosia enter.

34. The seizer (death,) lets not go his hold ; though his tongue and beak be scorched : where it deems a dainty, the *Chakor* devours the burning coals.

35. The *Chakor* (hill partridge,) in its passion for the moon, digests the burning coal ; Kabir declares it does not burn him, such is the fervour of his affection.

36. The village is on the top of a mountain, and so is the abode of the stout man. Choose, *Kabir*, one for your protector, who can really give you an asylum.

37. The crowd has taken the road travelled by the *Pandit : Kabir* has ascended the steep defile, where lies the abode of Ra'm.

38. What, ho ! *Kabir*, descend, together with your car and provender : your provender will fail, your feet will grow weary, and your life will be in the hands of another.

39. From the contest of swinging and being swung, no one has escaped. Gorak'h (the founder of the *Jogis*,) was stopped at the city of time : who shall be called exempt.

40. Gorak'h, enamoured as he was of Ra'ma, is dead ; his body was not burnt : (the Jogis bury the dead,) the flesh has decayed, and is turned to clay, and such rank as the *Kauravas* enjoy, does he obtain (bodily annihilation.)

41. The young camel flying from the wood, has fallen into the stream ; how shall the animal proclaim its misfortune, who shall learn it ?

42. After a search of many days, an empty shrine is raised : the camel's calf has strayed into a pit, and repents its heedlessness, when assistance is far off.

43. Kabir (mankind) has not escaped error, he is seized in various forms : without knowledge of its lord the heart will be but ashes.

44. Although not subject to fine, a heavy fine has been imposed upon the world : it has proved unprofitable : avarice has disposed of it ; the juice of the cane yields both clayed and candied sugar.

45. In the confines of the *Malaya* Mountain (where Sandal grows) the *Palás* (Butea) tree acquires fragrance ; were the *Bamboo* to grow there for ages, it would never gain perfume.

46. In the woods of the *Malaya* Mountain grow trees of every kind ; they may be called Sandal, but they yield not the Sandal of *Malaya*.

47. Walking, walking still, the feet are weary ; the city is yet far off, a tent is erected by the road side : say, who is to blame.

48. The end of the journey is sunset, but night comes on mid-way : it is from the embrace of many lovers that the wanton is barren.

49. *Man* (the pride of intellect) enquires, when may I be allowed to go ; the heart asks when shall I go : the village (truth) that I have been these six months in quest of (investigating in the six Dersanas, or systems), is not half a mile remote.

50. He has left his dwelling as an ascetic, and goes to the thickets to practise penance : tired of the *Pan*-box, he beats the betle-vender, and eats split pease.

51. When a man (intending, however, here a *Jogi*) becomes acquainted with the name of Ra'm, his body becomes a mere skeleton ; his eyes taste no repose ; his limbs retain no flesh.

52. He who sows Ra'm, never puts forth the buds of wrath : he attaches no value to the valueless ; he knows neither pleasure nor pain.

53. The cut mango will not blossom, the slit ear cannot be reunited ; whose loss is it, if they apply not the philosopher's stone, that Gorak'h had.

54. They have not regarded good advice, but have determined for themselves. *Kabir* says and cries aloud, the world has passed away like a dream.

55. When fire (evil) burns amidst the ocean, (the world) no one sees the smoke : he is conscious of the fire who lighted it, and he who perishes in the flame.

56. The incendiary orders the fire to be kindled, and he who lights

it singes his wings: he expiates his own act: the thatch escapes, but the house is burned.

57. When fire (truth) burns in the ocean (the mind), as it burns, it clears away the rubbish (worldly care). *Pandits* from the east and from the west have died in the discussion.

58. When fire blazes in the ocean, the thatch of the house falls to pieces. Mankind weep as they resign their breath, and the inestimable jewel is lost.

59. That a drop falls into the ocean, all can perceive; but that the drop and the ocean are but one, few can comprehend.

60. The poison still remains in the soil, although the latter has been a hundred times sprinkled with ambrosia—man quits not the evil practices to which he has been long addicted.

61. The bellows is applied to the damp wood, which calls aloud with pain: if again it is caught in the blacksmith's forge, it will be burned the second time.

62. The soul that pines in absence, vainly flies to medicaments for relief; sigh follows sigh: it faints repeatedly and recovers, to exist, restless and distressed.

63. The separated (spirit) is like the moist fuel which smokes and blazes by fits: then only will it be exempted from pain, when all is utterly consumed.

64. An invitation has been issued in metre, and no one has understood the stanza; fortunate is the scholar who comprehends the word.

65. Take the true word of *Kabir* to your heart; the mind has received, but not understood it, although it has been divulged throughout the four ages.

66. If you are a true dealer, open the market of veracity; keep clean your inward man, and repel oppression to a distance.

67. The house is of wood, fire is all around it; the *Pandit*, with his learning is burnt: the prudent man makes his escape.

68. Drops fall from heaven on the verdure of *Srávan*: all the world are *Vaishnavas*, no one listens to the teacher.

69. The bather dives nor comes up again; I think within myself, should sleep surprise him in the stream of fascination, what will befall him.

70. The *Sákhi* (text) is uttered, but not obeyed; the road is pointed

out, but not followed: the stream of fascination sweeps him away; he finds no place to put his feet.

71. Many there are that talk, but few that take care to be found: let him pass on without regard, who practices not what he professes.

72. One by one, let each be considered, and adhered to, so shall error be stopped: he who is double-faced like a drum, shall be slapped (like a drum) on both cheeks.

73. He who has no check upon his tongue, has no truth in his heart; keep him not company: he will kill you on the highway.

74. Life has been destroyed by the repeated falsehoods of the tongue; it has strayed the path of pride, and been whirled in the swing of time.

75. Put a check upon the tongue; speak not much: associate with the wise; investigate the words of the teacher.

76. The body is wounded by a spear, the head is broken off, and left in the flesh; it cannot be extracted without the loadstone: a thousand other stones are of no avail.

77. At first the ascent is difficult, but afterwards the way is easy; the beauty is behind the curtain, far from the pregnant woman.

78. Worldly existence is the season for reflecting what is the *Yoga:* the season is passing away; think, ye, who have understanding.

79. Doubt has overcome the world, and no one has triumphed over doubt: he will refute doubt, who has investigated the word.

80. The eyes see dimly from incessant babbling. *Kabir* cries aloud, and says, understand the word that is spoken.

81. Life is the philosopher's stone, the world is of iron: *Pársí (Máyá,)* comes from *Páras* (God,) the mintage is of the former.

82. Affection is the garment in which man dresses for the dance: consign yourself hand and foot to him, whose body and soul are truth.

83. In the concavity of the mirror, the image is formed: the dog seeing his likeness, barks at it till he dies.

84. But as a man viewing his reflexion in a mirror, knows that it and the original are but one, so should he know that *this* element is but *that* element, and that thus the world proceeds.

85. Kabir cries aloud to his fellows, ascend the sandal ridge; whether there be a road prepared or not, what matters it to me.

86. Truth, provided there be truth in the heart, is the best of all; there can be no happiness without truth, let man do as he will.

87 Let truth be your rate of interest, and fix it in your heart, a real diamond should be purchased, the mock gem is waste of capital.

88. Truth is the best of all, if it be known for truth—when truth combines with truth, then a real union is effected.

89. No act of devotion can equal truth, no crime is so heinous as falsehood: in the heart where truth abides, there is my abode.

90. The net of error catches the heron; the simpleton falls into the snare: KABIR declares, that *he* will escape the toils, who has discrimination in his heart.

91. Like the harlot companion of the minstrel is life, (*Jiv*) associated with intellect, (*Man*) at his command, she dances various steps, and is never separated from him.

92. This pride of intellect is manifold, now a swindler, now a thief, now a liar, now a murderer: men, sages, gods, have run after it in vain: its mansion has a hundred gates.

93. The snake of separation has attached itself to the body, and darted its fangs into the heart: into the body of the *Sád'h*, it finds no admission: prepare yourself for what may happen.

94. How is it possible to reach the city when the guide cannot point out the road: when the boat is crazy, how shall the passengers get clear of the *ghát*.

95. When the master is blind, what is to become of the scholar: when the blind leads the blind, both will fall into the well.

96. Yet the master is helpless when the scholar is unapt: it is blowing through a *bambu*, to teach wisdom to the dull.

97 The instruction of the foolish is waste of knowledge; a *maund* of soap cannot wash charcoal white.

98. The tree bears not fruit for itself, nor for itself does the stream collect its waters: for the benefit of others alone, does the sage assume a bodily shape.

99. I have wept for mankind, but no one has wept with me, *he* will join my tears, who comprehends the word.

100. All have exclaimed, master, master, but to me this doubt arises; how can they sit down with the master, whom they do not know.

The preceding will serve as exemplifications of the compositions of this school: they are necessarily unsatisfactory, as amongst some hundreds of similar passages, the business of selection, when confined to the few admissible in this place, is unavoidably perplexing and incomplete: they are, however, sufficient for the present purpose, as the perusal of the entire work from which they have been selected, would not convey any more positive notions of the doctrines of *Kabir:* these we shall now proceed to state according to the authority of the *Suk'h Nidhán.*

The *Suk'h Nidhán* is supposed to be addressed by *Kabir* himself to *Dhermadás* his chief pupil, and follower of *Rámánand's* doctrines, it is said to be the work of SRUTGOPAL, the first of KABIR's disciples.

From this authority it appears, that although the *Kabir Pant'his* have withdrawn, in such a very essential point as worship, from the Hindu communion, they still preserve abundant vestiges of their primitive source, and that their notions are in substance the same as those of the Pauranic sects, especially of the Vaishnava division. They admit of but one God, the creator of the world; and in opposition to the *Vedánta* notions of the absence of every quality and form, they assert that he has body, formed of the five elements of matter, and that he has mind endowed with the three *Gunas,* or qualities of being; of course of ineffable purity and irresistible power: he is free from the defects of human natures, and can assume what particular shape he will: in all other respects he does not differ from man, and the *pure* man, the Sádh of the *Kabir* sect, is his living resemblance, and after death is his associate and equal; he is eternal, without end or beginning, as in fact is the elementary matter of which he consists, and of which all things are made residing in him before they took their present form, as the parts of the tree abide in the seed, or flesh, blood and bone, may be considered to be present in the seminal fluid: from the latter circumstance, and the identity of their essential nature, proceeds the doctrine, that God and man are not only the same, but that they are both in the same manner, every thing that lives and moves and has its being: other sects have adopted these phrases literally, but the followers of *Kabir* do not mean by them to deny the individuality of being, and only intend these texts as assertions of all nature originally participating in common elementary principles.

The *Paramapurusha* was alone for seventy-two ages, for after the *Pauraniks* the *Kabir Pant'his* maintain successive and endless creations: he then felt a desire to renew the world, which desire became manifest in a female form,* being the *Máyá*, from whom all the mistaken notions current amongst mankind originate: with this female the *Adi Bhaváni*, *Prakriti* or *Sakti*, the *Parama Purusha*, or first male, cohabits, and begets the Hindu triad, *Brahma, Vishnu* and *Siva:* he then disappears, and the lady makes advances to her own sons: to their questions of her origin and character, she tells them, she was the bride of the first great invisible being, without shape and void, and whom she describes agreeably to the *Vedánta* notions; that she is now at liberty, and being of the same nature as themselves, is a fit associate for them: the deities hesitate, and *Vishnu*, especially putting some rather puzzling queries to *Máyá*, secured the respect of the *Kabir Pant'his*, and excited the wrath of the goddess: she appears as *Maha Máyá*, or *Durgá*, and frightens her sons into a forgetfulness of their real character, an assent to her doctrines, and compliance with her desires: the result of this, is the birth of *Saraswatí, Lakshmí* and *Umá*, whom she weds to the three deities, and then establishing herself at *Jwálamuk'hí*, leaves the three wedded pairs to frame the universe, and give currency to the different errors of practice and belief which they have learnt from her.

It is to the falsehood of *Máyá* and her criminal conduct that the *Kabir Pant'his* perpetually allude in their works, and in consequence of the deities pinning their faith upon her sleeve, that they refuse them any sort of reverential homage: the essence of all religion is to know *Kabir* in his real form, a knowledge which those deities and their worshippers, as well as the followers of Mohammed, are all equally strange to, although the object of their religion, and of all religions is the same.

Life is the same in all beings, and when free from the vices and defects of humanity assumes any material form it pleases: as long as it is ignorant of its source and parent, however, it is doomed to transmigration through various forms, and amongst others we have a new class of them, for it animates the planetary bodies, undergoing a fresh transfer, it is supposed, whenever a star or meteor falls: as to heaven and hell, they are the inventions of *Máyá*, and are therefore both ima-

* These notions are common to the whole Hindu system—diversified according to the favourite object of worship, but essentially the same in all sects; we shall have occasion to discuss them more fully under the division *Sáktas*, or worshippers of SAKTI.

ginary, except that the *Swerga* of the Hindus, and *Bihisht* of the Musselmans, imply worldly luxury and sensual enjoyment, whilst the *Narak* and *Jehannam* are those cares and pains which make a hell upon earth.

The moral code of the *Kabir Pant'his* is short, but if observed faithfully is of a rather favourable tendency. Life is the gift of God, and must not therefore be violated by his creatures. *Humanity* is, consequently, a cardinal virtue, and the shedding of blood whether of man or animal, a heinous crime. *Truth* is the other great principle of their code, as all the ills of the world, and ignorance of God, are attributable to original falsehood. *Retirement* from the world is desirable, because the passions and desires, the hopes and fears which the social state engenders, are all hostile to tranquillity and purity of spirit, and prevent that undisturbed meditation on man and God which is necessary to their comprehension. The last great point is the usual sum and substance of every sect amongst the Hindus,* implicit devotion in word, act, and thought to the *Guru*, or spiritual guide: in this, however, the characteristic spirit of the *Kabir Pant'his* appears, and the pupil is enjoined to scrutinize his teacher's doctrines and acts, and to be first satisfied that he is the sage he pretends to be, before he resigns himself to his controul. This sect, indeed, is remarkably liberal in this respect, and the most frequently recurring texts of *Kabir* are those which enforce an attentive examination of the doctrine, that he offers to his disciples. The chief of each community has absolute authority over his dependants: the only punishments he can award, however, are moral, not physical —irregular conduct is visited by reproof and admonition: if the offender does not reform, the *Guru* refuses to receive his salutation; if still incurable, the only further infliction is expulsion from the fraternity.

The doctrine of outward conformity, and the absence of visible objects of worship have prevented this sect from spreading very generally

* The *Bhágavat* declares the Deity and *Guru* to be the same. आचार्य्यं मां विजानीयान्नावमन्येत कर्हिचित्। नमर्त्यबु ास्सूयेत सर्व्वदेवमयोगुरुः॥ NA'BHA'JI declares the Deity, *Guru*, worshipper, and worship, to be four names and one substance. भक्तिभक्तभगवंत गुरु चतुर्नाम वपु ऐक॥

throughout India : it is, however, very widely diffused, and as I have observed, has given rise to many others, that have borrowed its phraseology, and caught a considerable portion of its spirit : the sect itself is split into a variety of subdivisions, and there are no fewer than twelve branches of it traced up to the founder, between which a difference of opinion, as well as descent prevails : the founders of these twelve branches, and the position of their descendants, are the following :—

1. SRUTGOPAL DA'S, the author of the *Suk'h Nidhán :* his successors preside over the *Chaura* at *Benares,* the *Samádh* at *Magar,* an establishment at *Jagannát'h,* and one at *Dwáraká.*

2. *Bhago Dás,* the author of the *Bíjek ;* his successors reside at *Dhancuti.*

3. *Narayan Dás,* and

4. *Churáman Dás :* these two were the sons of DHERMA DA'S, a merchant of the *Kasaundhya* tribe, of the *Sri Vaishnava* sect, and one of *Kabir's* first and most important converts ; his residence was at *Bandho* near *Jabbelpur,* where the *Mat'hs* of his posterity long remained : the *Mahants* were family men, thence termed *Bans Gurus :* the line of NA'RA'YAN DA'S is extinct, and the present successor of *Churáman,* being the son of a concubine, is not acknowledged as a *Mahant* by all the other branches.

5. *Jaggo Dás,* the Gaddi or Pillow at Cuttack.

6. *Jivan Dás,* the founder of the *Setnámi* sect, to whom we shall again have occasion to advert.

7. *Kamál.*—Bombay : the followers of this teacher practise the *Yoga.* *Kamal* himself, is said to have been the son of *Kabir,* but the only authority for this is a popular and proverbial phrase.*

8. *Tak Sáli.*—Baroda.

9. *Jnyáni.*—Majjhni near Sahasram.

10. *Saheb Dás.*—Cuttack : his followers have also some distinct notions, and form a sect called *Múla Pant'his.*

11. *Nityánand.*

* डुवा वंश कवीर का जोउपजा पुत कमाल ॥ "The race of *Kabir* became extinct when his son KAMA'L was born," KAMA'L adopting, on principle, a life of celibacy, or being a person of worldly appetites.—ROEBUCK's *Proverbs*, 2. 1. 656.

12. *Kamal Nád:* these two settled somewhere in the Dekhin, but my informant could not tell me exactly where. There are also some popular, and perhaps local distinctions of the sect, as *Hansa Kabiris, Dána Kabiris*, and *Mangréla Kabiris*, but in what respect, except appellation, they differ from the rest has not been ascertained.

Of these establishments the *Kabir Chaura*, at Benares, is pre-eminent in dignity, and it is constantly visited by wandering members of the sect, as well as by those of other kindred heresies: its Mahant receives and feeds these visitors whilst they stay, although the establishment has little to depend upon, except the occasional donations of its lay friends and followers. Balwant Sinh, and his successor, Cheit Sinh, were great patrons of it, and the latter granted to the *Chaura* a fixed monthly allowance. Cheit Sinh also attempted to form some estimate of the numbers of the sect, and if we may credit the result, they must be very considerable indeed, as at a grand meeting, or *Mela*, which he instituted near Benares, no fewer than 35,000 *Kabir Pant'his* of the Monastic and Mendicant class are said to have been collected. There is no doubt that the *Kabir Pant'his*, both clerical and lay, are very numerous in all the provinces of Upper and Central India, except, perhaps, in Bengal itself: the quaker-like spirit of the sect, their abhorrence of all violence, their regard for truth, and the inobtrusiveness of their opinions, render them very inoffensive members of the state: their mendicants also never solicit alms, and in this capacity even they are less obnoxious than the many religious vagrants, whom the rank soil of Hindu superstition and enervating operation of an Indian climate so plentifully engender.

KHAKIS.

This division of the *Vaishnavas* is generally derived, though not immediately, from Ra'ma'nand, and is undoubtedly connected in its polity, and practice, with his peculiar followers. The reputed founder is Ki'l, the disciple of Krishnada's, whom some accounts make the disciple of Asa'nand, the disciple of Ra'ma'nand; but the history of the *Khâki* sect is not well known, and it seems to be of modern origin, as no notice of it occurs in the *Bhakta Málá*, or in any other work that has been consulted: the sectaries, though believed to be rather numerous, appear to be either confined to a few particular districts, or to lead wholly an erratic life, in which latter character they are confounded with the class of *Bairágis:* as no written accounts have been procured, and the opportunities of obtaining oral information have been rare and imperfect, a very brief notice of this sect is all that can here be offered.

The *Khákis*, as the name implies, are distinguished from the other *Vaishnavas*, by the application of clay and ashes to their dress or persons: those who reside in fixed establishments generally dress like other *Vaishnavas*, but those who lead a wandering life, go either naked or nearly so, smearing their bodies with the pale grey mixture of ashes and earth, and making, in this state, an appearance very incompatible with the mild and decent character of the *Vaishnava* sects: the *Khákis* also frequently wear the *Jatá*, or braided hair, after the fashion of the votaries of *Siva*, and, in fact, it appears that this sect affords one of the many instances of the imitative spirit common amongst the Hindu polytheists, and has adopted, from the *Saivas*, some of their characteristic practices, blending them with the preferential adoration of Vishnu, as *Raghunáth* or *Ráma:* the *Khákis* also worship Sita', and pay particular veneration to Hanuma'n.

Many *Khákis* are established about Farakhabad, but their principal seat on this side of India is at *Hanuman Gérh*, near *Ayudhya*, in Oude: the *Samádh* or spiritual throne of the founder, is said to be at *Jaypur:* the term *Samádh* applied to it, however, would seem to indicate their adopting a like practice with the *Jogis*, that of burying their dead, as the word is more generally used to express a tomb or mausoleum.*

MALUK DASIS.

The *Maluk Dásis* form another subdivision of the *Rámánandi Vaishnavas*, of comparatively uncertain origin and limited importance: they

* The little information given in the text, was obtained from the Superior of a small, but neat establishment on the bank of the river, above *Bisránta Ghát*, at

are generally traced from *Rámánand* in this manner: 1, *Rámánand*. 2, *Asánand*. 3, *Krishna Dás*. 4, *Kil*. 5, *Malúk Dás*; making the last, consequently, contemporary with the author of the *Bhakta Málá*, and placing him in the reign of AKBER, or about 250 years ago.

We had occasion, in the notice taken of NA'BHA'JI, to shew that the spiritual genealogy now enumerated could scarcely be correct, for as RA'MA'NAND must have flourished prior to the year 1400, we have but three generations between him and the date even of AKBER's succession 1555, or a century and a half: it was then mentioned, however, that according to the *Bhakta Málá*, KRISHNA DA's was not the pupil of ASA'NAND, and consequently the date of succession was not necessarily uninterrupted: we might therefore place MALU'K DA's where there is reason to place NA'BHA'JI, about the end of AKBER's reign, as far as this genealogy is to be depended upon, but there is reason to question even its accuracy, and to bring down MALU'K DA's to a comparatively recent period: the uniform belief of his followers is indeed sufficient testimony on this head, and they are invariably agreed in making him contemporary with AURENGZEB.

The modifications of the *Vaishnava* doctrines introduced by MALU'K DA's, appear to have been little more than the name of the teacher, and a shorter streak of red upon the forehead: in one respect indeed there is an important distinction between these and the *Rámánandi* ascetics, and the teachers of the *Malúk Dásis* appear to be of the secular order, *Grihasthas*, or house-holders, whilst the others are all cœnobites: the doctrines, however, are essentially the same: VISHNU, as RA'MA, is the object of their practical adoration, and their principles partake of the spirit of quietism, which pervades these sects: their chief authority is the *Bhagavat Gita*, and they read some small Sanscrit tracts, containing the praise of *Ráma*: they have also some Hindi *Sák'his*, and *Vishnu Padas* attributed to their founder as also a work in the same language, entitled the *Dasratan*: the followers of this sect are said to be numerous

Farakhabad. The *Ghát* and *Mat'h* had been recently erected by a merchant of Lucknow: the tenants, three or four in number, were a deputation from *Ayudhya*, in Oude, and were but little acquainted with their own peculiarities, although not reluctant to communicate what they knew; other *K'hakis* encountered here were *Nágas* and *Brahmacharis*, with whom no satisfactory communication was attainable; there were other establishments, but time did not permit their being visited.

in particular districts, especially amongst the trading and servile classes, to the former of which the founder belonged.*

The principal establishment of the *Malúk Dásis* is at *Kara Manikpur*, the birth-place of the founder, and still occupied by his descendants;† the present *Mahant* is the eighth in descent from him: the series is thus enumerated.

1, Malu'k Da's. 2, Ra'msana'hi. 3, Krishnasna'hi. 4, Thakur Da's. 5, Gopa'l Da's. 6, Kunj Beha'ri. 7, Ramsa'hu'. 8, Seopresa'd Da's. 9, Ganga' Presa'd Da's, the present *Mahant*.

The *Mat'h* at *Kara* is situated near the river, and comprises the dwellings of the *Mahant*, and at the time it was visited, of fifteen resident *Chelas*, or disciples, accommodations for numerous religious mendicants who come hither in pilgrimage, and a temple dedicated to *Rámachandra:* the *Gaddi*, or pillow of the sect, is here, and the actual pillow originally used by Malu'k Da's, is said to be still preserved. Besides this establishment, there are six other *Mat'hs* belonging to this sect, at *Allahabad, Benares, Bindraban, Ayudhya, Lucknow*, which is modern, having been founded by *Gomati Das*, under the patronage of *Asef al Daula*, and *Jagannáth*, which last is of great repute as rendered sacred by the death of Malu'k Da's.

DADU PANT'HIS.

This class is one of the indirect ramifications of the *Rámánandi* stock, and is always included amongst the *Vaishnava* schisms: its

* A verse attributed to Malu'k Da's is so generally current, as to have become proverbial, it is unnecessary to point out its resemblance to Christian texts
अजगर करे न चाकरी पंछी करे न काम। दास मलूका यों कहे सब का दाता राम ॥ The snake performs no service, the bird discharges no duty. Malu'k Da's declares, Ra'm is the giver of all.

† There is some variety in the accounts here, Mat'hura Na'th says, the *Tomb* is at *Kara*; *Purán Dás* asserts, that it is at *Jagannáth*, and the birth-place at *Kara* —he has been at both: the establishment at *Jagannáth* is of great repute; it is near to a *Mat'h* of Kabir Pant'his, and all ascetics who go to this place of pilgrimage, consider it essential to receive the *Malúk Dás ka Tukra*, from the one, and *Kabír ka Tarani*, from the other, or a piece of bread and a spoonful of sour rice-water. This and most of the other particulars, were procured for me from the present *Mahant*, by a young officer, Lieut. Wilton, stationed for a short time at *Kara*.

founder is said to have been a pupil of one of the *Kabir Pant'hi* teachers, and to be the fifth in descent from RA'MA'NAND, according to the following genealogy :—

1.	*Kabir.*	4.	*Bimal.*
2.	*Kamál.*	5.	*Buddhan.*
3.	*Jamál.*	6.	*Dádu.*

The worship is addressed *to Ráma*, but it is restricted to the *Japa*, or repetition of his name, and the *Ráma* intended is the deity, negatively described in the *Vedánta* theology : temples and images are prohibited.

Dádu was a cotton cleaner by profession : he was born at *Ahmedabad*, but in his twelfth year removed to *Sambher*, in Ajmer : he thence travelled to *Kalyánpur*, and next removed to *Naraina*, in his thirty seventh year, a place four cos from *Sambher*, and twenty from *Jaypur*. When here, he was admonished, by a voice from heaven, to addict himself to a religious life, and he accordingly retired to *Baherana* mountain, five cos from *Naraina*, where, after some time, he disappeared, and no traces of him could be found. His followers believe he was absorbed into the deity. If the list of his religious descent be accurate, he flourished about the year 1600, at the end of *Akber's* reign, or in the beginning of that of *Jehangir*. The followers of *Dádu* wear no peculiar frontal mark nor *Málá*, but carry a rosary, and are further distinguished by a peculiar sort of cap, a round white cap, according to some, but according to others, one with four corners, and a flap hanging down behind ; which it is essential that each man should manufacture for himself.

The *Dádu Pant'his* are of three classes : the *Viraktas*, who are religious characters, who go bare-headed, and have but one garment and one water-pot. The *Nagas*, who carry arms, which they are willing to exercise for hire, and, amongst the Hindu princes, they have been considered as good soldiers. The third class is that of the *Bister Dháris*, who follow the occupations of ordinary life. A further subdivision exists in this sect, and the chief branches again form fifty-two divisions, or *Thambas*, the peculiarities of which have not been ascertained. The *Dádu Pant'his* burn their dead at dawn, but their religious members not unfrequently enjoin, that their bodies, after death, shall be thrown into some field, or some wilderness, to be devoured by the beasts and birds of prey, as they say, that in a funeral pile insect life is apt to be destroyed.

The *Dádu Pant'his* are said to be very numerous in *Marwar* and *Ajmer:* of the *Nága* class alone, the Raja of *Jaypur* is reported to entertain as soldiers more than ten thousand: the chief place of worship is at *Naraina,* where the bed of *Dádu,* and the collection of the texts of the sect are preserved and worshipped: a small building on the hill, marks the place of his disappearance—a *Mela,* or fair, is held annually, from the day of new moon to that of full moon in Phalgun, (Feb.-March) at *Naraina.* The tenets of the sect are contained in several *Bhásha* works, in which it is said a vast number of passages from the *Kabir* writings are inserted, and the general character of which is certainly of a similar nature.* The *Dádu Pant'his* maintain a friendly intercourse with the followers of Kabir, and are frequent visitors at the *Chaura.*

RAI DASIS.

Ra'i Da's was another of Ra'ma'nand's disciples, who founded a sect, confined, however, it is said, to those of his own caste, the *Chamars,* or workers in hides and in leather, and amongst the very lowest of the Hindu mixed tribes: the circumstance renders it difficult, if not impossible to ascertain whether the sect still exists: the founder must once have enjoyed some celebrity, as some of his works are included in the *Adi Grant'h* of the Sikhs; he is there named Ra'bi Da'sa, which is the Sanscrit form of his name: some of his compositions also form part of the collection of hymns and prayers used by that sect at Benares: there appears to be but little known of him of any authentic character, and we must be contented with the authority of the *Bhakta*

* I had prepared a list of the contents of one of their manuals, and a translation of a few passages, but the Manuscript has been mislaid. The work was lent me for a short time by one of the sect, who would on no account part with it. The above notice was taken partly from a statement in Hindi procured at *Naraina* by Lieut. Colonel Smith, and partly from verbal information obtained at Benares. *Dádu* is not mentioned in the *Bhakta Málá,* but there is some account of him in the *Dabistan.*

Málá, where he makes a rather important figure : the legend is as follows :—

One of RA'MA'NAND's pupils was a *Brahmáchári,* whose daily duty it was to provide the offering presented to the deity : on one of these occasions, the offering consisted of grain, which the pupil had received as alms from a shop-keeper, who supplied chiefly the butchers with articles of food, and his donation was, consequently, impure : when RA'MA'NAND, in the course of his devotions, attempted to fix his mind upon the divinity, he found the task impracticable, and suspecting that some defect in the offering occasioned such an erratic imagination, he enquired whence it had been obtained : on being informed, he exclaimed, *Há Chamár*, and the *Brahmáchári* soon afterwards dying, was born again as RAI DA's, the son of a worker in hides and leather.

The infant RAI DA's retained the impression left upon his mind by his old master's anger, and refused to take any nourishment : the parents, in great affliction, applied to RA'MA'NAND, who, by order of the deity, visited the child, and recognising the person at once, whispered into his ear the initiating *Mantra :* the effect was instantaneous : the child immediately accepted the breast, and throve, and grew up a pious votary of RA'MA.

For some time the profits of his trade maintained RAI DA's, and left him something to divide amongst the devout ; but a season of scarcity supervening, reduced him to great distress, when *Bhagaván*, in the semblance of a *Vaishnava,* brought him a piece of the philosopher's stone, and shewing him its virtue, made him a present of it. RAI DA's paid little regard to the donation, replying to the effect of the following *Pada,* as since versified by *Súr Dás.*

Pada. " A great treasure is the name of HARI to his people : it multiplieth day by day, nor doth expenditure diminish it : it abideth securely in the mansion, and neither by night nor by day, can any thief steal it. The Lord is the wealth of *Súr Dás*, what need hath he of a stone."

The miraculous stone was thrown aside, and when, thirteen months afterwards, *Vishnu* again visited his votary, he found no use had been made of it : as this expedient had failed, the deity scattered gold coin in places where RAI DA's could not avoid finding it : the discovery of this treasure filled the poor Currier with alarm, to pacify which *Krishna* appeared to him in a dream, and desired him to apply the money cither to his own use or that of the deity, and thus authorised, RAI DA's erected a temple, of which he constituted himself the high priest, and acquired great celebrity in his new character.

The reputation of RAI DA's was further extended by its attracting a persecution, purposely excited by *Vishnu* to do honour to his worshipper, the deity well knowing that the enmity of the malignant is the most effective instrument for setting open to the world, the retired glory of the pious: he therefore inspired the Brahmans to complain thus to the king.

Sloka (Sanscrit stanza). "Where things profane are reverenced, where sacred things are profanely administered, there three calamities will be felt, famine, death, and fear."

A *Chamár*, oh king, ministers to the *Sálagrám*, and poisons the town with his *Prasád*;* men and women, every one will become an outcast; banish him to preserve the honour of your people.

The king accordingly sent for the culprit, and ordered him to resign the sacred stone. RAI DA's expressed his readiness to do so, and only requested the *Raja's* presence at his delivery of it to the *Brahmans*, as, he said, if after being given to them it should return to him, they would accuse him of stealing it. The *Raja* assenting, the *Sálagrám* was brought, and placed on a cushion in the assembly. The Brahmans were desired to remove it, but attempted to take it away in vain: they repeated hymns and charms, and read the *Védas*, but the stone was immoveable. RAI DA's then addressed it with this *Pada*:—

Pada. "Lord of lords, thou art my refuge, the root of Supreme happiness art thou, to whom there is none equal: behold me at thy feet: in various wombs have I abided, and from the fear of death have I not been delivered. I have been plunged in the deceits of sense, of passion, and illusion; but now let my trust in thy name dispel apprehension of the future, and teach me to place no reliance on what the world deems virtue. Accept, oh God, the devotions of thy slave RAI DA's, and be thou glorified as the Purifier of the sinful.

The saint had scarcely finished, when the *Sálagrám* and cushion flew into his arms, and the king, satisfied of his holy pretensions, command-

* The *Prasad* is any article of food that has been consecrated by previous presentation to an Idol after which it is distributed amongst the worshippers on the spot, or sent to persons of consequence at their own houses.

ed the Brahmans to desist from their opposition. Amongst the disciples of RAI DA's was JHALI, the *Rani* of Chitore: her adopting a *Chamár*, as her spiritual preceptor, excited a general commotion amongst the Brahmans of her state, and, alarmed for her personal safety, she wrote to RAI DA's to request his counsel and aid. He repaired to her, and desired her to invite the Brahmans to a solemn feast: they accepted the invitation, and sat down to the meal provided for them, when between every two Brahmans, there appeared a RAI DA's. This miraculous multiplication of himself had the desired effect, and from being his enemies and revilers, they became his disciples.

Such are the legends of *Bhakta Málá*, and whatever we may think of their veracity, their tenor, representing an individual of the most abject class, an absolute outcast in Hindu estimation, as a teacher and a saint, is not without interest and instruction.

SENA PANT'HIS.

SENA', the barber, was the third of *Rámánand's* disciples, who established a separate schism; the name of which, and of its founder, are possibly all that now remain of it. SENA' and his descendants were, for sometime, however, the family *Gurus* of the Rajas of *Bandhogerh*, and thence enjoyed considerable authority and reputation: the origin of this connexion is the subject of a ludicrous legend in the *Bhakta Málá*.

SENA', the barber of the Raja of *Bandhogerh*, was a devout worshipper of VISHNU, and a constant frequenter of the meetings of the pious: on one of these occasions, he suffered the time to pass unheeded, when he ought to have been officiating in his tonsosial capacity, and VISHNU, who noticed the circumstance, and knew the cause, was alarmed for his votary's personal integrity. The god, therefore, charitably assumed the figure of SENA', and equipping himself suitably, waited on the Raja, and performed the functions of the barber, much to the Raja's satisfaction, and without detection, although, the prince perceived an unusual fragrance about his barber's person, the ambrosial odour that indicated present deity, which he supposed to impregnate the oil used in lubricating his royal limbs. The pretended barber had scarcely departed, when the real one appeared, and stammered out his excuses: his astonishment and the Raja's were alike, but the discernment of the latter was more acute, for he immediately comprehended the whole business, fell at his barber's feet, and elected for his spiritual guide, an individual so pre-eminently distinguished by the favour and protection of the deity.

RUDRA SAMPRADAYIS, OR
Vallabhácháris.

The sects of *Vaishnavas* we have hitherto noticed, are chiefly confined to professed ascetics, and to a few families originally from the South and West of India, or as in the case of the *Rámáwats* and *Kabir Pant'his*, to such amongst the mass of society, as are of a bold and curious spirit; but the opulent and luxurious amongst the men, and by far the greater portion of the women, attach themselves to the worship of Krishna and his mistress Ra'dha', either singly, or conjointly, as in the case of Vishnu and Lakshmi, amongst the *Ramánujas*, and Sita' and Ra'm, amongst the *Rámáwats*. There is, however, another form, which is perhaps more popular still, although much interwoven with the others. This is the Ba'la Gopa'la, the infant Krishna, the worship of whom is very widely diffused amongst all ranks of Indian society, and which originated with the founder of the *Rudra Sampradáyi* sect, Vallabha Acha'rya; it is, perhaps, better known, however, from the title of its teachers, as the religion of the *Gokulast'ha Gosains*.

The original teacher of the philosophical tenets of this sect, is said to have been Vishnu Swa'mi, a commentator on the texts of the *Védas*, who, however, admitted disciples from the Brahmanical caste only, and considered the state of the *Sanyási*, or ascetic, as essential to the communication of his doctrines. He was succeeded by Jnya'na Deva, who was followed by Na'ma Deva and Trilochana, and they, although whether immediately or not does not appear, by Vallabha Swa'mi, the son of Lakshmana Bhatt, a *Tailinga* Brahman: this *Sanyási* taught early in the sixteenth century: he resided originally at

Gokul, a village on the left bank of the Jumna, about three cos to the East of Mathura: after remaining here sometime, he travelled through India as a pilgrim, and amongst other places he visited, according to the *Bhakta Málá*, the court of KRISHNA DEVA, king of *Vijayanagar*, apparently the same as KRISHNA RAYALU, who reigned about the year 1520, where he overcame the *Smárta* Brahmans in a controversy, and was elected by the *Vaishnavas*, as their chief, with the title of *Achárj*: hence he travelled to *Ujayin*, and took up his abode under a *Pipal* tree, on the banks of the *Sipra*, said to be still in existence, and designated as his *Beit'hek*, or station. Besides this, we find traces of him in other places. There is a *Beit'hek* of his amongst the *Ghats* of *Muttra*, and about two miles from the fort of *Chunar*, is a place called his well, *Achárj kuän*, comprising a temple and *Mat'h* in the court-yard of which is the *well* in question; the Saint is said to have resided here sometime. After this peregrination, VALLABHA returned to *Vrindavan*, where, as a reward for his fatigues and his faith, he was honoured by a visit from KRISHNA in person, who enjoined him to introduce the worship of *Bála Gopál*, or *Gopál Lál*, and founded the faith which at present exists in so flourishing a condition. VALLABHA is supposed to have closed his career in a miracle: he had finally settled at *Jét'han Ber*, at Benares, near which a *Mat'h* still subsists; but at length, having accomplished his mission, he is said to have entered the *Ganges*, at *Hanumán Ghát*, when, stooping into the water, he disappeared: a brilliant flame arose from the spot, and, in the presence of a host of spectators, he ascended to heaven, and was lost in the firmament.

The worship of KRISHNA as one with VISHNU, and the Universe, dates evidently from the *Mahábhárat*,* and his more juvenile forms are brought pre-eminently to notice in the account of his infancy, contained in the *Bhágavat*,† but neither of these works discriminates him from VISHNU, nor do they recommend his infantine or adolescent state to particular veneration. At the same time some hints may have been derived from them, for the institution of this division of the HINDU

* The well known passage in the *Bhágavad Gitá*, in which ARJUNA sees the universe in the mouth of KRISHNA, establishes this identity.

† Particularly in the tenth book, which is appropriated to the life of KRISHNA. The same subject occupies a considerable portion of the *Hari Bans* section of the *Mahábhárat*, of the *Pátála* section of the *Padma Purána*, the sixth section of the *Vishnu Purána*, and the whole of the *Adi Upapurána*.

faith.* In claiming, however, supremacy for Krishna, the *Brahma Vaivertta Purána* is most decided, and this work places Krishna in a heaven, and society exclusively his own, and derives from him all the objects of existence.

According to this authority, the residence of Krishna is denominated *Goloka* ; it is far above the three worlds, and has, at five hundred millions of Yojanas below it, the separate *Lokas* of Vishnu and Siva, *Vaikuntha*, and *Kailás*. This region is indestructible, whilst all else is subject to annihilation, and in the centre of it abides Krishna, of the colour of a dark cloud, in the bloom of youth, clad in yellow raiment, splendidly adorned with celestial gems, and holding a flute. He is exempt from *Máyá*, or delusion, and all qualities, eternal, alone, and the *Paramátmá*, or supreme soul of the world.

Krishna being alone in the *Goloka*, and meditating on the waste of creation, gave origin to a being of a female form endowed with the three *Gunas*, and thence the primary agent in creation. This was *Prakriti*, or *Máyá*, and the system so far corresponds with that of the other Vaishnavas, and of the Puránas generally speaking. They having adopted, in fact, the *Sánkhya* system, interweaving with it their peculiar sectarial notions.

Crude matter, and the five elements, are also made to issue from Krishna, and then all the divine beings. Na'ra'yana, or Vishnu pro-

* Thus in the *Vana Parva* of the *Mahábhárat*; Ma'rkandeya Muni, at the time of a minor destruction of the world, sees, "amidst the waters, an Indian fig tree of vast size, on a principal branch of which was a bed ornamented with divine coverings, on which lay a child with a countenance like the moon." The Saint, though acquainted with the past, present, and future, cannot recognise the child, who therefore appears of the hue, and with the symbols, of Krishna, and desires the Sage to rest within his substance from his weary wanderings over the submerged world.

In the *Bhágavat* it is stated, that when first born, Vasudeva beheld the child of the hue of a cloud, with four arms, dressed in a yellow garb, and bearing the weapons, the jewels, and the diadem of Vishnu.

तमद्भुतं बालकमंबुजेक्षणं चतुर्भुजं शंखगदाद्युदायुधं श्रीवत्सलक्ष्मं गलशोभिकौस्तुभं पीतांबरं सांद्रपयोदसौभगं। महार्हवैदूर्यकिरीट कुंडलत्विषापरिष्वक्तसहस्रकुंतलं उद्दामकांच्यंगदकंकणादिभिर्वि रोचमानं वसुदेव ऐक्षत ॥

And the same work describes Yasoda', his adoptive mother, as seeing the universe in the mouth of the child.

ceeds from his right side, MAHA'DEVA from his left, BRAHMA' from his hand, DHARMA from his breath, SARASWATI' from his mouth, LAKSHMI' from his mind, DURGA' from his understanding, RA'DHA' from his left side. Three hundred millions of *Gopis*, or female companions of RA'DHA', exude from the pores of her skin, and a like number of *Gopas*, or companions of KRISHNA, from the pores of his skin: the very cows and their calves, properly the tenants of *Goloka*, but destined to inhabit the Groves of *Vrindavan*, are produced from the same exalted source.

In this description of creation, however, the Deity is still spoken of as a young man, and the *Purána* therefore affords only indirect authority in the marvels it narrates of his infancy, for the worship of the child. Considering, however, that in this, or in any other capacity, the acts of the Divinity are his *Lílá*, or sport, there is no essential difference between those who worship him either as a boy or as a man, and any of his forms may be adored by this class of *Vaishnavas*, and all his principal shrines are to them equally objects of pilgrimage. As the elements and chief agents of creation are thus said to proceed from the person of KRISHNA, it may be inferred that the followers of this creed adopt the principles of the *Vedánta* philosophy, and consider the material world as one in substance, although in an illusory manner with the Supreme. Life is also identified with spirit, according to the authority of a popular work.* None of the philosophical writings of the chief teachers of this system have been met with.

Amongst other articles of the new creed, VALLABHA introduced one, which is rather singular for a Hindu religious innovator or reformer: he

* According to the *Vártté*, VALLABHA advocated this doctrine with some reluctance, by the especial injunction of the juvenile *Krishna*.

तव श्री आचार्य्य जी ने कही। जो तुम जीव को स्वभाव जानती हो दोष वंत है। तो तुम सो सम्बन्ध कसे होय। तव श्री आचार्य्य जी सो श्री ठाकुर जी कहे। जो तुम जीव को ब्रह्म सम्बन्ध करो हों तिन को अङ्गीकार करोंगों॥

"Then *Achárj Ji* said, 'you know the nature of life, it is full of defects, how can it be combined with you:' to which *Sri Thákur Ji* (KRISHNA) replied; 'do you unite *Brahme* and *life* in what way you will, I shall concur, and thence all its defects will be removed.'"

taught, that privation formed no part of sanctity, and that it was the duty of the teachers and his disciples to worship their Deity, not in nudity and hunger, but in costly apparel and choice food; not in solitude and mortification, but in the pleasures of society, and the enjoyment of the world. The *Gosains*, or teachers, are almost always family men, as was the founder VALLABHA, for after he had shaken off the restrictions of the monastic order to which he originally belonged, he married, by the particular order, it is said, of his new god. The *Gosains* are always clothed with the best raiment, and fed with the daintiest viands by their followers, over whom they have unlimited influence: part of the connexion between the *Guru* and teacher, being the three-fold *Samarpan*, or consignment of *Tan*, *Man*, and *Dhan;* body, mind, and wealth, to the spiritual guide. The followers of the order are especially numerous amongst the mercantile community, and the *Gosains* themselves are often largely engaged, also, in maintaining a connexion amongst the commercial establishments of remote parts of the country, as they are constantly travelling over India, under pretence of pilgrimage, to the sacred shrines of the sect, and notoriously reconcile, upon these occasions, the profits of trade, with the benefits of devotion: as religious travellers, however, this union of objects renders them more respectable than the vagrants of any other sect.

The practices of the sect are of a similar character with those of other regular worshippers: their temples and houses have images of GOPAL, of KRISHNA and RA'DHA', and other divine forms connected with this incarnation, of metal chiefly, and not unfrequently of gold: the image of KRISHNA represents a chubby boy, of the dark hue of which VISHNU is always represented: it is richly decorated and sedulously attended; receiving eight times a day the homage of the votaries. These occasions take place at fixed periods and for certain purposes, and at all other seasons, and for any other object, except at stated and periodical festivals, the temples are closed and the Deity is invisible. The eight daily ceremonials are the following:—

1. *Mangala:* the morning levee. The image being washed and dressed, is taken from the couch, where it is supposed to have slept during the night, and placed upon a seat, about half an hour after sunrise: slight refreshments are then presented to it, with betel and *Pan:* lamps are generally kept burning during this ceremony.

2. *Sringára:* the image having been anointed and perfumed with oil, camphor, and sandal, and splendidly attired, now holds his public court: this takes place about an hour and a half after the preceding, or when four *Gheris* of the day have elapsed.

3. *Gwala:* the image is now visited, preparatory to his going out to attend the cattle along with the cow-herd; this ceremony is held about forty-eight minutes after the last, or when six *Gheris* have passed.

4. *Raja Bhóga:* held at midday, when Krishna is supposed to come in from the pastures, and dine; all sorts of delicacies are placed before the image, and both those, and other articles of food dressed by the ministers of the temple, are distributed to the numerous votaries present, and not unfrequently sent to the dwellings of worshippers of some rank and consequence.

5. *Utthápan:* the calling up. The summoning of the god from his siesta: this takes place at six *Gheris*, or between two and three hours before sunset.

6. *Bhóga;* the afternoon meal: about half an hour after the preceding.

7. *Sandhya;* about sunset: the evening toilet of the image, when the ornaments of the day are taken off, and fresh unguent and perfume applied.

8. *Sayan;* retiring to repose: the image, about eight or nine in the evening, is placed upon a bed, refreshments and water in proper vases, together with the betel-box and its appurtenances, are left near it, when the votaries retire, and the temple is shut till the ensuing morning.

Upon all these occasions the ceremony is much the same, consisting in little more than the presentation of flowers, perfumes, and food by the priests and votaries; and the repetition, chiefly by the former, of Sanscrit stanzas in praise of Krishna, interspersed with a variety of prostrations and obeisances. There is no established ritual, indeed, in the Hindu religion, for general use, nor any prescribed form of public adoration.

Besides the diurnal ceremonials described, there are several annual festivals of great repute observed throughout India: of these, in Bengal and Orissa, the *Rath Játra*, or procession of Jaganna'th in his car, is the most celebrated, but it is rarely held in Upper India, and then only by natives of Bengal, established in the provinces: the most popular festival at Benares, and generally to the Westward, is the

Janamashtamí, the nativity of KRISHNA on the eighth day of *Bhádra*, (August.*) Another is the *Rás Yátra*, or annual commemoration of the dance of the frolicksome Deity with the sixteen GOPIS. This last is a very popular festival, and not an uninteresting one: vast crowds, clad in their best attire, collecting in some open place in

* Great difference of practice prevails on occasion of this observance. KRISHNA was born on the eighth lunar day of the waning moon of *Bhádra*, at midnight, upon the moon's entrance into *Rohini*, in commemoration of which a fast is to be held on the day preceding his birth, terminating, as usual, in a feast; but the day of his birth is variously determinable, according to the adoption of the civil, the lunar, or lunar-sydereal computations, and it rarely happens that the eighth lunation comprises the same combination of hours and planetary positions, as occurred at KRISHNA's birth. Under these circumstances, the followers of the *Smriti*, with the *Saivas* and *Sáktas*, commence their fast with the commencement of the lunation, whenever that takes place: the *Rámánujas* and *Mádhwas*, observe such part of the eighth day of the moon's age as includes sunrise, and forms the eighth day of the calendar, or civil day, whilst some of the *Rámánujas*, and the *Nimáwats* regulate the duration of their fast by the moon's passage through the asterism *Rohini*. The consequence is, that the *Smartas* often fast on the 7th, one set of *Vaishnavas* on the 8th, and another on the 9th, whilst those who affect great sanctity, sometimes go thirty hours without food. An extract from last year's calendar will very well exemplify these distinctions.

"3rd Bhádra, 17th August 1825, Tuesday, Saptamí, 10 Dandas, 17 Palas. The Janmáshtamí Vrata and a fast.

"4th Bhádra, 18th August, Wednesday, Ashtamí, 9 Dandas, 18 Palas. Fast according to the Vaishnavas of Vruj.

"5th Bhádra, 19th August, Thursday, Navamí, 7 Dandas, 4 Palas. Rohiní Nakshatra, till 10 Dandas, 52 Palas, at which hour *Párana*, the end of the fast."

Now the 3rd day of the *Solar Bhádra* was the 7th of the *Lunar* month, but it comprised little more than ten *Dandas* or four hours of that lunation: as it included sunrise, however, it was the 7th of the calendar, or *civil* day. The eighth *Tithi*, or lunation, therefore, began about that time, or four hours after sunrise, and the *Smártas, Saivas*, and *Sáktas*, observed the fast on that day; they began with sunrise, however, as there is a specific rule for the *Sankalpa*, or pledge, to perform the usual rite at dawn. This *Ashtami* comprised midnight, and was the more sacred on that account.

The 4th of *Bhádra* was the *Ashtami*, or eighth of the *Vaishnavas*, although the lunation only extended to 9 *Dandas*, or less than four hours after sunrise, but they are particularly enjoined to avoid the *Suptami*, or the *Ashtami* conjoined with it, and therefore they could not commence their fast earlier, although they lost thereby the midnight of the eighth lunation, which they were, consequently, compelled to extend into the night of the ninth. They fasted till the next morning, unless they chose to eat after midnight, which, on this occasion, is allowable.

The 5th of *Bhádra* was the *Navami*, or ninth of the calendar, but it included a portion of the moon's passage through *Rohini*, and the strict *Vaishnavas* of the different sects should not have performed the *Párana*, the close of the fast, earlier, or before 10 Dandas and 52 Palas after sunrise, or about nine o'clock. Those *Vaishnavas*, however, who wholly regulate their observance by the Asterism, and referring also to the necessity of commencing it with sunrise, would only have begun their fast on the calendar *Navami*, and have held the *Párana* on Friday the 10th, the third day after the proper birth-day of their Deity.

the vicinity of the town, and celebrating the event with music, singing, and dramatic representations of KRISHNA's sports: all the public singers and dancers lend their services on this occasion, and trust for a remuneration to the gratuities of the spectators: at Benares, the *Rás Yátra* is celebrated at the village of *Sivapur*, and the chief dancers and musicians, ranging themselves under the banners of the most celebrated of the profession, go out in formal procession: tents, huts, and booths are erected, swings and roundabouts form a favourite amusement of the crowd, and sweetmeats and fruits are displayed in tempting profusion: the whole has the character of a crowded fair in Europe, and presents, in an immense concourse of people, an endless variety of rich costume, and an infinite diversity of picturesque accompaniment, a most lively and splendid scene. The same festival is held from the tenth day of the light half of *Kuär* (Sept.-Oct.), to the day of the full moon, at *Bindraban*, where a stone plat-form, or stage, has been built for the exhibition of the mimic dance, in a square near the river side. Besides their public demonstrations of respect, pictures and images of GOPA'LA are kept in the houses of the members of the sect, who, before they sit down to any of their meals, take care to offer a portion to the idol. Those of the disciples who have performed the triple *Samarpana*, eat only from the hands of each other; and the wife or child that has not exhibited the same mark of devotion to the *Guru*, can neither cook for such a disciple, nor eat in his society.

The mark on the forehead consists of two red perpendicular lines, meeting in a semicircle at the root of the nose, and having a round spot of red between them. The *Bhaktas* have the same marks as the *Sri Vaishnavas* on the breasts and arms, and some also make the central spot on the forehead with a black earth, called *Syámabandi*, or any black metallic substance: the necklace and rosary, are made of the stalk of the *Tulasí*. The salutations amongst them are, *Srikrishna* and *Jaya Gopál*.

The great authority of the sect is the *Bhágavat*, as explained in the *Subodhiní*, or Commentary of VALLABHA'CHA'RYA: he is the author also of a *Bháshya* on part of VYA'SA's *Sútras*, and of other Sanscrit works, as the *Siddhánta Rahasya*, *Bhágavat Lílá Rahasya*, and *Ekánta Rahasya*; these, however, are only for the learned, and are now very rare. Amongst the votaries in general, various works upon the history of KRISHNA are current, but the most popular are the *Vishnu Padas*, stanzas in *Bhásha*, in praise of VISHNU, attributed to VALLABHA himself; the *Bruj Bilas*, a *Bhákha* poem of some length, descriptive of KRISHNA's life, during his residence at *Vrindaban*, by BRUJ BA'SI DA's; the *Ash'ta Chháp*, an account of VALLABHA's eight chief disciples, and the *Vártá*, or *Bártá*, a collection in *Hindustani* of marvellous and insipid anecdotes of VALLABHA and his primitive followers, amounting to the number of eighty-four, and including persons of both sexes, and every class of Hindus. The *Bhakta Málá* also contains a variety of legends regarding the different teachers of this sect, but it is less a text-book with this sect than any other class of *Vaishnavas*, as the *Bártá* occupies its place amongst the worshippers of *Gopál*. The following are specimens of this work, and by no means the most unfavourable :—

DA'MODAR DA's, of *Kanoj*, was a disciple of SRI' ACHA'RYA, (VALLABHA'CHA'RYA.) Like the rest of the members of this sect, he had an image of KRISHNA in his house. One day it was exceedingly hot, and when night came, *Srí Thákur Jí* (the image,) woke the maid servant, and desired her to open the doors of his chamber, as it was very warm. She obeyed, and taking a *pankha*, fanned him—early in the morning DA'MODAR DA's observed the doors of the chamber open, and enquired how this had happened : the girl mentioned the circumstance, but her master was much vexed that she had done this, and that *Srí Thákur Jí* had not called him to do it. *Srí Thákur Jí*, knowing his thoughts, said; 'I told her to open the doors, why are you displeased with her; you shut me up here in a close room, and go to sleep yourself on an open and cool terrace.' Then DA'MODAR DA's made a vow, and said, 'I will not taste consecrated food until I have built a new temple :' but his wife advised him, and urged, 'this is not a business of five or six days, why go without the consecrated food so long.' Then he said, 'I will not partake of the consecrated sweetmeats, I will only eat the fruits ;' and so he did, and the temple was completed, and *Srí Thákur Jí* was enshrined in it, and DA'MODAR DA's distributed food to the *Vaishnavas*, and they partook thereof.

Srí Thákur Jí had a faithful worshipper in a Mahratta lady, whom, with the frolicsomeness of boyhood, he delighted to tease. One day, a woman selling vegetables having passed without the *Bai* noticing her, *Srí Thákur Jí* said to her, 'will you not buy any vegetables for me to-day :'

she replied, 'whenever any one selling them comes this way, I will buy some;' to which he answered, 'one has just now passed.' The *Bai* replied; 'no matter if one has gone by, another will presently be here:' but this did not satisfy the little deity, who leaping from his pedestal, ran after the woman, brought her back, and, after haggling for the price with her himself, made his protectress purchase what he selected.

As RA'NA'VYA's and JAGANNA'TH, two of VALLABHA'CHA'RYA's disciples, were bathing, a woman of the *Rajput* caste came down to the river to burn herself with her husband; on which JAGANNA'TH said to his companion, 'what is the fashion of a woman becoming a *Sati*:' RA'NA'VYA's shook his head, and said, 'the fruitless union of beauty with a dead body.' The *Rajputani* observing RA'NA'VYA's shake his head, her purpose at that moment was changed, and she did not become a *Sati*, on which her kindred were much pleased. Some time afterwards, meeting with the two disciples, the *Rajputani* told them of the effect of their former interview, and begged to know what had passed between them. RA'NA'VYA's being satisfied, that the compassion of *Srí Achárj* was extended to her, repeated what he had said to JAGANNA'TH, and his regret that her charms should not be devoted to the service of *Srí Thákur Jí*, rather than be thrown away upon a dead body. The *Rajputani* enquired how the service of *Thákur Jí* was to be performed, on which RA'NA'VYA's, after making her bathe, communicated to her the initiating prayer, and she thenceforth performed the menial service of the deity, washing his garments, bringing him water, and discharging other similar duties in the dwelling of RA'NA'VYA's with entire and fervent devotion, on which account, she obtained the esteem of *Srí Achárj*, and the favour of the deity.

RA'M DA's was married in his youth, but adopting ascetic principles, he refused to take his wife home: at last, his father-in-law left his daughter in her husband's dwelling, but RA'M DA's would have nothing to say to her, and set off on a pilgrimage to *Dwáraká*: his wife followed him, but he threw stones at her, and she was compelled to remain at a distance from him. At noon, he halted and bathed the god, and prepared his food, and presented it, and then took the *Prasád* and put it in a vessel, and fed upon what remained; but it was to no purpose, and he was still hungry. Thus passed two or three days, when RANACHHOR appeared to him in a dream, and asked him why he thus ill-treated his wife. He said, he was *Virakta,* (a cœnobite), and what did he want with a wife. Then RANACHHOR asked him, why he had married, and assured him that such an unsocial spirit was not agreeable to *Srí Achárya,* and desired him to take his wife unto him; for RANACHHOR could not bear the distress of the poor woman, as he has a gentle heart, and his nature has been imparted to the *Achárya* and his disciples. When morning came, RA'M DA's called to his wife, and suffered her to accompany him, by which she was made happy. When the time for preparing their food arrived, RA'M DA's prepared it himself, and after presenting the portion to the image, gave a part of it to his wife. After a few days, RANACHHOR again appeared, and asked him, why he did not allow his wife to cook, to which RA'M DA's replied, that she had not received the initiating name from *Srí Achárya,* and was, therefore, unfit to prepare his food. RANACHHOR, therefore, directed him to communicate the *Nám* (*the* name) to his wife, and after returning to the *Achárya,* get him to repeat it. Accordingly, RA'M DA's initiated his wife, and this being confirmed by the *Achárya,* she also became his disciple, and, with her husband, assiduously worshipped *Srí Thákur Jí.*

VALLABHA was succeeded by his son VITTALA NA'TH, known amongst the sect by the appellation of *Srí Gosain Jí;* VALLABHA's designation being *Srí Achárj Jí.* VITTALA NA'TH, again, had seven sons, GIRDHARI RAI, GOVIND RAI, BA'LA KRISHNA, GOKUL NA'TH, RAGHUNA'TH, YADUNA'TH, and GHANASSYA'MA; these were all teachers, and their followers, although in all essential points the same, form as many different communities. Those of GOKUL NA'TH, indeed, are peculiarly separate from the rest, looking upon their own *Gosains* as the only legitimate teachers of the faith, and withholding all sort of reverence from the persons and *Mat'hs* of the successors of his brethren: an exclusive preference that does not prevail amongst the other divisions of the faith, who do homage to all the descendants of all VITTALA NA'TH's sons.

The worshippers of this sect are very numerous and opulent, the merchants and bankers, especially those from Guzrat and Malwa, belonging to it: their temples and establishments are numerous all over India, but particularly at Mathura and Bindraban, the latter of which alone is said to contain many hundreds, amongst which are three of great opulence. In Benares are two temples of great repute and wealth, one sacred to *Lál Jí*, and the other to *Purushottama Jí*.* *Jagannáth* and *Dwáraká*, are also particularly venerated by this sect, but the most celebrated of all the *Gosain* establishments is at *Srí Náth Dwár*, in Ajmer. The image at this shrine is said to have transported itself thither from *Mathurá*, when *Aurengzeb* ordered the temple it was there placed in to be destroyed. The present shrine is modern, but richly endowed, and the high priest, a descendant of Gokul Na'th, a man of great wealth and importance.† It is a matter of obligation with the members of this sect to visit *Srí Náth Dwár*, at least once in their lives; they receive there a certificate to that effect, issued by the head *Gosain*, and, in return, contribute according to their means to the enriching of the establishment: it is not an uncurious feature in the notions of this sect, that the veneration paid to their *Gosain* is paid solely to their descent, and unconnected with any idea of their sanctity or learning; they are not unfrequently destitute of all pretensions to individual respectability, but they not the less enjoy the homage of their followers: the present chief, at *Srináth Dwár*, is said not to understand the certificate he signs.

MIRA BAIS.

These may be considered as forming a subdivision of the preceding, rather than a distinct sect, although, in the adoption of a new leader, and the worship of Krishna under a peculiar form, they differ essentially from the followers of Vallabha: at the same time, it is chiefly amongst those sectarians, that Mi'ra' Bai and her deity, Ranachhor, are held in high veneration, and, except in the West of India, it does not appear that she has many immediate and exclusive adherents.

* Many of the bankers of this city, it is said, pay to one or other of the temples a tax of one-fourth of an *ana*, on every bill of exchange, and the cloth merchants, half an *ana* on all sales.

† Every temple is said to have three places of offering; the image, the pillow of the founder, and a box for *Sri Náth Dwár*.

MI'RA' BAI is the heroine of a prolix legend in the *Bhakta Málá*, which is a proof at least of her popularity: as the author of sacred poems addressed to the deity, as *Vishnu*, she also enjoys a classical celebrity, and some of her odes are to be found in the collections which constitute the ritual of the deistical sects, especially those of *Nának* and *Kabir*: according to the authority cited, she flourished in the time of *Akbar*, who was induced, by her reputation, to pay her a visit, accompanied by the famous musician *Tán Sen*, and it is said, that they both acknowledged the justice of her claim to celebrity.

MI'RA' was the daughter of a petty Raja, the sovereign of a place called *Mertá*; she was married to the *Rána* of *Udayapur*, but soon after being taken home by him, quarrelled with her mother-in-law, a worshipper of *Deví*, respecting compliance with the family adoration of that goddess, and was, in consequence of her persevering refusal to desert the worship of KRISHNA, expelled the *Rana's* bed and palace: she appears to have been treated, however, with consideration, and to have been allowed an independent establishment, owing, probably, rather to the respect paid to her abilities, than a notion of her personal sanctity, although the latter was attested, if we may believe our guide, by her drinking unhesitatingly a draught of poison presented to her by her husband, and without its having the power to do her harm. In her uncontrouled station, she adopted the worship of RANAÇHHOR, a form of the youthful KRISHNA; she became the patroness of the vagrant *Vaishnavas*, and visited, in pilgrimage, *Bindraban* and *Dwáraká*: whilst at the latter, some persecution of the *Vaishnavas*, at *Udayapur*, appears to have been instituted, and Brahmans were sent to bring her home from *Dwáraká*: previously to departing, she visited the temple of her tutelary deity, to take leave of him, when, on the completion of her adorations, the image opened, and MI'RA' leaping into the fissure, it closed, and she finally disappeared. In memory of this miracle it is said, that the image of MI'RA' BAI is worshipped at *Udayapur*, in conjunction with that of RANACHHOR. The *Padas* that induced this marvel, and which are current as the compositions of MI'RA' BAI, are the two following:

Pada 1.—Oh, sovereign RANACHHOR, give me to make *Dwáraká* my abode: with thy shell, discus, mace, and lotus, dispel the fear of YAMA: eternal rest is visiting thy sacred shrines; supreme delight is the clash of thy shell and cymbals: I have abandoned my love, my possessions, my principality, my husband. MI'RA', thy servant, comes to thee for refuge: oh, take her wholly to thee.

Pada 2.—If thou knowest me free from stain, so accept me: save thee, there is none other that will show me compassion: do thou, then, have mercy upon me: let not weariness, hunger, anxiety, and restlessness, consume this frame with momentary decay. Lord of MI'RA', GIRDHARA her beloved, accept her, and never let her be separated from thee.

BRAHMA SAMPRADAYIS, OR MADHWACHARIS.

This division of the *Vaishnavas* is altogether unknown in Gangetic Hindustan. A few individuals belonging to it, who are natives of Southern India, may be occasionally encountered, but they are not sufficiently numerous to form a distinct community, nor have they any temple or teachers of their own. It is in the peninsula, that the sect is most extensively to be found, and it is not comprised, therefore, in the scope of this sketch: as, however, it is acknowledged to be one of the four great *Sampraḍayas*, or religious systems, such brief notices of it as have been collected will not be wholly out of place.

The institution of this sect is posterior to that of the *Sri Vaishnavas*, or *Ramanujas:* the founder was MADHWA'CHARYA,* a Brahman, the son of MADHIGE, BHATTA, who was born in the Saka year 1121 (A. D. 1199,) in *Tuluva:* according to the legendary belief of his followers, he was an incarnation of *Váyu*, or the god of air, who took upon him the human form, by desire of NA'RA'YANA, and who had been previously incarnate as *Hanumán* and *Bhíma*, in preceding ages. He was educated in the convent established at *Ananteswar*, and, in his ninth year, was initiated into the order of Anchorets, by ACHYUTA PRACHA, a descendant of SANAKA, son of BRAHMA. At that early age also he composed his

* In the *Sarvadersana Sangraha*, he is cited by the name *Purna Prajna*—a work is also quoted as written by him under the name of *Medhya Mandira*. Reference is also made to him by the title, most frequently found in the works ascribed to him, of *Ananda Tirtha*.

Bháshya, or Commentary on the *Gítá*, which he carried to *Badarikásrama*, in the Himalaya, to present to VEDAVYASA, by whom he was received with great respect, and presented with three *Sálagráms*, which he brought back and established as objects of worship, in the Mat'hs of *Udipi*, *Madhyatala*, and *Subrahmanya*—he also erected and consecrated at *Udipi*, the image of KRISHNA, that was originally made by ARJUNA, of which he became miraculously possessed.

A vessel from *Dwáraká*, trading along the Malabar coast, had taken on board, either accidentally or as ballast, a quantity of *Gopichandana*, or the sacred clay, from that city, in which the image was immersed: the vessel was wrecked off the coast of *Tuluva*, but MADHWA, receiving divine intimation of the existence of the image, had it sought for, and recovered from the place where it had sunk,* and established it as the principal object of his devotion at *Udipi*, which has since continued to be the head-quarters of the sect. He resided here for some time himself, and composed, it is said, thirty-seven works.† After some time, he went upon a controversial tour, in which he triumphed over various teachers, and amongst others, it is said, over *Sankara Achárya*—he finally, in his 79th year, departed to *Badarikásrama*, and there continues to reside with VYA'SA, the compiler of the Vedas and Puranas.

Before his relinquishing charge of the shrine he had established, MADHWA'CHA'RYA had very considerably extended his followers, so that he was enabled to establish eight different temples, in addition to the principal temple, or that of *Krishna*, at *Udipi*: in these were placed images of different forms of *Vishnu*,‡ and the superintendence of them was entrusted to the brother of the founder, and eight *Sanayásis*, who were Brahmans, from the banks of the *Godaveri*. These establishments still exist, and, agreeably to the code of the founder, each *Sanyási*, in turn, officiates as superior of the chief station at *Udipi* for two years,

* This story is rather differently told by the late Colonel Mackenzie in his account of the Marda Gooroos, published in the Asiatic Annual Register, for 1804.

† The principal of these are—the Gítá Bhsábya, Sútra Bhsáhya, Rig-Bháshya, Desopanishadh Bháshya—Anuvákanunaya Viverna, Anuvedanta Rasa Prakarana, Bhárata Tátparya Nirnaya, Bhágavat-tátparya, Gitátátparya—Krishnámrita Mahárnava, Tantra Sára.

‡ Ráma with Sítá—2. Sítá and Lakshman—3. Kálíya Mardana, with two arms—4. Kálíya Mardana, with four arms—5. Suvitala—6. Sukara—7. Nrisinha—8. Vasanta Vitala.

or two years and a half. The whole expense of the establishment devolves upon the superior for the time being, and, as it is the object of each to outvie his predecessor, the charges* are much heavier than the receipts of the institution, and, in order to provide for them, the *Sanyásis* employ the intervals of their temporary charge in travelling about the country, and levying contribution on their lay votaries, the amount of which is frequently very large, and is appropriated for the greater part to defray the costs of the occasional pontificate.

The eight *Mat'hs* are all in *Tuluva*, below the Ghats,† but, at the same time, MADHWA'CHA'RYA authorised the foundation of others above the Ghats, under PADMANA'BHA TIRTHA, to whom he gave images of RA'MA, and the *Vyása Sálagrám*, with instructions to disseminate his doctrines, and collect money for the use of the shrine at *Udipi:* there are four establishments under the descendants of this teacher above the Ghats, and the superiors visit *Udipi* from time to time, but never officiate there as pontiffs.

The superiors, or *Gurus* of the *Mádhwa* sect, are Brahmans and *Sanyásis*, or profess cœnobitic observances: the disciples, who are domesticated in the several *Mat'hs*, profess also perpetual celibacy. The lay votaries of these teachers, are members of every class of society, except the lowest, and each *Guru* has a number of families hereditarily attached to him, whose spiritual guidance he may sell or mortgage to a Brahman of any sect.

The ascetic professors of MADHWA'CHA'RYA's school, adopt the external appearance of *Dandis*, laying aside the Brahmanical cord, carrying a staff and a water-pot, going bare-headed, and wearing a single wrapper stained of an orange colour with an ochry clay: they are usually adopted into the order from their boyhood, and acknowledge no social affinities nor interests. The marks common to them, and the lay votaries of the order, are the impress of the symbols of *Vishnu*, upon their shoulders and breasts, stamped with a hot iron, and the frontal mark, which consists of two perpendicular lines made with *Gopichandana*, and joined at the root of the nose like that of the *Sri Vaishnavas;* but instead of a red line down the centre, the *Mádhwácháris* make a

* Buchanan states them at 13,000 rupees at least, and often exceeding 20,000.

† They are at Kánúr, Pejáwer, Admár, Phalamár, Krishnapur, Sirúr, Sode, and Putti.

straight black line, with the charcoal from incense offered to *Náráyana*, terminating in a round mark made with turmerick.

The essential dogma of this sect, like that of the *Vaishnavas* in general, is the identification of *Vishnu* with the Supreme Spirit, as the pre-existent cause of the universe,* from whose substance the world was made.† This primeval *Vishnu*, they also affirm to be endowed with real attributes,‡ most excellent, although indefinable and independent. As there is one independent, however, there is also one dependent, and this doctrine is the characteristic dogma of the sect, distinguishing its professors from the followers of RA'MA'NUJA as well as SANKARA, or those who maintain the qualified or absolute unity of the deity. The creed of the *Mádhwas*, is *Dwaita*, or duality.§ It is not, however, that they discriminate between the principles of good and evil, or even the difference between spirit and matter, which is the duality known to other sects of the Hindus. Their distinction is of a more subtle character, and separates the *Jivátmá* from the *Paramátmá*, or the principle of life from the Supreme Being. Life, they say, is one and eternal, dependent upon the Supreme, and indissolubly connected with, but not the same with him.|| An important consequence of this

* In proof of these doctrines, they cite the following texts from the SRUTI, or VEDAS: एको नारायण आसीत् न ब्रह्मा न च शङ्करः। *Náráyana* alone was; not *Brahma* nor *Sankara*. आनन्द एकएवाग्र आसीन्नारायणः प्रभुः। Happy and alone before all was *Nárdyana* the Lord.

† The whole world was manifest from the body of VISHNU, विष्णोर्देहाज्जगत्सर्वमाविरासीत्।

‡ VISHNU is independent, exempt from defects, and endowed with all good qualities.—*Tatwa Vivek*, स्वतन्त्रो भगवान् विष्णुर्निर्दोषोऽशेष सद्गुणः।

§ Independent and dependent, is declared to be the two-fold condition of being.—*Tatwa Vivek.* स्वतन्त्रमस्वतन्त्रंच द्विविधंतत्वमिष्यते।

|| As the bird and the string, as juices and trees, as rivers and oceans, as fresh water and salt, as the thief and his booty, as man and objects of sense, so are God and Life distinct, and both are ever indefinable.—*Mahopanishat.* यथा पक्षीसूत्रंच नानावृक्षरसायथा नद्यः समुद्राश्च शुद्धोद लवणे यथा। चोरोपहार्य्यौंच यथा पुंविषयावपि तथा जीवेश्वरौभिन्नौ सर्व्वदैवविलक्षणौ॥

doctrine is the denial of *Moksha,* in its more generally received sense, or that of absorption into the universal spirit, and loss of independent existence after death. The *Yoga* of the *Saivas,* and *Sáyujyam* of the *Vaishnavas,* they hold to be impracticable.*

The Supreme Being resides in *Vaikuntha,* invested with ineffable splendour, and with garb, ornaments, and perfumes of celestial origin, being the husband also of *Lakshmí,* or *glory, Bhúmì,* the earth, and *Nilá,* understood to mean *Devì,* or *Durgá,* or personified matter. In his primary form, no known qualities can be predicated of him, but when he pleases to associate with *Máyá,* which is properly his desire, or wish, the three attributes of purity, passion, or ignorance, or the *Satwa, Raja* and *Tama Gunas,* are manifested, as *Vishnu, Brahmá,* and *Siva,* for the creation, protection, and destruction of the world. These deities, again, perform their respective functions through their union with the same delusive principle to which they owed their individual manifestation. This account is clearly allegorical, although the want of some tangible objects of worship has converted the shadows into realities, and the allegory, when adapted to the apprehensions of ordinary intellects, has been converted into the legend known to the followers of *Kabir,* of the Supreme, begetting the Hindu TRIAD by MA'YA', and her subsequent union with her sons.† Other legends are current

* In confirmation of which they adduce texts from the *Puránas* and *Vedas.*

"From the difference between Omniscience and partial knowledge, Omnipotence and inferior power, supremacy and subservience, the union of God and Life cannot take place."—*Garura Purána.* सर्व्वज्ञाल्पज्ञाभेदात्सर्व्वशक्त्यल्पशक्तिनः । स्वतान्त्र्यपारतान्त्र्भ्यां सम्भोगो नेशजीवयोः । गां पुरं ॥ "Spirit is Supreme, and above qualities; Life is feeble and subordinate."—*Bhúllavaga Upanishad.*

आत्मा हि परमस्वतन्त्रोऽधिगुणो जीवोऽल्पशक्तिरस्वतन्त्रो । भां ॥

† Colonel MacKenzie, in his account of the sect, gives this legend in a different and rather unusual form, and one that indicates some relation to the *Saiva* sects. It is not, however, admitted as orthodox by those members of the sect whom I have encountered, nor do any traces of it appear in the works consulted.

"The Lord of the Creation, by whose supremacy the world is illuminated, and who is infinitely powerful, creating and destroying many worlds in a moment, that Almighty Spirit, in his mind, contemplating the creation of a world for his pleasure, from his wishes sprung a goddess, named Itcha Sacktee; at her request, he directed her to create this world. Then the Sacktee, by the authority of God, immediately created three divine persons, generally called by Hindus, the Moortee-trium, by their several amongst the MA'DHWAS, founded on this view of the creation, in which BRAHMA and SIVA, and other divinities, are described as springing from his mind, his forehead, his sides, and other parts of his body. They also receive the legends of the *Vaishnava Puránas*, of the birth of BRAHMA from the *Lotus*, of the navel of VISHNU, and of RUDRA, from the tears shed by BRAHMA' on being unable to comprehend the mystery of creation.

The modes in which devotion to VISHNU is to be expressed, are declared to be three, *Ankana*, *Námákarana*, and *Bhajana*, or marking the body with his symbols,* giving his names to children, and other objects of interest, and the practice of virtue in word, act, and thought; truth, good council, mild speaking, and study belong to the first; liberality, kindness, and protection, to the second; and clemency, freedom from envy, and faith, to the last. These ten duties form the moral code of the *Mádhwas*.

The usual rites of worship,† as practised by the *Vaishnavas* of this sect, are observed, and the same festivals. In the *Pújá*, however, there

names of Brahma, Vishnu and Siva, committing to them separately, their respective charges in the expected world; Surstee, Sthutee and Sayom, or the power of creating, nourishing, and destroying. When she had made these three lords, she requested of one after the other, that they might be her consort; but Brahma and Vishnu, disapproving of her request, she consumed them with the fire of her third eye, and proposed the same thing to Siva; then Sadaseevû, considering in his mind that her demands were not agreeable to the divine law, replied that he could not be her consort, unless she granted her third eye to him. The goddess was pleased with his prudence, and adorned him with her third eye. So soon as Siva was possessed of that, he immediately destroyed her by a glance of the flaming eye, and revived Brahma and Vishnu, and of her ashes made three goddesses, Saraswatee, Latchmi, and Paravatee, and united one of them to each of the Trimoortee."

[*Account of the Marda Gooroos.—Asiatic Annual Register*, 1804.]

This legend is probably peculiar to the place where it was obtained, but the ideas and the notions adverted to in the text appear to have been misunderstood by Dr. Buchanan, who observes, that the MARDAS believe in the generation of the gods, in a literal sense, thinking VISHNU to be the father of BRAHMA, and BRAHMA the father of SIVA.—Mysore, vol. i. 14.

* Especially with a hot iron, which practice they defend by a text from the VEDAS Whose body is not cauterised, does not obtain liberation. अतप्ततनुर्नतदामोच्चमश्नुते। To which, however, *Sankarácharya* objects, that *Tapta* does not mean cauterised, but purified with *Tapas*, or ascetic mortification.

† The daily ceremonies at *Udipi* are of nine descriptions: *Malavisarjana*, cleaning the temple; 2, *Upasthána*, awaking Krishna; 3, *Panchámrita*, bathing him with milk, &c. 4, *Udverttana*, cleaning the image; 5, *Tírttha Pújá*, bathing it with holy water; 6, *Alankára*, putting on his ornaments; 7, *Avritta*, addressing prayers and hymns to

is one peculiarity which merits notice, as indicative of a friendly leaning towards the *Saiva* sects; the images of SIVA, DURGA', and GANESA, are placed on the same shrine with the form of VISHNU, and partake in the adoration offered to his idol. Rites are conducive to final happiness only, as they indicate a desire to secure the favour of VISHNU. The knowledge of his supremacy is essential to the zeal with which his approbation may be sought, but they consider it unnecessary to attempt an identification with him by abstract meditation, as that is unattainable.* Those who have acquired the regard of VISHNU are, thereby, exempted from future birth, and enjoy felicity in *Vaikuntha* under four conditions, as *Sárupya*, similarity of form, *Sálokya*, visible presence, *Sánnidhya*, proximity, and *Sársht'hi*, equal power.

Besides the writings of the founder, the following works are considered as forming the *Sástra*, or scriptural authority of this sect. The four Vedas, the *Mahábhárat*, the *Páncharátra*, and the genuine or original *Rámáyana*.

It seems not improbable, that the founder of the *Mádhwa* sect was, originally, a *Saiva* priest, and, although he became a convert to the *Vaishnava* faith, he encouraged an attempt to form a kind of compromise or alliance between the *Saivas* and *Vaishnavas*. MA'DHWA was first initiated into the faith of SIVA, at *Ananteswar*, the shrine of a *Linga*, and one of his names, ANANDA TIRT'HA, indicates his belonging to the class of *Dasnámi Gosains*, who were instituted by SANKARA'CHA'RYA; one of his first acts was to establish a *Sálágram*, a type of VISHNU, at the shrine of SUBRAHMANYA, the warrior son of SIVA, and, as observed above, the images of SIVA are allowed to partake, in the *Mádhwa* temples, of the worship offered to VISHNU. The votaries of the *Mádhwa Gurus*, and of the *Sankaráchari Gosains*, offer the *Namaskár*, or reverential obeisance, to their teachers mutually, and the *Sríngeri* Mahant visits *Udipi*, to perform his adorations at the shrine of KRISHNA. It

him; 8, *Mahápújá*, presenting fruits, perfumes, &c. with music and singing; 9, *Rátri Pújá*, nocturnal worship, waving lamps before the image, with prayers, offerings, and music.

* Emancipation is not obtained without the favour of VISHNU. His favour is obtained from knowledge of his excellence, and not from a knowledge of his identity. —*Sruti.*

मोक्षस्तु विष्णुप्रसादान्तरेण न लभ्यते प्रसादश्चगुणोत्कर्षज्ञानादेव नाभेदज्ञानात्।

is evident, therefore, that there is an affinity between these orders, which does not exist between the *Saivas* and *Vaishnavas* generally, who are regarded by the *Mádhwas*, even without excepting the *Rámánujas*, as *Páshandis*, or *heretics*, whether they profess the adoration of VISHNU or of SIVA.

SANAKADI SAMPRADAYIS, OR NIMAWATS.

This division of the *Vaishnava* faith is one of the four primary ones, and appears to be of considerable antiquity: it is one also of some popularity and extent, although it seems to possess but few characteristic peculiarities beyond the name of the founder, and the sectarial mark.

NIMBA'DITYA is said to have been a *Vaishnava* ascetic, originally named *Bháskara Achárya*, and to have been, in fact, an incarnation of the *sun*, for the suppression of the heretical doctrines then prevalent: he lived near *Vindrávan*, where he was visited by a *Dandí*, or, according to other accounts, by a *Jaina* ascetic, or *Jati*, whom he engaged in controversial discussion till sunset: he then offered his visitant some refreshment, which the practice of either mendicant renders unlawful after dark, and which the guest was, therefore, compelled to decline: to remove the difficulty, the host stopped the further descent of the sun, and ordered him to take up his abode in a neighbouring *Nimb* tree, till the meat was cooked and eaten: the sun obeyed, and the saint was ever after named *Nimbárka*, or *Nimbáditya*, or the *Nimb* tree sun.

The *Nímáwats* are distinguished by a circular black mark in the centre of the ordinary double streak of white earth, or *Gopichandan*: they use the necklace and rosary of the stem of the *Tulasi*; the objects of their worship are KRISHNA and RA'DHA' conjointly: their chief authority is the *Bhágavat*, and there is said to be a *Bháshya* on the *Védas* by NIMBA'RKA: the sect, however, is not possessed of any books peculiar to the members, which want they attribute to the destruction of their works at *Mathura* in the time of Aurengzeb.

The *Nímáwats* are scattered throughout the whole of Upper India. They are met with of the two classes cœnobitical and secular, or

Viraktas and *Grihasthas*, distinctions introduced by the two pupils of NIMBA'RKA, KESAVA BHATT, and HARI VYA'S: the latter is considered as the founder of the family which occupies the pillow of NIMBA'RKA at a place called *Dhruva Kshetra*, upon the Jumna close to *Mathura*: the *Mahant*, however, claims to be a lineal descendant from NIMBA'RKA himself, and asserts the existence of the present establishment for a past period of 1400 years: the antiquity is probably exaggerated: the *Nímáwats* are very numerous about *Mathura*, and they are also the most numerous of the *Vaishnava* sects in Bengal, with the exception of those who may be considered the indigenous offspring of that province.

VAISHNAVAS OF BENGAL.

The far greater number of the worshippers of VISHNU, or more properly of KRISHNA, in Bengal, forming, it has been estimated, one-fifth of the population of the province,* derive their peculiarities from some *Vaishnava* Brahmans of *Nadiya* and *Santipur*, who flourished about the end of the fifteenth century. The two leading men in the innovation then instituted, were ADWAITA'NAND and NITYA'NAND, who, being men of domestic and settled habits, seem to have made use of a third, who had early embraced the ascetic order, and whose simplicity and enthusiasm fitted him for their purpose, and to have set up CHAITANYA as the founder and object of a new form of *Vaishnava* worship.

The history of CHAITANYA has been repeatedly written, but the work most esteemed by his followers is the *Chaitanya Charitra* of VRINDA'VAN DA'S, which was compiled from preceding works by MURA'RI GUPTA and DA'MODARA, who were the immediate disciples of CHAITANYA, and who wrote an account, the first of his life as a *Grihastha*, or the *Adi Lílá*, and the second of his proceedings as a pilgrim and ascetic, or the *Madhya* and *Anta Lílá*. An abridgement of the composition of VRINDA'VAN DA'S, under the title of *Chaitanya Charitámrita*, was made by KRISHNA DA'S about 1590: although described by the author as an abridgement, it is a most voluminous work, comprising, besides

* Ward on the Hindus, 2. 175. In another place he says five-sixteenths, p. 448.

anecdotes of CHAITANYA and his principal disciples, the expositions of the doctrines of the sect: it is written in Bengali, but it is interspersed most thickly with the Sanscrit texts on which the faith is founded, and which are taken from the *Brahma Sanhitá*, the *Vishnu Purán*, the *Bhágavat Gítá*, and, above all, the *Sri Bhágavat*, the work that appears about this period to have given a new aspect to the Hindu faith, throughout the whole of Hindustan: the accounts we have to offer of CHAITANYA and his schism, are taken from the *Chaitanya Charitámrita*.

CHAITANYA was the son of a Brahman settled at *Nadiya*, but originally from *Srihatta*, or Silhet. His father was named JAGANNA'TH MISRA, and his mother SACHI: he was conceived in the end of Magha 1484, but not born till *Phalgun* 1485, being thirteen months in the womb: his birth was accompanied by the usual portentous indications of a super-human event, and, amongst other circumstances, an eclipse of the moon was terminated by his entrance into the world. CHAITANYA was, in fact, an incarnation of KRISHNA, or *Bhagaván*, who appeared for the purpose of instructing mankind in the true mode of worshipping him in this age: with the like view he was, at the same time, incarnate in the two greater teachers of the sect as principal *Ansas*, or portions of himself, animating the form of ADWAITA'NAND, whilst NITYA'NAND was a personal manifestation of the same divinity, as he had appeared formerly in the shape of BALARA'MA: the female incarnation was not assumed on this occasion, being, in fact, comprised in the male, for RA'DHA', as the *Purna-Sakti*, or comprehensive energy, and KRISHNA, as the *Purna-Saktimán*, or possessor of that energy, were both united in the nature of the *Nadiya* saint.

The father of CHAITANYA died in his son's childhood, and his elder brother, VISWARU'PA, had previously assumed the character of an ascetic: to take care of his mother, therefore, CHAITANYA refrained from following his inclinations, and continued in the order of the *Grihastha*, or householder, till the age of twenty-four, during which time he is said to have married the daughter of VALLABHA'CHA'RYA. At twenty-four,* he shook off the obligations of society, and becoming a *Bairágí*, spent the next six years in a course of peregrinations between *Mathura* and *Jagannáth*, teaching his doctrines, acquiring followers, and extending

* Not forty, as stated by Mr. Ward, (2. 173.) his whole life little exceeded that age, as he disappeared at forty-two.

the worship of KRISHNA. At the end of this period, having nominated ADWAITA'CHA'RYA and NITYA'NAND to preside over the *Vaishnavas* of Bengal, and RUPA and SANA'TANA over those of *Mathura*, CHAITANYA settled at *Nilâchal*, or *Cuttack*, where he remained twelve years, engaging deeply in the worship of *Jagannâth*, to whose festival he seems at least to have communicated great energy and repute.* The rest of his time was spent in tuition and controversy, and in receiving the visits of his disciples, who came annually, particularly the Bengalis, under ADWAITA and NITYA'NAND, to *Nilâchal*, in the performance of acts of self-denial, and in intent meditation on KRISHNA: by these latter means he seems to have fallen, ultimately, into a state of imbecility approaching to insanity, which engendered perpetually beatific visions of KRISHNA, RA'DHA', and the GOPIS: in one of these, fancying the sea to be the *Jumna*, and that he saw the celestial cohort sporting in its blue waters, he walked into it, and fainting with ecstasy, would have been drowned, if his emaciated state had not rendered him buoyant on the waves: he was brought to shore in a fisherman's net, and recovered by his two resident disciples, SWARUPA and RA'MA'NAND: the story is rendered not improbable, by the uncertain close of CHAITANYA's career: he disappeared; how, is not known: of course his disciples suppose he returned to *Vaikunt'ha*, but we may be allowed to conjecture the means he took to travel thither, by the tale of his marine excursion, as it is gravely narrated by KRISHNA DA's: his disappearance dates about A. D. 1527.

Of ADWAITA'NAND and NITYA'NAND, no marvels, beyond their divine pervasion, are recorded: the former, indeed, is said to have predicted the appearance of KRISHNA as CHAITANYA; a prophecy that probably wrought its own completion: he sent his wife to assist at the birth of the saint, and was one of his first disciples. ADWAITA'NAND resided at *Santipur*, and seems to have been a man of some property and respectability: he is regarded as one of the three *Prabhus*, or *masters* of the

* It may be observed, that in the frequent descriptions of the celebration of the *Rath Yátra*, which occur in the work of KRISHNA DA's, no instance is given of self-sacrifice, amongst the numerous votaries collected, neither is there any passage that could be interpreted, as commendatory of the practice: it is, in fact, very contrary to the spirit of *Vaishnava* devotion, and is probably a modern graft from *Saiva* or *Sákta* superstition. ABULFAZL does not notice the practice, although he mentions that those who assist in drawing the car, think thereby to obtain remission of their sins.

sect, and his descendants, who are men of property, residing at *Santipur*, are the chief *Gosains*, or spiritual superiors, conjointly with those of NITYA'NAND, of the followers of this faith. NITYA'NAND was an inhabitant of *Nadiya*, a *Rárhiya* Brahman, and a householder : he was appointed especially by CHAITANYA, the superior of his followers in Bengal, notwithstanding his secular character, and his being addicted to mundane enjoyments :* his descendants are still in existence, and are divided into two branches : those of the male line reside at *Kharda*, near Barrackpore ; and those of the female at *Bálagor*, near *Suk'hságar* : there are other families, however, of nearly equal influence in various parts of Bengal, descended from the other *Gosains*, the *Kavirájas* and original *Mahants*.

Besides the three *Prabhus*, or CHAITANYA, ADWAITA, and NITYA'NAND, the *Vaishnavas* of this order acknowledge six *Gosains* as their original and chief teachers, and the founders, in some instances, of the families of the *Gosains* now existing, to whom, as well as to the *Gokulast'ha Gosains*, hereditary veneration is due. The six *Gauriya*, or Bengal *Gosains*, appear to have all settled at *Vrindavan* and *Mathura*, where many of their descendants are still established, and in possession of several temples : this locality, the agreement of dates, and the many points of resemblance between the institutions of VALLABHA and CHAITANYA, render it extremely probable that their origin was connected, and that a spirit of rivalry and opposition gave rise to one or other of them.

The six *Gosains* of the Bengal *Vaishnavas*, are RU'PA, SANA'TAN, JIVA, RAGHUNA'TH BHATT, RAGHUNA'TH DA'S, and GOPA'L BHATT. RU'PA and SANA'TAN,† were brothers in the employ of the Mohammedan

* Thus, according to KRISHNA DA'S, when RAGHUNATH DA'S visits him, he finds him at a feast with his followers, eating a variety of dainties; amongst others a dish called *Pulína*, and when he good humouredly notices it, NITYA'NAND replies :—

গোপজাতি আমি বহুগোপসঙ্গে। আমি সুখপাই এ পুলীন ভোজনরঙ্গে ॥

"I am of the *Gopa* caste, (i. e. fig : a companion of KRISHNA, the cow-herd,) and am amidst many *Gopas*, and such as we are, consider *Pulína* a delicacy." A verse is also ascribed to him, said to have become proverbial ; মৎস্যের ঝোল্ কামিনীর কোল্ । আনন্দে তোরাসবে হরিহরি বোল্ ॥ Let all enjoy fish, broth, and woman's charms—be happy, and call upon HARI.

† From the indistinct manner in which they are conjointly described in the *Bhakta Málá*, it might be thought that *Rupa Sanátana* was but a single individual ; but, in

governor of Bengal, and were hence regarded as little better than *Mlech'has*, or outcasts, themselves: the sanctity of CHAITANYA's life and doctrine induced them to become his followers, and as it was a part of his system to admit all castes, even Mussulmans, amongst his disciples, they were immediately enlisted in a cause, of which they became the first ornaments and supports: they were men of learning, and were very indefatigable writers as we shall hereafter see, and the foundation of two temples at *Vindraban*, the most respectable reliques of the Hindu faith existing in Upper Hindustan, is ascribed to their influence and celebrity.* JIVA was the nephew of the preceding, the son of their younger brother: he was likewise an author, and the founder of a temple at *Vindraban*, dedicated to *Rádhá Dámodara*. RAGHUNA'TH BHATT and RAGHUNA'TH DA's were both Brahmans of Bengal, but they established themselves in the vicinity of *Mathura* and *Vindraban*. GOPAL BHATT founded a temple and establishment at *Vindraban*, which are still maintained by his descendants: the presiding deity is RA'DHA' RAMANA.

Next to the six *Gosains*, several learned disciples and faithful companions of CHAITANYA are regarded with nearly equal veneration: these are SRINIBA's, GADA'DHAR *Pandit*, SRI SWARU'PA, RA'MA'NAND, and others, including HARI DA's: the last, indeed, has obtained almost equal honour with his master, being worshipped as a divinity in some places in Bengal—it is recorded of him, that he resided in a thicket for many years, and during the whole time he repeated the name of KRISHNA three hundred thousand times daily. In addition to these chiefs, the sect enumerates eight *Kavi Rajas*, or eminent and orthodox bards, amongst

one passage, the work indicates their being two brothers, conformably to the *Charitámrita*, and the tradition in general currency.

* The temples of *Govind Deva* and *Madanmohan*, both in ruins; a Sanscrit inscription in the former, however, attributing it to MAN SINH DEVA, a descendant of PRITHU RAO, is dated Sambat 1647, or A.D. 1591. Besides the authority of KRISHNA DA's, for these two brothers being cotemporary with CHAITANYA, who died in 1527, I have a copy of the *Vidagdha Mádhava*, of which RUPA is the author, dated 1525; it is not therefore likely, that SANATAN actually founded the temple of *Govind Deva*, although he may have been instrumental to its being undertaken. The interior of this temple is far superior to any of the religious structures to be met with along the *Ganges* and *Jumna*, and may almost be considered handsome: the exterior of that of *Madanmohan* is remarkable for its being built something after the plan of the pyramidical temples of *Tanjore*; or rather its exterior corresponds with that of the temples at *Bhuvaneswara* in *Cuttack*. *As. Res.* vol. xv. plate.

whom is KRISHNA DA's, the author of the *Chaitanya Charitámrita*, and they also specify sixty-four *Mahantas*, or heads of religious establishments.

The object of the worship of the CHAITANYAS is KRISHNA : according to them he is *Paramátmá*, or supreme spirit, prior to all worlds, and both the cause and substance of creation : in his capacity of creator, preserver, and destroyer, he is BRAHMA, VISHNU, and SIVA, and in the endless divisions of his substance or energy, he is all that ever was or will be : besides these manifestations of himself, he has, for various purposes, assumed specific shapes, as *Avatárs*, or descents; *Ansas*, or portions; *Ansansas*, portion of portions, and so on ad infinitum : his principal appearance, and, in fact, his actual sensible manifestation, was as KRISHNA, and in this capacity he again was present in CHAITANYA, who is therefore worshipped as the deity, as are the other forms of the same god, particularly as GOPA'L, the cow-herd, or GOPINA'TH, the lord of the milk-maids of *Vindraban ;* his feats, in which juvenile characters are regarded, are his *Lílá*, or sport.

It is not worth while to enter upon the prolix series of subtle and unmeaning obscurities in which this class of KRISHNA's worshippers envelop their sectarial notions : the chief features of the faith are the identification of *Vishnu* with *Brahme*, in common with all the *Vaishnava* sects, and the assertion of his possessing, in that character, sensible and real attributes, in opposition to the *Vedanta* belief of the nagative properties of God : these postulates being granted, and the subsequent identity of KRISHNA and CHAITANYA believed, the whole religious and moral code of the sect is comprised in one word, *Bhákti*, a term that signifies a union of implicit faith with incessant devotion, and which as illustrated by the anecdote of HARI DA's, above given, is the momentary repetition of the name of KRISHNA, under a firm belief, that such a practice is sufficient for salvation.

The doctrine of the efficacy of *Bhákti* seems to have been an important innovation upon the primitive system of the Hindu religion. The object of the *Vedas*, as exhibiting the *Vedanta*, seems to have been the inculcation of fixed religious duties, as a general acknowledgement of the supremacy of the deities, or any deity, and, beyond that, the necessity of overcoming material impurities, by acts of self-denial and profound meditation, and so fitting the spiritual part for its return to its original sources; in a word, it was essentially the same system that was diffused throughout the old pagan world. But the fervent adoration of any one deity superseded all this necessity, and broke down practice and speculation, moral duties, and political distinctions. KRISHNA himself declares, in the *Bhágavat*, that to his worshipper, that worship presents whatever he wishes—paradise, liberation, godhead, and is infinitely more efficacious than any or all observances, than abstraction, than knowledge of the divine nature, than the subjugation of the passions, than the practice of the *Yoga*, than charity, than virtue, or than any thing that is deemed most meritorious.* Another singular and important consequence results from these premises, for as all men are alike capable of feeling the sentiments of faith and devotion, it follows, that all castes become by such sentiments equally pure. This conclusion indeed is always admitted, and often stoutly maintained in theory, although it may be doubted whether it has ever been acted upon, except by CHAITANYA himself and his immediate disciples, at a period when it was their policy to multiply proselytes.† It is so

* यत् कर्म्मभिर्यत्तपसा ज्ञानवैराग्यतश्च यत् योगेन दानधर्म्मेण श्रेयोभिरितरैरपि। सर्व्वं मद्भक्तियोगेन मद्भक्तो लभतेऽञ्जसा। स्वर्गापवर्गं मद्धामकथञ्चित् यदि वाञ्छतं॥ *Bhágavat*, 11th Section.

† CHAITANYA admitted amongst his followers five *Pat'háns*—who purposed to attack and plunder him, but were stopped by his sanctity, and converted by his arguments: one of these, who was a *Pír*, he new-named RA'M DA's; another, their leader, was a young prince *(a Rájákumár,)* whom he named *Bijjili Khán.* CHAITANYA communicated the *Upadesa*, or initiating *Mantra* to them, and they all became famous *Vaishnavas;* পাঠান বৈষ্ণবনিহৈল তাঁরখ্যাতি॥ CHAITANYA uniformly maintains the pre-eminence of the faith over caste: the mercy of God, he says, regard neither tribe nor family; ঈশ্বরের কৃপাজাতি কুলনাহি মানে॥ KRISHNA did not disdain to eat in the house of *Vidura*, a *Sudra*, বিদুরের ঘরে কৃষ্ণ করিল ভোজন॥ and he cites *Sanscrit* texts for his authority—as शुचिसद्भक्तिदीप्ताग्निः दग्धदुर्जाति कल्मषः। श्वपा कोऽपिवुधैः श्लाघ्यो नवेदज्ञोऽपि नास्तिकः॥ "The *Chándála*, whose impurity is consumed by the chastening fire of holy faith, is to be reverenced by the wise, and not the unbelieving expounder of the *Vedas.*" Again; न मे भक्तश्चतुर्वेदी मद्भक्तः श्वपचः प्रियः। तस्मै देयं ततो ग्राह्यं स च पूज्यो यथा ह्यहं॥ The teacher of the four

far observed, however, that persons of all castes and occupations are admitted into the sect, and all are at liberty to sink their civil differences in the general condition of mendicant and ascetic devotees, in which character they receive food from any hands, and of course eat and live with each other, without regard to former distinctions. As followers of one faith, all individuals are, in like manner, equally entitled to the *Prasád*, or food which has been previously presented to the deity, and it is probably the distribution of this, annually, at *Jagannáth*, that has given rise to the idea, that at this place all castes of Hindus eat together: any reservation, however, on this head is foreign to the tenets of this sect, as well as of the *Rámánandi Vaishnavas*,* and in both, community of schism is a close connecting link, which should, in deed, as well as word, abrogate every other distinction.

The *Bhakti* of the followers of this division of the Hindu faith is supposed to comprehend five *Rasas* or *Ratis*, tastes or passions: in its simplest form it is mere *Sánta*, or quietism, such as was practised by the *Yógendras*, or by sages, as SANAKA and his brethren, and other saints: in a more active state, it is servitude, or *Dásya*, which every votary takes upon himself; a higher condition is that of *Sákhya*, a personal regard or friendship for the deity, as felt by BHI'MA, ARJUNA, and others, honoured with his acquaintance. *Bátsalya*, which is a higher station, is a tender affection for the divinity, of the same nature as the love of parents for their children, and the highest degree of *Bhakti* is the *Mádhúrya*, or such passionate attachment as that which pervaded the feelings of the *Gopis*, towards their beloved KRISHNA.

The modes of expressing the feelings thus entertained by his votaries towards KRISHNA, do not differ essentially from those prevalent amongst the followers of the *Gokulast'ha Gosains*: the secular worshippers, however, pay a less regular homage in the temples of KRISHNA, and in most parts of Bengal, his public adoration occurs but twice a day, or between nine and twelve in the morning, and six and ten at night: occasionally, however, it does take place in a similar manner, or eight times a day. The chief ritual of the Bengal *Vaishnavas*

Vedas is not my disciple; the faithful *Chándála* enjoys my friendship; to him be given, and from him be received: let him be reverenced, even as I am reverenced. These passages are from the *Chaitanya Charitámrita*, where many others of similar purport may be found.

* See remark on the *Rámánandi Vaishnavas*; page 37.

of the class is a very simple one, and the *Náma Kírt'tana*, or constant repetition of any of the names of KRISHNA, or his collateral modifications, is declared to be the peculiar duty of the present age, and the only sacrifice the wise are required to offer; it is of itself quite sufficient to ensure future felicity: however, other duties, or *Sádhanas*, are enjoined, to the number of sixty-four, including many absurd, many harmless, and many moral observances; as fasting every eleventh day, singing and dancing in honour of KRISHNA, and suppressing anger, avarice, and lust. Of all obligations, however, the *Guru Pádásraya*, or servile veneration of the spiritual teacher, is the most important and compulsory: the members of this sect not only are required to deliver up themselves and every thing valuable to the disposal of the *Guru*, they are not only to entertain full belief of the usual *Vaishnava* tenet, which identifies the votary, the teacher, and the god, but they are to look upon the *Guru* as one and the present deity, as possessed of more authority even than the deity, and as one whose favour is more to be courted, and whose anger is more to be deprecated, than even that of KRISHNA himself.* We have already had occasion to observe that this veneration is hereditary, and is paid to the successor of a deceased *Gosain*, although, in the estimation perhaps of his own worshippers, he is in his individual capacity more deserving of reprobation than of reverence. This blind and extravagant adoration of the *Guru* is, perhaps, the most irrational of all Hindu irrationalities, and it is but justice to the founders of the system to acquit them of being immediately

* On this subject, the following text occurs in the *Upásana Chandrámrita*, योमन्त्रः सगुरुः साक्षात् यो गुरुः स हरिस्स्वयं ॥ The *Mantra* is manifest in the *Guru*, and the *Guru* is HARI himself. प्रथमं तु गुरुः पूज्यस्ततश्चैव ममार्चनं । "First, the *Guru* is to be worshipped, then I am to be worshipped." गुरुरेव सदाराध्यः श्रेष्ठोमन्त्रादभेदतः गुरौ तुष्टेहरिस्तुष्टः नान्यथा कल्प कोटिभिः । "The *Guru* is always to be worshipped: he is most excellent from being one with the *Mantra*. HARI is pleased when the *Guru* is pleased; millions of acts of homage else will fail of being accepted." Again, हरौ रुष्टे गुरुस्त्राता गुरौ रुष्टे नकश्चन: । "When HARI is in anger, the *Guru* is our protector; when the *Guru* is in anger, we have none." These are from the *Bhajanámrita*.

the authors of this folly. The earliest works inculcate, no doubt, extreme reverence for the teacher, but not divine worship; they direct the disciple to look upon his *Guru* as his second father, not as his God: there is great reason to suppose, that the prevailing practice is not of very remote date, and that it originates chiefly with the *Sri Bhágavat*: it is also falling into some disrepute, and, as we shall presently see, a whole division of even CHAITANYA's followers have discarded this part of the system.

Liberation from future terrestrial existence is the object of every form of Hindu worship. The prevailing notion of the means of such emancipation is the re-union of the spiritual man, with that primitive spirit, which communicates its individual portions to all nature, and which receives them, when duly purified, again into its essence. On this head, however, the followers of CHAITANYA, in common with most of the *Vaishnava* sects, do not seem to have adopted the *Vedánta* notions; and, although some admit the *Sáyujya*, or identification with the deity, as one division of *Mukti*, others are disposed to exclude it, and none acknowledge its pre-eminence: their *Moksha* is of two kinds; one, perpetual residence in *Swerga*, or Paradise, with possession of the divine attributes of supreme power, &c. and the other, elevation to *Vaikunt'ha* —the heaven of VISHNU, which is free from the influence of *Máyá*, and above the regions of the *Avatárs*, and where they enjoy one or all of the relations to KRISHNA, which have been enumerated when speaking of the followers of RA'MA'NUJA and MADHWA'CHA'RYA.

The doctrines of the followers of CHAITANYA are conveyed in a great number of works, both in Sanscrit and Bengali. The sage himself, and the two other *Maháprabhus*, NITYA'NAND and ADWAITA, do not appear to have left any written compositions, but the deficiency was amply compensated by RU'PA and SANA'TAN, both of whom were voluminous and able writers. To RU'PA are ascribed the following works: the *Vidagdha Mádhava*, a drama; the *Lalitá Madhavá*, *Ujjala Nilamani*, *Dána Kéli Kaumudi*, poems in celebration of KRISHNA and RA'DHA'; *Bahustavávali*, hymns; *Ashtádasa Lílá Khánd*; *Padmávali*, *Govinda Virudávali*, and its *Lakshana*, or exposition; *Mathura Máhátmya*, panegyrical account of *Mathurá*, *Nátaka Lakshana*, *Laghu Bhágavat*, an abridgement of the *Sri Bhágavat*, and the *Vruja Vilás Vernanam*, an account of KRISHNA's sports in *Vrindávan*. SAN'ATAN was the author of the *Hari Bhakti Vilás*, a work on the nature of the deity and devotion the *Rásámrita Sindhu*, a work of high authority on the same subjects, the *Bhágavat Amrita*, which contains the observances of the sect, and the *Siddhánta Sára*, a commentary on the 10th Chapter of the *Sri Bhágavat*. Of the other six *Gosains*, JIVA wrote the *Bhágavat Sanderbha*, the *Bhakti Siddhánta*, *Gopála Champu*, and *Upadesámrita*, and RAGHUNATH DA'S, the *Manassíkshá* and *Gunalesa Suk'hara*. These are all in Sanscrit. In Bengali, the *Rága Maya Kóna*, a work on subduing the passions, is ascribed to RU'PA, and *Rasamaya Kaliká*, on devotedness to KRISHNA, to SANA'TAN. Other Sanscrit works are enumerated amongst the authorities of this sect, as the *Chaitanya Chandrodaya*, a drama, *Stava Málá*, *Stavámrita Laharí*, by VISWANA'TH CHAKRAVERTI ; *Bhajanámrita*, *Sri Smarana Derpana, by* RAMCHANDRA *Kavirája* ; the *Gopipremámrita*, a comment on the *Krishna Kernámrita*, by KRISHNA DA's *Kavirája* ; and the *Krishna Kírtana*, by GOVIND DA's and VIDYA'PATI. The biographical accounts of CHAITANYA have been already specified in our notice of the *Chaitanya Charitámrita*, and besides those, there enumerated, we have the *Chaitanya Mangala*, a history of the saint, by LOCHANA, and the *Gauraganóddesa dípiká*, an account of his chief disciples. The principal works of common reference, and written in *Bengali*, though thickly interspersed with *Sanscrit* texts, are the *Upásanáchandrámrita*, a ritual, by LA'L DA's, the *Prémábhákti Chandriká*, by THAKUR *Gosain*, the *Páshanda Dalana*, a refutation of other sects, by RA'DHA'MA'DHAVA, and the *Vaishnava Verddhana*, by DAIVAKI NANDANA. There are no doubt many other works circulating amongst this sect, which is therefore possessed of a voluminous body of literature of its own.*

The *Vaishnavas* of this sect are distinguished by two white perpendicular streaks of sandal, or *Gopichandana*, down the forehead, uniting at the root of the nose, and continuing to near the tip ; by the name of *Rádhá Krishna* stamped on the temples, breast and arms ; a close necklace of *Tulasi* stalk of three strings, and a rosary of one hundred and eight or sometimes even of a thousand beads made of the stem of the *Tulasi* ; the necklace is sometimes made of very minute beads,

* The particulars of the above are taken chiefly from the CHAITANYA CHARITA'MRITA, others from the *Upásaná Chandrámrita*, and a few from the list given by *Mr. Ward*—Account of the Hindus, Vol. 2. 448.

and this, in upper India, is regarded as the characteristic of the *Chaitanya* sect, but in Bengal it is only worn by persons of the lowest class. The *Chaitanya* sectaries consist of every tribe and order, and are governed by the descendants of their *Gosains*. They include some *Udásínas*, or *Vairágis*, men who retire from the world, and live unconnected with society in a state of celibacy and mendicancy: the religious teachers are, however, married men, and their dwellings, with a temple attached, are tenanted by their family and dependants. Such cœnobitical establishments as are common amongst the *Rámánandis* and other ascetics, are not known to the great body of the *Chaitanya Vaishnavas*.

Besides the divisions of this sect arising from the various forms under which the tutelary deity is worshipped, and thence denominated *Rádháramanis, Rádhípális, Vihárijí* and *Govindji*, and *Yugala Bhaktas*, and which distinctions are little more than nominal, whilst also they are almost restricted to the Bengal *Vaishnavas* about *Mathura* and *Vindravan*, there are in Bengal three classes of this sect, that may be regarded as seceders from the principal body, these are denominated *Spashtha Dáyakas, Karta Bhajas* and *Sahujas*.

The *Spashtha Dáyakas* are distinguished from perhaps every other Hindu sect in India by two singularities—denial of the divine character, and despotic authority of the *Guru*, and the, at least professedly, platonic association of male and female cœnobites in one conventual abode.*

The secular followers of this sect are, as usual, of every tribe, and of the *Grihast'ha*, or householder order: the teachers, both male and female, are *Udásína*, or mendicants and ascetics, and lead a life of celibacy: the sectarial marks are a shorter *Tilaka* than that used by the other *Chaitanyas*, and a single string of *Tulasi* beads worn close round the neck: the men often wear only the *Kaupína*, and a piece of cloth round the waist, like an apron, whilst the women shave their heads, with the exception of a single slender tress: those amongst them who are most rigid in their conduct, accept no invitations nor food from any but persons of their own sect.

The association of men and women is, according to their own assertions, restricted to a residence within the same inclosure, and leads to no other than such intercourse as becomes brethren and sisters, or than

* Like the brethren and sisters of the free spirit, who were numerous in Europe in the 13th century—See Mosheim 3. 379.

the community of belief and interest, and joint celebration of the praise of KRISHNA and CHAITANYA, with song and dance: the women act as the spiritual instructors of the females of respectable families, to whom they have unrestricted access, and by whom they are visited in their own dwellings: the institution is so far political, and the consequence is said to be actually, that to which it obviously tends, the growing diffusion of the doctrines of this sect in Calcutta, where it is especially established.

The *Karta Bhajas,* or worshippers af the Creator, are a sect of very modern origin, having been founded no longer than thirty years ago by RA'MA SARAN PA'LA, a *Gwála,* an inhabitant of *Ghospara,* a village near *Sukh Sagar,* in Bengal.* The chief peculiarity of this sect, is the doctrine of the absolute divinity of the *Guru,* at least as being the present *Krishna,* or deity incarnate, and whom they therefore, relinquishing every other form of wroship, venerate as their *Ishta Devata,* or elected god: this exclusive veneration is, however, comprehended within wide limits: we have seen that it prevails amongst the followers of *Ghaitanya* generally, and it need scarcely have been adopted as a schismatical distinction: the real difference, however, is the person, not the character of the *Guru,* and the innovation is nothing, in fact, but an artful encroachment upon the authority of the old hereditary teachers or *Gosains,* and an attempt to invest a new family with spiritual power: the attempt has been so far successful, that it gave affluence and celebrity to the founder, to which, as well as his father's sanctity, the son, RA'MDULA'L PA'L has succeeded. It is said to have numerous disciples, the greater proportion of whom are women. The distinctions of caste are not acknowledged amongst the followers of this sect, at least when engaged in any of their religious celebrations, and they eat

† See *Mr. Ward's* account of this sect, Vol. 2. 175.; in a note he has given a translation of the *Mantra,* "Oh! sinless Lord—Oh! great Lord, at thy pleasure I go and return, not a moment am I without thee, I am even with thee, save, Oh! great Lord:" the following is the original:

কর্ত্তা আউলে মহাপ্রভু আমি তোমার স্বখে চলি ফিরি তিলার্দ্ধ তোমা ছাড়া নহি আমি তোমারসঙ্গে আছি দোহাই মহা প্রভু॥ This is called the *Solah ana Mantra,* the *Neophyte* paying that sum, or sixteen annas for it: it is, perhaps, one singularity in the sect, that this *Mantra* is in *Bengali,* a common spoken language—in all other cases it is couched in Sanscrit, the language of the gods.

together in private, once or twice a year: the initiating *Mantra* is supposed to be highly efficacious in removing disease and barrenness, and hence many infirm persons and childless women are induced to join the sect.

The remaining division of the Bengal *Vaishnavas* allow nothing of themselves to be known: their professions and practices are kept secret, but it is believed that they follow the worship of *Sakti*, or the female energy, agreeably to the left handed ritual, the nature of which we shall hereafter have occasion to describe.

The chief temples of the Bengal *Vaishnavas*, besides those which at *Dwáraká* and *Vrindavan*, and particularly at *Jagannáth*, are objects of universal reverence, are three, one at *Nadiya*, dedicated to Chaitanya, one at *Ambiká*, to Nitya'nand and the same, and one at *Agradwipa*, dedicated to Gopina'th: at the latter a celebrated *Méla*, or annual fair, is held in the month of March, at which from 50 to 100,000 persons are generally collected.

RADHA VALLABHIS.

Although the general worship of the female personifications of the Hindu deities forms a class by itself, yet when individualised as the associates of the divinities, whose energies they are, their adoration becomes so linked with that of the male power, that it is not easy, even to their votaries, to draw a precise line between them: they, in fact, form a part of the system, and *Lakshmí* and *Sítá* are the preferential objects of devotion to many of the followers of Ra'ma'nuja and Ra'ma'nand, without separating them from the communion of the sect.

In like manner Ra'dha', the favourite mistress of Krishna, is the object of adoration to all the sects who worship that deity, and not unfrequently obtains a degree of preference that almost throws the character from whom she derives her importance into the shade: such seems to be the case with the sect now noticed, who worship Krishna as *Rádhá Vallabha*, the lord or lover of Ra'dha'.

The adoration of Ra'dha' is a most undoubted innovation in the Hindu creed, and one of very recent origin. The only Ra'dha' that is named in the *Mahábhárat* is a very different personage, being the wife of DURYODHANA's charioteer, and the nurse of KERNA. Even the *Bhágavat* makes no particular mention of her amongst the *Gupis* of *Vrindavan*, and we must look to the *Brahma Vaivertta Purána*, as the chief authority of a classical character, on which the pretensions of RA'DHA' are founded; a circumstance which is of itself sufficient to indicate the comparatively modern date of the *Purána*.

According to this work, the primeval being having divided himself into two parts, the right side became KRISHNA, and the left RA'DHA', and from their union, the vital airs and mundane egg were generated. RA'DHA' being, in fact, the *Ich'chá Sakti*, the will or wish of the deity, the manifestation of which was the universe.

RA'DHA' continued to reside with KRISHNA in *Goloka*, where she gave origin to the *Gopís*, or her female companions, and received the homage of all the divinities. The *Gopas*, or male attendants of KRISHNA, as we have formerly remarked, were in like manner produced from his person. The grossness of Hindu personification ascribes to the KRISHNA of the heavenly *Goloka*, the defects of the terrestial cowherd, and the RA'DHA' of that region is not more exempt from the causes or effects of jealousy than the nymph of *Vrindavan*. Being on one occasion offended with KRISHNA for his infidelity, she denied him access to her palace, on which she was severely censured by SUDA'MA', a *Gopa*, and confidential adviser of KRISHNA. She therefore cursed him, and doomed him to be born on earth as an *Asura*, and he accordingly appeared as SANKHACHURA. He retaliated by a similar imprecation, in consequence of which RA'DHA' was also obliged to quit her high station, and was born at *Vrindavan* on earth, as the daughter of a *Vaisya*, named VRISHABHA'NU, by his wife KALAVATI. KRISHNA having, at the same time, become incarnate, was married to her at *Vrindavan*, when he was fourteen, and she was twelve years of age: as a further result of the imprecation, she was separated from him after he attained maturity, until the close of his earthly career; when she preceded him to the celestial *Goloka*, and was there re-united with him. The following is a further illustration of the notions of RA'DHA' entertained by this sect. It is the address of GANESA to her, in the *Brahma Vaivertta Purána*, after she had set the example of presenting offerings to him.

"Mother of the universe, the worship thou hast offered affords a lesson to all mankind. Thou art of one form with *Brahme,* and abidest on the bosom of KRISHNA. Thou art the presiding goddess of his life, and more dear than life to him, on the lotus of whose feet meditate the gods *Brahmá, Siva, Sesha,* and the rest, and *Sanaka* and other mighty munis, and the chiefs of the sages, and holy men, and all the faithful. RA'DHA' is the created left half, and MA'DHAVA the right, and the great *Lakshmí,* the mother of the world, was made from thy left side. Thou art the great goddess, the parent of all wealth, and of the *Védas,* and of the world. The primœval *Prakriti,* and the universal *Prakriti,* and all the creations of the will, are but forms of thee. Thou art all cause and all effect. That wise *Yogi,* who first pronounces thy name, and next that of KRISHNA, goes to his region; but he that reverses this order, incurs the sin of Brahminicide.* Thou art the mother of the world. The *Paramátmá* HARI is the father. The *Guru* is more venerable than the father, and the mother more venerable than the *Guru.* Although he worship any other god, or even KRISHNA, the cause of all, yet the fool in this holy land who reviles RA'DHIKA', shall suffer sorrow and pain in this life, and be condemned to hell, as long as the sun and moon endure. The spiritual preceptor theaches wisdom, and wisdom is from mystical rites and secret prayers; but they alone are the prayers of wisdom, that inculcate faith in KRISHNA and in you. He who preserves the *Mantras* of the gods through successive births, obtains faith in DURGA', which is of difficult acquisition. By preserving the *Mantra* of DURGA', he obtains SAMBHU, who is eternal happiness and wisdom. By preserving the *Mantra* of SAMBHU, the cause of the world, he obtains your lotus feet, that most difficult of attainments. Having found an asylum at your feet, the pious man never relinquishes them for an instant, nor is separated from them by fate. Having with firm faith received, in the holy land of *Bharata,* your *Mantra* (initiating prayer,) from a *Vaishnava,* and adding your praises *(Stava)* or charm, *(Kavacha)* which cleaves the root of works, he delivers himself (from future births) with thousands of his kindred. He who having properly worshipped his *Guru* with clothes, ornaments, and sandal, and assumed thy *Kavacha,* (a charm or prayer, carried about

* Accordingly the formula used by the *Rádhá Vallabhi* sect, and the like, is always RA'DHA' KRISHNA, never KRISHNA RA'DHA'.

the person in a small gold or silver casket,) is equal to VISHNU himself."

In what respect the *Rádhá Vallabhis* differ from those followers of the Bengali *Gosains*, who teach the worshp of this goddess in conjunction with KRISHNA, does not appear, and perhaps there is little other difference than that of their acknowledging separate teachers. Instead of adhearing to any of the hereditary *Gosains*, the members of this sect consider a teacher named HARI VANS, as their founder. This person settled at *Vrindavan*, and established a *Math* there, which in 1822 comprised between 40 and 50 resident ascetics. He also erected a temple there that still exists, and indicates, by an inscription over the door, that it was dedicated to *Sri Rádhá Vallabha* by HARI VANS, in *Samvat* 1641, or A.D. 1585. A manual, entitled *Rádhá Sudha Nidhi*, which is merely a series of Sanscrit verses in praise of RA'DHA', is also ascribed to the same individual. A more ample exposition of the notions of the sect, and of their traditions and observances, as well as a collection of their songs or hymns, is the *Seva Sakhi Váni*, a work in *Bhákha*, in upwards of forty sections. There are other works in the vernacular dialects, and especially in that of *Bruj*, or the country about *Mathura* and *Vrindavan*, which regulate or inspire the devotion of the worshippers of *Rádhá Vallabha*.

SAKHI BHAVAS.

The sect is another ramification of those which adopt KRISHNA and RA'DHA' for the objects of their worship, and may be regarded as more particularly springing from the last named stock, the *Rádhá Vallabhis*. As RA'DHA' is their preferential and exclusive divinity, their devotion to this personification of the *Sakti* of RRISHNA is ridiculously and disgustingly expressed. In order to convey the idea of being as it were her followers and friends, a character obviously incompatible with the difference of sex, they assume the female garb, and adopt not only the dress and ornaments, but the manners and occupations of women: the preposterous nature of this assumption is too apparent, even to

Hindu superstition, to be regarded with any sort of respect by the community, and, accordingly, the *Sak'hi Bhávas* are of little repute, and very few in number: they occasionally lead a mendicant life, but are rarely met with: it is said that the only place where they are to be found, in any number, is *Jaypur:* there are a few at Benares, and a few in Bengal.

CHARAN DASIS.

Another *Vaishnava* sect conforming with the last, in the worship of *Rádhá* and *Krishna*, was instituted by Charan Da's, a merchant of the *Dhusar* tribe, who resided at *Dehli* in the reign of the second Alemgir. Their doctrines of universal emanation, are much the same as those of the *Vedanta* school, although they correspond with the *Vaishnava* sects in maintaining the great source of all things, or *Brahme*, to be Krishna: reverence of the *Guru*, and assertion of the pre-eminence of faith, above every other distinction, are also common to them with other *Vaishnava* sects, from whom, probably, they only differ in requiring no particular qualification of caste, order, nor even of sex, for their teachers: they affirm, indeed, that originally they differed from other sects of *Vaishnavas*, in worshipping no sensible representations of the deity, and in excluding even the *Tulasi* plant and *Sálagrám* stone from their devotions: they have, however, they admit, recently adopted them, in order to maintain a friendly intercourse with the followers of Ra'ma'nand: another peculiarity in their system is the importance they attach to morality, and they do not acknowledge faith to be independent of works: actions, they maintain, invariably meet with retribution or reward: their moral code, which they seem to have borrowed from the *Mádhwas*, if not from a purer source, consists of ten prohibitions. They are not to lie, not to revile, not to speak harshly, not to discourse idly, not to steal, not to commit adultery, not to offer violence to any created thing, not to imagine evil, not to cherish hatred, and not to indulge in conceit or pride. The other obligations enjoined, are, to discharge the duties of the profession or caste to which a person belongs, to associate with pious men, to put implicit faith in the spiritual preceptor, and to adore HARI as the original and indefinable cause of all, and who, through the operation of MA'YA', created the universe, and has appeared in it occasionally in a mortal form, and particularly as KRISHNA at *Vindravan.*

The followers of CHARAN DA's are both clerical and secular; the latter are chiefly of the mercantile order; the former lead a mendicant and ascetic life, and are distinguished by wearing yellow garments, and a single streak of sandal, or *Gopichandana*, down the forehead; the necklace and rosary are of *Tulasi* beads: they wear also a small pointed cap, round the lower part of which they wrap a yellow turban. Their appearance in general is decent, and their deportment decorous; in fact, although they profess mendicity, they are well supported by the opulence of their disciples; it is possible, indeed, that this sect, considering its origin, and the class by which it is professed, arose out of an attempt to shake off the authority of the *Gokulast'ha Gosains.*

The authorities of the sect are the *Sri Bhágavat* and *Gítá,* of which they have *Bhásha* translations: that of the former is ascribed, at least in parts, to CHARAN DA's himself: he has also left original works, as the *Sandeha Ságar* and *Dharme Jiháj*, in a dialogue between him and his teacher, SUKH DEVA, the same, according to the *Charan Dásis*, as the pupil of VYAS, and narrator of the *Purános*. The first disciple of CHARAN DA's was his own sister, SAHAJI BAI, and she succeeded to her brother's authority, as well as learning, having written the *Sahaj Prakás* and *Solah Tat Nirnaya:* they have both left many *Sabdas* and *Kavits:* other works, in *Bhásha*, have been composed by various teachers of the sect.

The chief seat of the *Charan Dásis* is at *Delhi*, where is the *Samádh,* or monument of the founder: this establishment consists of about twenty resident members: there are also five or six similar *Mat'hs* at *Dehli,* and others in the upper part of the *Doab*, and their numbers are said to be rapidly increasing.

HARISCHANDIS, SADHNA PANT'HIS, AND MADHAVIS.

These sects may be regarded as little more than nominal. The two first have originated, apparently, in the determination of some of the classes considered as outcaste, to adopt new religious as well as civil distinctions for themselves, as they were excluded from every one actually existing. The *Harischandis* are *Doms*, or sweepers, in the western provinces: their name bears an allusion to the *Paurânik* prince *Harischandra*,* who, becoming the purchased slave of a man of this impure order, instructed his master, it is said, in the tenets of the sect. What they were, however, is not known, and it may be doubted whether any exist.

Sadhna, again, was a butcher, but it is related of him, that he only sold, never slaughtered meat, but purchased it ready slain. An ascetic rewarded his humanity with the present of a stone, a *Sálágram*, which he devoutly worshipped, and, in consequence, Vishnu was highly pleased with him, and conferred upon him all desires. Whilst on a pilgrimage, the wife of a Brahman fell in love with him, but he replied to her advances, by stating, that a throat must be cut before he would comply, which she misinterpreting, cut off her husband's head: finding Sadhna regarded her on this account with increased aversion, she accused him of the crime, and as he disdained to vindicate his innocence, his hands were cut off as a punishment, but they were restored to him by Jaganna'th. The woman burnt herself, on her husband's funeral pile, which Sadhna observing, exclaimed; "No one knows the ways of women, she kills her husband, and becomes a *Sati*," which phrase has passed into a proverb. What peculiarity of doctrine he introduced amongst the *Vaishnavas* of his tribe, is no where particularised.

Ma'dho is said to have been an ascetic, who founded an order of mendicants called *Mádhavis*: they are said to travel about always with a *Saroda* or *Balian*, stringed instruments of the guitar kind, and to accompany their solicitations with song and music: they are rarely if ever to be met with, and their peculiarity of doctrine is not known. The founder appears to be the same with the Ma'dhoji of the *Bhakta Málá*, who was an inhabitant of *Garagerh*, but there are several celebrated ascetics of the same name, especially a Ma'dho Da's, a Brahman of *Kanoj*, who was a man of considerable learning, and spent some time in *Orissa* and *Vrindavan*. He was probably a follower of Chaitanya.

* See the Story of *Harischandra* in Ward, Vol. 1, p. 16. Note.

SANYASIS, VAIRAGIS, &c.

Much confusion prevails in speaking of the mendicant and monastic orders of the Hindus, by the indiscriminate use of the terms prefixed to this division of our subject, and from considering them as specific denominations. They are, on the contrary, generic terms, and equally applicable to any of the erratic beggars of the Hindus, be they of what religious order they may: they signify, in fact, nothing more than a man, who has abandoned the world, or has overcome his passions, and are therefore equally suitable to any of the religious vagrants we meet with in Hindustan: the term *Fakir* is of equally general application and import, although it is of Mohammedan origin, and in strictness, more descriptive of the holy beggars of that faith.

Although, however, *Sanyásis* and *Vairágis*, and other similar denominations are used, and correctly used in a wide acceptation, yet we occasionally do find them limited in meaning, and designating distinct and inimical bodies of men. When this is the case, it may be generally concluded, that the *Sanyásis* imply the mendicant followers of Siva, and the *Vairágis* those of Vishnu.

The distinction thus made requires, at its outset, a peculiar exception, for besides the indiscriminate application of the term *Sanyási* to the *Vaishnavas*, as well as other mendicants; there is a particular class of them to whom it really appertains, these are the *Tridandis*, or *Tridandi Sanyásis*.

The word *Danda* originally imports a *staff*, and it figuratively signifies moral restraint; exercised in three ways especially, or in the control of speech, body, and mind; or word, deed, and thought: a joint reference to the literal and figurative sense of the term has given rise to a religious distinction termed *Danda Grahanam*, the taking up of the staff, or adopting the exercise of the moral restraints above-mentioned, and carrying, as emblematic of such a purpose, either one, or, as in the present instance, three small wands or staves. *Tridandi* designates both these characteristics of the order.

Tridandi Sanyásis are such members of the *Rámánuja*, or *Sri Vaishnava* sect, as have past through the two first states of the Brahmanical order, and entered that of the *Sanyási*, or the ascetic life: their practices are, in some other respects, peculiar: they never touch metals nor fire, and subsist upon food obtained as alms from the family Brahmans of the *Sri Vaishnava* faith alone: they are of a less erratic disposition than most other mendicants, and are rarely met with in upper India: they are found in considerable numbers, and of high character, in the South: in their general practices, their religious worship, and philosophical tenets, they conform to the institutes and doctrines of RA'MA'NUJA.

VAIRAGIS.

The term *Vairági* implies a person devoid of passion,* and is therefore correctly applicable to every religious mendicant, who affects to have estranged himself from the interests and emotions of mankind. *Virakta*, the dispassionate, and *Avadhúta*, the liberated, have a similar import, and are therefore equally susceptible of a general application: they are, indeed, so used in many cases, but it is more usual to attach a more precise sense to the terms, and to designate by them the mendicant *Vaishnavas* of the *Rámánandi* class, or its ramifications, as the disciples of KABIR, DADU, and others.

The ascetic order of the *Rámánandi Vaishnavas*, is considered to have been instituted especially by the twelfth disciple of RA'MA'NAND, SRI ANAND: they profess perpetual poverty and continence, and subsist upon alms: the greater number of them are erratic, and observe no form of worship, but they are also residents in the *Mat'hs* of their respective orders,† and the spiritual guides of the worldly votaries; it is almost impossible, however, to give any general character of these *Vairágis*, as, although united generally by the watch-word of VISHNU, or his incarnations, there are endless varieties both of doctrine and

* From *Vi* privative prefix, and *Rága* passion.

† The *Rámánandi Vairágis*, although indigenous in upper India, have established themselves in the Dekhin, as mentioned by *Buchanan*, (Mysore, 2. 76.) the account he gives there of the *Dekhini Vairágis*, is an excellent illustration of the confusion that prevails respecting the application of the term; as he has blended with the *Rámánandi* ascetics, who are accurately entitled to the designation, a variety of religious vagrants, to some of whom the name is rarely, and to others never applied: as *Paramahansas, Digambaras*, or *Nágas, Urddhaváhus*, and even *Aghoris;* the latter are not named, but they, or similar *Saiva* mendicants are the only individuals "who extort compassion by burning themselves with tourches, and cutting themselves with swords."

practice amongst them : those who are collected in *Mat'hs*, are of more fixed principles than their vagrant brethren, amongst whom individuals are constantly appearing in some new form with regard to the deity they worship, or the practices they follow.*

NAGAS.

All the sects include a division under this denomination. The *Nágas* are of the same description as the *Vairágis*, or *Sanyásis*, in all essential points, but in their excess of zeal, they carry their secession from ordinary manners so far, as to leave off every kind of covering, and, as their name signifies, go naked; there are, however, other points in which they differ from the general character of Hindu mendicants, and they are unquestionably the most worthless and profligate members of their respective religions.

A striking proof of their propensities is their use of arms. They always travel with weapons, usually a matchlock and sword and shield, and that these implements are not carried in vain has been shewn on various occasions : the sanguinary conflicts of opposite sects of Hindu mendi-

* Such are the *Sitá Padres*, *Ramati Ráms*, and others; also the new and scarcely yet known sects *Gulál Dásis*, and *Derya Dásis* : mention is also made in the *Dabistan*, of a number of Hindu mendicants, who are no longer numerous, if ever to be encountered. It is not possible in general, however, to discriminate the classes to which they belong, as in the descriptions given by the writer, he usually confines himself to a few peculiarities of practice that afford no guide to the principles of the sect, and as in the case of the *Dhers*, he confounds the distinction of caste, or occupation with that of religious belief. Many of the vagrant ascetics whom he notices belong also rather to the Mohammedan, than the Hindu religion, as in the followers of SHEIKH BEDIA AL DIN MEDAR—who, although they credit the divine mission of Mohammed, disregard the established forms of the Musselman faith, chew *Bheng*, and go naked, smearing their bodies with *Vibhut*, or the ashes of burnt cow-dung, and twisting their hair into the *Jatá*, or braid worn by Hindu ascetics—except as professed worshippers of *Niranjan*, or the indescribable deity, and a belief in magic, these mendicants have little in common with the Hindu religion, or perhaps with any, although, with a facility of which innumerable instances occur in Hindustan, they have adopted many of the Hindu practices. The tomb of *Skeikh Medar* is still to be seen at *Makhenpur*, near *Firozabad*, in the *Doab*—where, at the time of the *Dabistan*, an annual meeting of his disciples was held. The tomb is an extensive building, though in decay. The *Dabistan*, although it contains many curious, and some correct notices of the Hindu religion, affords too loose and inaccurate a description to be consulted with advantage.

cants, have been described in several publications, with the customary indistinctness as to the parties concerned: these parties are the *Vaishnava* and *Saiva Nágas* chiefly, assisted and probably instigated by the *Vairágí* and *Sanyási* members of those two sects, and aided by abandoned characters from all the schisms connected respectively with the one or the other:* it would, however, be doing an injustice to the mendicant orders of any sect, to suppose that they are universally or even generally implicated in these atrocious affrays.

* As. Res. vi. 317, and xii. 455; an occurrence of a similar nature is recorded by the author of the Dabistan, who mentions, that in 1050 of the Hijra, a severe conflict took place at Dwaraka, between a set of Vaishnava ascetics termed *Mundis*, from shaving their heads, and the *Sanyásis*, in which a great number of the former were slain.

PART SECOND.

SAIVAS.

In the former communication on this subject, which I had the honour to lay before the Society, I attempted to convey a notion of the different classes amongst which the numerous worshippers of Vishnu are distributed. In my present, I propose to complete my task, and commencing with the followers of Siva and of Sakti, conclude with those sects which are of a miscellaneous and less orthodox description.

The worship of Siva in the districts along the Ganges, presents itself under a very different aspect from that of Vishnu, and with some singular anomalies. It appears to be the most prevalent and popular of all the modes of adoration, to judge by the number of shrines dedicated to the only form under which Siva is reverenced, that of the *Linga;* yet it will be generally observed, that these temples are scarcely ever the resort of numerous votaries, and that they are regarded with comparatively little veneration by the Hindus. *Benares*, indeed, furnishes exception, and the temple of *Visweswara** is thronged with a never-ceasing crowd of adorers. There is, however, little solemnity or veneration in the hurried manner in which they throw their flowers or

* "The Lord of all," an epithet of Siva, represented as usual by a *Linga*. It is one of the twelve principal emblems of this description, and has been, for many centuries, the chief object of veneration at *Kási* or *Benares*. The old temple was partially destroyed by the Mohammedans in the reign of Aurengzeb: the present was built by Ahalya Bai, the Mahratta Princess, and although small and without pretension to magnificence, is remarkable for the minute beauty of its architectural embellishments.

fruits before the image ;* and there are other temples, the dwellings of other divinities, that rival the abode of *Visweswara* in popular attraction.

The adoration of SIVA, indeed, has never assumed, in upper India, a popular form. He appears in his shrines only in an unattractive and rude emblem, the mystic purpose of which is little understood, or regarded by the uninitiated and vulgar, and which offers nothing to interest the feelings or excite the imagination. No legends are recorded of this deity of a poetic and pleasing character ; and above all, such legends as are narrated in the Puranas and Tantras, have not been presented to the Hindus in any accessible shape. The *Saivas* have no works in any of the common dialects, like the *Rámáyana*, the *Bártta*, or the *Bhakta Málá*. Indeed, as far as any enquiry has yet been instituted, no work whatever exists, in any vernacular dialect, in which the actions of SIVA, in any of his forms, are celebrated. It must be kept in mind, however, that these observations are intended to apply only to Gangetic Hindustan, for in the South of India, as we shall hereafter see, popular legends relating to local manifestations of SIVA, are not uncommon.

Corresponding to the absence of multiplied forms of this divinity, as objects of worship, and to the want of those works which attach importance to particular manifestations of the favourite god, the people can scarcely be said to be divided into different sects, any farther than as they may have certain religious mendicants for their spiritual guides. Actual divisions of the worshippers of SIVA are almost restricted to these religious personages, collected sometimes, in opulent and numerous associations ; but for the greater part detached, few, and indigent. There are no establishments amongst the *Saivas* of Hin-

* A Hindu temple comprises an outer court, usually a quadrangle, sometimes surrounded by a piazza ; and a central edifice constituting the shrine. This, which in upper India is generally of small dimensions, is divided into two parts, the *Sabhá*, or vestibule ; and the *Garbhagriha*, or adytum, in which the Image is placed. The course of worship is the circumambulating of the temple, keeping the right hand to it, as often as the devotee pleases : the worshipper then enters the vestibule, and if a bell is suspended there, as is commonly the case, strikes two or three times upon it. He then advances to the threshhold of the shrine, presents his offering, which the officiating Brahman receives, mutters inaudibly a short prayer, accompanied with prostration, or simply with the act of lifting the hands to the forehead, and departs. There is nothing like a religious service, and the rapid manner in which the whole is performed, the quick succession of worshippers, the gloomy aspect of the shrine, and the scattering about of water, oil, and faded flowers, inspire any thing but feelings of reverence or devotion.

dustan, like those of *Srináth* or *Puri;* no individuals as wealthy as the *Gokulastha Gosains,* nor even as influential as the descendants of ADWAITA and NITYA'NAND. There are no teachers of ancient repute except SANKARA ACHA'RYA, and his doctrines are too philosophical and speculative to have made him popular.

The worship of SIVA continues, in fact, to be what it appears to have been from a remote period, the religion of the *Brahmanas.** SAMBHU is declared, by MENU, to be the presiding deity of the Brahmanical order, and the greater number of them, particularly those who practice the rites of the *Vedas*, or who profess the study of the *Sastras*, receive SIVA as their tutelary deity, wear his insignia, and worship the *Linga*, either in temples, in their houses, or on the side of a sacred stream, providing, in the latter case, extempore emblems kneaded out of the mud or clay of the river's bed. The example of the Brahmans, and the practice of ages, maintain the veneration universally offered to the type of SIVA; but it is not the prevailing, nor the popular condition of the Hindu faith, along the banks of the Ganges. We shall now proceed to specify the different classes into which the worshippers of SIVA, as distinct from the mass of Brahmans, may be distinguished.

DANDIS AND DASNAMIS.

It is customary to consider these two orders as forming but one division. The classification is not, in every instance, correct, but the practices of the two are, in many instances, blended, and both denominations are accurately applicable to the same individual. It will not be necessary, therefore, to deviate from the ordinary enumeration.

The *Dandis,* properly so called, and the *Tridandis* of the *Vaishnavas,* are the only legitimate representatives of the fourth *Asrama,* or mendicant life, into which the Hindu, according to the instructions of his inspired legislators, is to enter, after passing through the previous

* See a preceding Note—A. R. vol. XVI. page 2.

stages of student, householder and hermit.* It is not necessary, however, to have gone through the whole of the previous career, as the Brahman may pass from any one of the first orders to the last at once;† he is then to take up his staff and water pot, to derive from begging such a portion of food as is sufficient for his mere sustenance, and to devote the remainder of his day to holy study and pious meditation.‡

Adopting, as a general guide, the rules of original works, the *Dandí* is distinguished by carrying a small *Dand,* or wand, with several processes or projections from it, and a piece of cloth dyed with red ochre, in which the Brahmanical cord is supposed to be enshrined, attached to

* Thus MENU, 6, 33.

वनेषु तु विहृत्यैवन्तृतीयम्भागमायुषः ।
चतुर्थमायुषो भागंत्यक्त्वा सङ्गान् परिव्रजेत् ॥

"Having thus performed religious acts in a forest during the third portion of his life, let him become a *Sanyási*, for the fourth portion of it, abandoning all sensual affection.

† So MENU, as expounded by KULLUKA BHATTA, 6, 38.

प्रजापत्यां निरूप्येष्टिं सर्व्ववेदसदक्षिणाम्
आत्मन्यग्नीन् समारोप्य ब्राह्मणः प्रव्रजेद्गृहात् ॥
ब्रह्मचर्य्यादेव प्रव्रजेत् गृहाद्वा वनद्वा इति टीका ।

"Having performed the sacrifice of *Prájápati,* &c. a Brahman may proceed from his house, that is, from the second order, or he may proceed even from the first to the condition of a *Sanyási.*" Indeed the intermediate stage of the *Vanaprastha* is amongst the prohibited acts in the *Kali* age.

‡ Agreeably to the high authority already quoted, 6, 41, &c.

आगारादभिनिष्क्रान्तः पवित्रोपचितोमुनिः
समुपोढेषु कामेषु निरपेक्षः परिव्रजेत् ॥
अनग्निरनिकेतः स्याद्ग्राम मन्नार्थं माश्रयेत्
उपेक्षकोऽसंकुसुको मुनिर्भावसमाहितः ।

"Departing from his house, taking with him pure implements, his water-pot, and staff, keeping silence, unallured by desire of objects near him, let him enter into the fourth order."

"Let him have no culinary fire, no domicile, let him when very hungry, go to the town for food, let him patiently bear disease, let him study to know God, and fix his attention on God alone."

it: he shaves his hair and beard, wears only a cloth round his loins, and subsists upon food obtained ready-dressed from the houses of the Brahmanas once a day only, which he deposits in the small clay pot that he carries always with him: he should live alone, and near to, but not within a city; but this rule is rarely observed, and in general the *Dandís* are found in cities collected like other mendicants in *Maths.** The *Dandí* has no particular time or mode of worship, but spends his time in meditation, or in practices corresponding with those of the *Yoga*, and in the study of the *Vedanta* works, especially according to the comments of SANKARA'CHA'RYA. As that teacher was an incarnation of SIVA,† the *Dandís* reverence that deity and his incarnations, in preference to the other members of the Triad, whence they are included

* These are all founded on the following texts of MENU:—

क्लृप्तकेशनखश्मश्रुः पात्रीदण्डी कुसुम्भवान्
विचरेन्नियतोनित्यं सर्व्वभूतान्यपीडयन् ॥
एककालञ्चरेद्भैक्षं न प्रसज्जेत विस्तरे ।
भैक्षे प्रसक्तो हि यतिर्विषयेष्वपि सज्जति ।
विधूमे सन्नमुसले व्यङ्गारे भुक्तवज्जने
वृत्ते सरावसम्पाते भिक्षान्नित्यं यतिश्चरेत् ॥
अलाभे न विषादी स्याल्लाभे चैव न हर्षयेत्
प्राणयात्रिकमात्रः स्यान्मात्रासङ्गाद्विनिर्गतः ॥

"His hair, nails and beard being clipped, bearing with him a dish, a staff, and a water-pot, let him wander about continually without giving pain to any being." 52.

"Only once a day let him demand food, let him not habituate himself to eat much at a time, for an anchorite habituated to eat much, becomes inclined to sensual gratification." 55.

"At the time when the smoke of kitchen fires has ceased, when the pestle lies motionless, when the burning charcoal is extinguished, when people have eaten and when dishes are removed, that is, late in the day, let the *Sanyási* always beg food."

"For missing it let him not be sorrowful, nor for gaining it, let him be glad, let him care only for a sufficiency to support life, but let him not be anxious about his utensils." 57, MENU 6.

† This character is given to him in the *Sankara Vijaya* of MA'DHAVA ACHA'RYA; his followers in the *Dekhin* assert that SIVA's descent as SANKARA, was foretold in the *Skanda Purána*: a prophecy which, if found in that work, will assist to fix its date, but the passage has not been met with.

amongst his votaries; and they so far admit the distinction as not unfrequently to bear the *Saiva* mark upon the forehead, smearing it with the *Tripundra*, a triple transverse line made with the *Vibhùti*, or ashes which should be taken from the fire of an *Agnihotra Brahman*, or they may be the ashes of burnt cowdung from an oblation offered to the god.* They also adopt the initiating *Mantra* of all the *Saiva* classes, either the five or six syllable Mantra, "*Nama Sivâya*," or, "*Om, Nama Sivâya.*" The genuine *Dandí*, however, is not necessarily of the *Saiva* or any other sect; and in their establishments it will be usually found that they profess to adore *Nirguna* or *Niranjana*, the deity devoid of attribute or passion.†

* The material, or *Vibhùti*, and the efficacy of the mark, the *Tripundra*, are thus described in the *Kásikhanda*—

आग्नेयमुच्यते भस्मदग्ध गोमयसम्भवं
तदेव द्रव्यमित्युक्तं त्रिपुण्ड्रस्य महामुने ॥

The ashes of fire made with burnt cowdung, are the material fittest for the *Tripundra*.

त्रिपुण्ड्रं कुरुते यस्तु भस्मना विधिपूर्वकम् ।
महापातकसङ्घातैर्मुच्यते चोपपातकैः
अमन्त्रेणापि यः कुर्य्यादज्ञात्वा महिमोन्नतिं
त्रिपुण्ड्रं भालफलके मुचयते सर्व्वपातकैः ।

Whoever marks the *Tripundra* with ashes, agreeably to rule, is purified from sins of the first and second degree: who makes it on his forehead without the *Mantras*, being ignorant of its virtue, will be purified from every simple sin. The mode of making it is thus laid down:

भ्रुवोर्मध्ये समारभ्य यावदन्तो भवेद्भ्रुवोः ।
मध्यमानामिकाङ्गुल्योर्मध्येतु प्रतिलोमतः ॥
अंगुष्ठेन कृता रेखा त्रिपुण्ड्राख्योभिधीयते ।

Beginning between the eye-brows, and carrying it to their extremity, the mark made with the thumb reverted between the middle and third fingers, is called the *Tripundra*.

† The *Dandis* of the North of India are the *Sanyásis*, or monastic portion of the *Smartal Brahmanas* of the South, of whom Buchanan gives the following account; "The most numerous class here, and which comprehends about one-half of all the Brahmans in the Lower Carnatic, is called the *Smartal* sect, and its members are the followers of SANKARA ACHA'RYA. They are commonly said to be of the sect of

The *Dandís*, who are rather practical than speculative, and who have little pretence to the appellation beyond the epithet and outward signs of the order, are those most correctly included amongst the *Saiva* sects. Amongst these, the worship of SIVA, as BHAIRAVA, is the prevailing form, and in that case part of the ceremony of initiation consists in inflicting a small incision on the inner part of the knee, and drawing the blood of the novice as an acceptable offering to the god. The *Dandís* of every description, have also a peculiar mode of disposing of their dead, putting them into coffins and burying them; or when practicable, committing them to some sacred stream. The reason of this is their being prohibited the use of fire on any account.*

Any Hindu of the three first classes may become *Sanyási* or *Dandí*, or, in these degenerate days, a Hindu of any caste may adopt the life and emblems of this order. Such are sometimes met with, as also are Brahmans, who, without connecting themselves with any community, assume the character of this class of mendicants. These constitute the *Dandís* simply so termed, and are regarded as distinct from the primitive members of the order, to whom the appellation of *Dasnámis* is also applied, and who admit none but Brahmans into their fraternity.

The *Dasinámi Dandís*, who are regarded as the descendants of the original members of the fraternity, are said to refer their origin to SANKARA ACHA'RYA, an individual who appears to have performed a part of some importance in the religious history of Hindustan; and to whom an influence has been often attributed much exceeding that which he really exercised. His biography, like that of most of the Hindu saints, is involved in considerable obscurity; but a few facts may be gleaned from such accounts as we have of him, upon which reliance may be placed, and to which it may not be uninteresting here briefly to advert.

SIVA, but they consider BRAHMA, VISHNU and ISWARA to be the same as the creator, preserver, and destroyer of the universe. They are readily distinguished by three horizontal stripes on the forehead, made with the ashes of cowdung." (Buch. 1. 13) "The *Sanyásis* are the *Gurus* of this sect;" (Ibid, 305) and the *Dandis* have great influence and authority amongst *Saiva* Brahmans of the North of India.

* In the South, the ascetic followers of both SIVA and VISHNU bury the dead; (Dubois, 56) so do the *Vaishnava Vairágis* and *Sanyásis* in the North of India, and the *Saiva Jogis*. The class of Hindu weavers called *Yogis*, have adopted a similar practice; (Ward 1, 201) all the castes in the South, that wear the *Linga*, do the same, (Buch. I. 27.)

A number of works are current in the South of India relating to this teacher, under the titles of *Sankara Cheritra, Sankara Kathá, Sankara Vijaya,* or *Sankara Digvijaya,* following much the same course of narration, and detailing little more than SANKARA's controversial victories over various sects; in most cases, no doubt, the fictions of the writers. Of the two principal works of the class, one attributed to ANANDAGIRI, a pupil of *Sankara*, has already been noticed.* The other is the work of MA'DHAVA ACHA'RYA, the minister of some of the earliest chiefs of *Vijayanagar*, and who dates, accordingly, in the fourteenth century. This is a composition of high literary and polemical pretension, but not equally high biographical value. Some particulars of SANKARA's birth and early life are to be found in the *Kerala Utpatti*, or political and statistical description of *Malabar*, although the work is sometimes said to have been composed by SANKARA himself.

With regard to the place of SANKARA's birth, and the tribe of which he was a member, most accounts agree to make him a native of *Kerala*, or *Malabar*, of the tribe of *Namburi* Brahmans, and in the mythological language of the sect, an incarnation of SIVA. According to other traditions, he was born at *Chidambaram*, although he transferred his residence to *Malabar*; whilst the *Kerala Utpatti* recognises *Malabar* as his native place, and calls him the offspring of adultery, for which his mother SRI MAHADEVI was expelled her caste.

In *Malabar*, he is said to have divided the four original castes into seventy-two, or eighteen sub-divisions each, and to have assigned them their respective rites and duties. Notwithstanding this, he seems to have met with particular disrespect, either on account of his opinions, origin, or his wandering life. On his return home, on one occasion, his mother died, and he had to perform the funeral rites, for which his relations refused to supply him with fire, and at which all the Brahmans declined to assist. SANKARA then produced fire from his arm, and burnt the corpse in the court yard of the house, denouncing imprecations on the country, to the effect, that the Brahmans there should not study the Vedas, that religious mendicants should never obtain alms, and that the dead should always be burned close to the houses in which they had resided—a custom which is said to have survived him.

* See Asiatic Researches, vol. XVI. page 10.

All accounts concur in representing SANKARA as leading an erratic life, and engaging in successful controversy with various sects, whether of the *Saiva*, *Vaishnava*, or less orthodox persuasions. In the course of his peregrinations, he established several *Maths*, or convents, under the presidence of his disciples, particularly one still flourishing at *Sringeri*, or *Sringagiri*, on the western Ghats, near the sources of the *Tungabhadrá*. Towards the close of his life, he repaired as far as to *Kashmir*, and seated himself, after triumphing over various opponents, on the throne of SARASWATI. He next went to *Badarikásrama*, and finally to *Kedarnáth*, in the *Himalaya*, where he died at the early age of thirty-two. The events of his last days are confirmed by local traditions, and the *Pítha*, or throne of SARASWATI, on which SANKARA sat, is still shown in *Kashmir*; whilst at the temple of SIVA, at *Badari*, a Malabar Brahman, of the *Namburi* tribe, has always been the officiating priest.*

The influence exercised by SANKARA in person, has been perpetuated by his writings, the most eminent of which are his *Bháshyas*, or Commentaries on the *Sútras*, or Aphorisms of VYA'SA. A Commentary on the *Bhagavad Gita*, is also ascribed to him, as is one on the *Nrisinha Tapaníya Upanishad*: a cento of verses in praise of DURGA, the *Saundaryá Laharí*, is likewise said to be his composition, as sometimes is the *Amru Sataka*, a collection of amatory stanzas, written in the name of AMRU, a Prince, whose dead body SANKARA is fabled to have animated, that by becoming familiarised with sensual enjoyments, he might argue upon such topics with the wife of *Madana Misra*, who was more than equal to him in discussions of this nature, and was the only disputant he was unable to subdue, until the period of his transmigration had expired, and he had thence become practised in the gratification of the passions.

Although no doubt of SANKARA's existence, or of the important part performed by him in the partial re-modelling of the Hindu system, can be entertained, yet the exact period at which he flourished can by no means be determined. I have, in another place, expressed my belief that he may have existed about the eighth or ninth century.† Subsequent enquiry has failed to add any reasons to those assigned for such an

* Asiatic Researches, vol. XII. page 536.

† Preface to the Sanscrit Dictionary, page XVII.

inference; but it has offered nothing to weaken or invalidate the conclusion there proposed.*

The spiritual descendants of SANKARA, in the first degree, are variously named by different authorities, but usually agree in the number. He is said to have had four principal disciples, who, in the popular traditions, are called *Padmapáda*, *Hastámalaka*, *Sureswara* or *Mandana*, and *Trotaka*. Of these, the first had two pupils, *Tírtha* and *Asrama*; the second, *Vana* and *Aranya*; the third had three, *Saraswatí*, *Purí*, and *Bhárati*; and the fourth had also three, *Giri* or *Gir*, *Párvata*, and *Ságara*. These, which being all significant terms, were no doubt adopted names, constitute collectively the appellation *Dasnámi*, or the *ten-named*, and when a Brahman enters into either class, he attaches to his own denomination that of the class of which he becomes a member; as *Tírtha*, *Purí*, *Gír*, &c.† The greater proportion of the ten

* A *Hálakánara* Manuscript, in the possession of the late Col. Mackenzie, entitled *Sankara Vijaya*, (Mackenzie Collection II, 34) gives the following list of the spiritual heads of the *Sríngeri* establishment.

1. Góvinda Páda.
2. Sankara Achárya.
3. Sanandana Achárya.
4. Surásura Achárya.
5. Trotaka Achárya.
6. Hastámalaka Achárya.
7. Jnyánaghana Achárya.
8. Jnyánottama Achárya.
9. Sinhagiríswara Achárya.
10. Iswaratírtha Achárya.
11. Nrisinha Múrtti Achárya.
12. Vitarana Achárya.
13. Vidyásankara Achárya.
14. Bháratí Krishna Achárya.
15. Vidyásanya Achráya.
16. Chandra Sekhara Achárya.
17. Nrisinha Bháratí Achárya.
18. Sankara Bharatí Achárya.
19. Nrisinha Bháratí Achárya.
20. Purushottoma Bháratí Achárya.
21. Ramachandra Bháratí Achárya.
22. Nrisinha Bháratí Achárya.
23. Immadi Bháratí Achárya.
24. Abhinava Nrisinha Bháratí Achárya.
25. Sachchidánanda Bháratí Achárya.
26. Nrisinha Bháratí Achárya.
27. Immádi Sachchidananda Bháratí Achárya.
28. Abhinava Sachchidánanda Bháratia Achárya.
29. Nrisinha Bháratí Achárya.

This gives 27 descents from SANKARA. As the *Mahant* is elected from the disciples, either by the *Guru* when about to die, or by the *Swámalu*, the spiritual chiefs of other establishments of the same sect, he is raised probably to the station in the prime of manhood, and in the ease and dignity of his sanctity has a favourable prospect of a long life. Twenty-five years to a *Guru* may therefore be but a fair average allowance, and the above list comprises at that rate an interval of 657 years: at what period it closes does not appear; but the *Halakanara* language is obsolete, and the work is possibly not less than two or three centuries old. This series of *Gurus* is so far corroborative of the view else where taken of SANKARA's date; but as it has been extracted by a Pandit, from a work which I could not consult myself, it is by no means certain that it is correct, and I do not wish to attach any undue importance to the authority.

† It is scarcely worth while perhaps to translate words of such common occurrence, but to prove what I have stated in the text, I subjoin their signification: *Tírtha*,

classes of mendicants, thus descended from SANKARA ACHA'RYA, have failed to retain their purity of character, and are only known by their epithets as members of the original order. There are but three, and part of a fourth mendicant class, or those called *Tírtha* or *Indra*, *Asrama*, *Saraswatí*, and *Bhárati*, who are still regarded as really SANKARA''s *Dandís*. These are sufficiently numerous, especially in and about Benares. They comprehend a variety of characters; but amongst the most respectable of them, are to be found very able expounders of the *Vedanta* works. Other branches of Sanscrit literature owe important obligations to this religious sect.* The most sturdy beggars are also members of this order, although their contributions are levied particularly upon the Brahmanical class, as whenever a feast is given to the Brahmanas, the *Dandís* of this description present themselves unbidden guests, and can only be got rid of by bestowing on them a due share of the cates provided for their more worldly-minded brethren. Many of them practice the *Yoga*, and profess to work miracles, although with less success than some members of the order in the days of the author of the *Dábistán*, who specifies one *Dandadhári*, as able to suspend his breath for three hours, bring milk from his veins, cut bones with hair, and put eggs into a narrow mouthed bottle without breaking them.

The remaining six and a half members of the *Dasnámi* class, although considered as having fallen from the purity of practice necessary to the *Dandí*, are still, in general, religious characters, and are usually denominated *Atíts*:† the chief points of difference between them and

a place of pilgrimage; *Asrama*, an order, as that of student, householder, &c.; *Vana*, a wood; *Aranya*, a wood; *Saraswáti*, the goddess of speech and eloquence; *Purí*, a city; *Bhárati*, speech, or its goddess; *Giri*, a mountain; in common use it always occurs *Gir*, which implies speech; *Párvata*, a mountaineer; *Ságara*, an ocean; the names are always compounded with different terms. One of SANKARA''s disciples we have seen, called ANANDA GIRI. The famous MA'DHAVA, when he became a *Dandi*, adopted the appellation of VI'DYA'RANYA. PU'RANGIR, has been elsewhere adverted to, and other like names occur in some of the following notes. *Bhárati* is the prevailing title of the latter *Sringagiri Gurus*.

* SANKARA' and MA'DHAVA are well known by their numerous and excellent works. The chief Vedanta writers, in like manner, were *Dandis*; and the author of the *Dasakumára*, RA'MASRAMA, the Commentator on AMERA, and VIJNYA'NESWARA, the Commentator on the texts of YAJNAVALKYA, were of the same class of ascetics.

† From अतिथि *Atithi*, a guest, a temporary dweller upon earth; or अतीत *Atíta*, past away, liberated from worldly cares and feelings.

the preceding, are their abandonment of the staff, their use of clothes, money, and ornaments; their preparing their own food, and their admission of members from any order of Hindus. They are often collected in *Maths*, as well as the *Dandís*, but they mix freely in the business of the world; they carry on trade, and often accumulate property, and they frequently officiate as priests at the shrines of some of the deities:* some of them even marry, but in that case they are distinguished by the term *Samyogí*, from the other *Atíts*.

The chief practices and designations of the *Dandís*, as generally characteristic of them, have been already adverted to, but a great variety prevails in the details.† Their philosophical tenets in the main, are those of the *Vedanta* system, as taught by SANKARA' and his disciples; but they generally superadd the practice of the *Yoga*, as taught by the followers of PATANJALI, and many of them have latterly adopted the doctrines of the *Tantras*. Besides SANKARA', the different orders of *Dandís* hold in high veneration the MUNI DATTATREYA, the son of ATRI and ANASUYA'. By virtue of a boon bestowed upon ATRI, or according to one legend, on his wife, by the three deities BRAHMA', VISHNU, and SIVA, that sage had three sons, SOMA, DATTA, and DURVA'SAS, who were severally portions of the deities themselves.‡ DATTA, or DATTATREYA, was eminent for his practice of the *Yoga*, and hence is held in high estimation by the *Jogis*, of whom we are next to speak, whilst, as an incarnation of a portion of VISHNU, he is likewise venerated by the *Vaishnavas*.

YOGIS OR JOGIS.

The *Dandís* are to the *Saiva* sects, what the followers of RA'MA'NUJA are to those of the *Vaishnava* faith, and a like parallel may be drawn

* The officiating priests at the celebrated shrine of ANNAPU'RNA, in Benares, are *Atits*.

† A specimen of the independent but scarcely orthodox *Dandi*, is presented in the well know personage *Puran Gir*, of whom Mr. Duncan published an account in the 5th volume of the Asiatic Researches.

‡ *Bhágavat*, Book IV, and *Márkandeya Purána*, Chapter XVI.

between the disciples of RA'MA'NAND and those of GORAKHNA'TH, or the *Kánphata Jogis*, the first pair being properly restricted to the Brahmanical order, intended chiefly for men of learning; the two latter admitting members from every description of people, and possessing a more attractive popular character.

The term *Jogi*, or *Yogi* is properly applicable to the followers of the *Yoga*, or *Pátanjala* school of philosophy, which, amongst other tenets, maintained the practicability of acquiring, even in life, entire command over elementary matter, by means of certain ascetic practices. The details of these it is unnecessary to particularize, and accounts of them and of the *Yoga* philosophy, will be best derived from the translation of BHOJA DEVA's' Comment on the *Pátanjala Sútras*, in Ward's Account of the Hindus, and Mr. Colebrooke's Essay on the *Sánkkya* and *Pátanjala* doctrines, in the 1st volume of the Transactions of the Royal Asiatic Society. It is sufficient here to observe, that the practices consist chiefly of long continued suppressions of respiration; of inhaling and exhaling the breath in a particular manner; of sitting in eighty-four different attitudes; of fixing the eyes on the top of the nose, and endeavouring, by the force of mental abstraction, to effect a union between the portion of vital spirit residing in the body and that which prevades all nature, and is identical with SIVA, considered as the supreme being, and source and essence of all creation. When this mystic union is effected, the *Yogi* is liberated in his living body, from the clog of material incumbrance, and acquires an entire command over all worldly substance. He can make himself lighter than the lightest substances, heavier than the heaviest; can become as vast, or as minute as he pleases, can traverse all space, can animate any dead body, by transferring his spirit into it from his own frame, can render himself invisible, can attain all objects, becomes equally acquainted with the past, present, and future, and is finally united with SIVA, and consequently exempted from being born again upon earth. The superhuman faculties are acquired, in various degrees, according to the greater or less perfection with which the initiatory processes have been performed.

According to standard authorities, the perfect fulfilment of the rites which the *Yogi* has to accomplish, requires a protracted existence and repeated births, and it is declared to be unattainable in the present or

Kali age.* The attempt is therefore prohibited, and the *Yoga* is prescribed in modern times. This inhibition is, however, disregarded, and the individuals who are the subjects of our enquiry, endeavour to attain the super-human powers which the performance of the *Yoga* is supposed to confer. They especially practice the various gesticulations and postures of which it consists, and labour assiduously to suppress their breath and fix their thoughts until the effect does somewhat realise expectation, and the brain, in a state of over-wrought excitement, bodies forth a host of crude and wild conceptions, and gives to airy nothings a local habitation and a name.† A year's intense application is imagined enough to qualify the adept,‡ whilst inferior faculties may be obtained by even a six month's practice.

* The *Khsikhanda* thus enumerates the difficulty or impossibility of completing the *Yoga* in the present age.

चञ्चलेन्द्रिय वृत्तित्वात्कलिकल्मषजृम्भणात् ।
अल्पायुष्यात्तथा नृणां केह योगमहोदयः ॥

"From the unsteadiness of the senses, the prevalence of sin in the *Kali*, and the shortness of life, how can Exaltation by the *Yoga* be obtained."

Again—

न सिध्यति कलौ योगो न सिध्यति कलौ तपः ।

In the *Kali* age, the *Yoga* and severe penance are impracticable.

† Some who have commenced their career in this line, have carried the practice to several hours duration, at which time they have described themselves as becoming perfectly exhausted, with strange objects passing before them, and sparks of fire flashing in their eyes. One individual quitted it from having at last a figure resembling himself always before him, and knowing this to be a deception, he wisely inferred the similar character of any other visionary creature of his contemplation, and the absurdity of the practice. Dubois has some amusing anecdotes on this subject, (page 357, &c.) they are fully authenticated by the similar accounts which many *Vairágis*, in upper India, will readily furnish. The worthy Abbe may indeed be generally trusted when he confines himself to what he saw or knew: in much that he heard he was misled, and in almost every thing connected with the language and literature, and the religion or philosophy, as taught by classical authority, he commits egregious blunders.

‡ ब्रह्मचारी मिताहारी योगी योगपरायणः ।
अब्दादूर्द्ध्वं भवेत्सिद्धो नात्र कार्य्या विचारणा ॥

Leading a life of chastity and abstemiousness, and diligent in the practice of the *Yoga*, the *Yogi* becomes perfect after a year: of this there is no doubt. *Hatha Prodipa*.

There are few *Jogis*, however, who lay claim to perfection, and their pretensions are usually confined to a partial command over their physical and mental faculties. These are evinced in the performance of low mummeries, or juggling tricks, which cheat the vulgar into a belief of their powers. A common mode of display is by waving a *Chowri*, or bunch of peacock's feathers, over a sick or new-born infant, to cure it of any morbid affection, or guard it against the evil eye. A trick of loftier pretence has, of late, attracted some notice in the person of a Brahman at Madras, who, by some ingenious contrivance, appeared to sit in the air, and who boasted of being able to remain for a considerable period under water. He and his followers ascribed the possession of these faculties to his successful practice of the observances of the *Yoga.**

In referring to the origin of this system, we must, no doubt, go back to some antiquity, although the want of chronological data renders it impossible to specify the era at which it was first promulgated. That it was familiarly known and practised in the eighth century, we may learn from the plays of BHAGABHU'TI, particularly the *Málatí* and *Mádhava*,† and from several of the *Saiva Puránas*, in some of which, as the *Kúrma Purána*, we have a string of names which

* "*Sitting in the Air.*—An exhibition at Madras has excited considerable curiosity. A Brahmin, old and slightly made, represented to be of high caste, contrives to poise himself in a most extraordinary manner in the air. He performs this feat at any gentleman's house, not for money, but as an act of courtesy. The following is a description, from an eye-witness, given in a Calcutta paper.—'The only apparatus seen is a piece of plank, which, with four pegs, he forms into a kind of long stool; upon this, in a little brass saucer or socket, he places, in a perpendicular position, a hollow bamboo, over which he puts a kind of crutch, like that of a walking crutch, covering that with a piece of common hide: these materials he carries with him in a little bag which is shown to those who come to see him exhibit. The servants of the house hold a blanket before him, and when it is withdrawn, he is discovered poised in the air, about four feet from the ground, in a sitting atitude, the outer edge of one hand merely touching the crutch, the fingers of that hand deliberately counting beads: the other hand and arm held up in an erect posture. The blanket was then held up before him, and they heard a gurgling noise like that occasioned by wind escaping from a bladder or tube, and when the screen was withdrawn he was again standing on terra firma. The same man has the power of staying under water for several hours. He declines to explain how he does it, merely saying he has been long accustomed to do so.' The length of time for which he can remain in his aerial station is considerable. The person who gave the above account says that he remained in the air for twelve minutes; but before the Governor of Madras he continued on his baseless seat for *forty minutes*"—*Asiatic Monthly Journal for March*, 1829.

† See especially the opening of the 5th Act, and Notes.

appear to be those of a succession of teachers.* The cavern temples of the South of India, in the subjects of their sculptures, and the decorations of SIVA and his attendants, belong to the same sect;† whilst the philosophical tenets of *Patanjali* are as ancient perhaps as most of the other philosophical systems, and are prior to the *Purânas*, by which they are inculcated in a popular form. The practices of the *Yoga* are also frequently alluded to, and enforced in the *Mahâbhârat*.‡ There is little reason to question therefore the existence and popularity of the *Yoga* in the early centuries of the Christian era, but whether it was known and cultivated earlier must be matter of vague conjecture alone. As represented in the *Sankaravijaya*, (Section 41) the *Yogis* vindicate their doctrine by texts from the *Vedas*, but the applicability of the texts is there denied, and is certainly far from conclusive or satisfactory.

The principal mode in which the *Yoga* takes a popular shape in upper India, is probably of comparatively recent origin. This is the

* SIVA, it is said, appeared in the beginning of the *Kali* age as SWETA, for the purpose of benefiting the Brahmanas. He resided on the *Himalaya* mountains and taught the *Yoga*. He had four chief disciples, one also termed SWETA, and the others SWETASIKHA, SWETASWA, and SWETALOHITA. They had twenty-eight disciples—*Sutâra*, *Madana*, *Suhotra*, *Kankana*, and twenty-four others. Of these four, whose names are not mentioned, had ninety-seven disciples, masters of the *Yoga* and inferior portions of SIVA. Those Brahmanas who recite the names of the teachers and offer to them libations acquire *Brahmavidyâ*, or knowledge of spirit. That this long string of one hundred and twenty-five names is wholly fictitious, seems improbable, although the list is possibly not very accurate. The four primitive teachers may be imaginary; but it is a curious circumstance that the word *Sweta*, *white*, should be the leading member of each appellation, and that in the person of SIVA, and his first disciple, it should stand alone as SWETA, *the white*. SIVA, however, is always painted white, and the names may be contrived accordingly; but we are still at a loss to understand why the god himself should have a European complexion.

† In the temples of *Salsette*, *Elephanta*, and *Ellora*, the principal figure is mostly SIVA, decorated with ear-rings, such as are still worn by the *Kânphata Jogis*; the walls are covered with ascetics in the various *Asanas*, or positions in which the *Yogi* is to sit; a favourite subject of sculpture at *Elephanta* and *Ellora* is the sacrifice of DAKSHA disconcerted, and the guests, though saints and gods, put to rout, bruised and mutilated, by VIRABHADRA, and the *Ganas* of SIVA, in revenge for that deity's not having been invited, a story told in most of the *Purânas* which inculcate the *Yoga* tenets. The cells attached to some of the temples are also indicative of *Jogi* residence, and one of the caves of *Salsette* is named that of *Jogiswara*, or SIVA, as lord of the *Jogis*. *Transactions of the Literary Society of Bombay.* Vols. 1 and 2.

‡ These allusions occur in the *Vana Parva* chiefly; whilst in the *Udyoga Parva*, the observances of the *Yoga* are detailed at considerable length, and strenuously enjoined.

sect of *Kánphata Jogis*, who acknowledge as their founder a teacher named GORAKHNA'TH, traces of whom are found in a *Gorakhkshetra* at *Peshawer*, mentioned by ABULFAZL, and in the district and town of *Gorakhpur*, where also exist a temple and religious establishment of his followers. They hold also in veneration a plain near *Dwáraka*, named *Gorakhkhetr*; and a cavern or subterraneous passage at *Haridwar*. The *Saiva* temples of *Nepal*, those of *Sambunath*, *Pasupatináth*, and others, belong to the same system, although local legends attached to them, have combined in a curious manner the fictions of the *Bauddha* with those of the Brahmanical mythology.*

From a *Ghoshti*,† or controversial dialogue between KABI'R and GORAKHNA'TH, it would seem that they were personally known to each other, but various texts in the *Bijek* allude to him as if recently deceased. In either case these two teachers may have been cotemporaries, or nearly so, and the latter therefore flourished in the beginning of the 15th century. According to his followers, he was an incarnation of SIVA; but in the controversial tract above named, he calls himself the son of MATSYENDRA NA'TH, and grandson of ADINA'TH.‡ MATSYENDRA NA'TH appears to have been the individual who introduced the *Yoga Saivism* into *Nepal*: one of the works of the sect, the *Hatha Pradípa*, makes MATSYENDRA prior to GORAKH by five spiritual descents.§ and this would place the former in the 14th century, supposing the *Kabir* work to be correct in the date it attributes to the latter.

* See Asiatic Researches, Vol. XVI. page 471, and Note.

† This has been printed in the first volume of Hindee and Hindustani Selections, for the use of the Interpreters of the Bengal Army, compiled by Captain Price. The discussion, in the form of a dialogue, occurs page 140.

‡ आदिनाथके नाती मच्छन्द्रनाथ के पूत ।
मैं योगी गोरख् अवधूत ॥

§ The list of teachers is thus particularised:

1. *Adináth.*	10. *Vileso.*
2. *Matsyendra.*	11. *Manthana Bhairava.*
3. *Sambara.*	12. *Siddhabuddha.*
4. *Ananda.*	13. *Kanthada.*
5. *Bhairava.*	14. *Paurandaka.*
6. *Chourángi.*	15. *Suránanda.*
7. *Ména.*	16. *Siddhapáda.*
8. *Goraksha.*	17. *Churpati.*
9. *Virúpáksha.*	18. *Káneri.*

If the date assigned by Hamilton to the migration of the Hindu tribes from *Chitaur*, the beginning of the 14th century, be accurate,* it is probable that this was the period at which the worship of SIVA, agreeably to the doctrines of MATSYENDRA, or GORAKH, was introduced there, and into the eastern provinces of Hindustan.

The temple of GORAKHNA'TH at *Gorakhpur*, according to the local tradition, was founded by SIVA in the second, or *Treta* age. Of its revolutions subsequent to that period, no account was preserved, until it was converted into a Mohammedan mosque by ALA-ADDIN. The temple, after some interval, was re-built in a different situation by an association of the followers of GORAKHNA'TH, and this was possibly the period at which the sect assumed its present form. A similar fate, however, attended this edifice, and it was appropriated by AURANGZEB to the Mohammedan religion. A second interval elapsed before a shrine was again erected to GORAKHNA'TH, when it was re-built on the spot on which it now stands, by BUDDHANA'TH, according to instructions communicated to him by GORAKHNA'TH in person. The present temple is situated to the west of the City of *Gorakhpur*, and attached to it on the south are three temples, consecrated to MAHA'DEVA, PASUPATINA'TH and HANUMA'N. The inclosure also comprehends the tombs of several eminent members of this communion, and the dwellings of the Mahant and his resident disciples.

GORAKHNA'TH was a man of some acquirement, and has left specimens of his scholarship in two Sanscrit Compositions, the *Goraksha sataka* and *Goraksha kalpa:* third, the *Goraksha sahasra Náma* is, probably, of his writing. The celebrated BHARTRIHARI, the brother of VEIKRAMA'DITYA, is said to have been one of his disciples, but chronology

19. *Pujyapáda.*
20. *Nityanátha.*
21. *Niranjana.*
22. *Kapála.*
23. *Bindu.*
24. *Kákachandiswara.*
25. *Allamá.*
26. *Prabhudeva.*
27. *Goráchili.*
28. *Dindima.*
29. *Bháluki.*
30. *Nágabodha.*
31. *Chandakapálika*

The author of the *Hatha Pradipa*, ATMA RA'MA, states that these and many more *Mahasiddhas*, or perfect *Yogis*, are in existence. His names are possibly those of the *Mahants*, of a particular establishment: some of them are very unlike Hindu appellatives. If the date assigned to *Goraknáth* in the text be rightly conjectured, we cannot assign much more than fifteen years to each of his successors.

* *Hamilton's Nepal*, page 14.

will not admit of such an approximation. According to the authorities of the sect, GORAKH is but one of nine eminent teachers, or *Náths*. Of the perfect *Yogis*, or *Siddhas*, eighty-four are enumerated; but it is said, that there have been many more, of whom several are still upon the surface of the earth.

The *Jogis* of GORAKHNA'TH are usually called *Kánphatas*, from having their ears bored, and rings inserted in them at the time of their initiation. They may be of any caste; they live as ascetics, either singly or in *Maths*.* SIVA is the object of their worship—they officiate indeed, as the priests of that deity, in some places, especially at the celebrated *Lát*, or Staff, of BHAIRAVA, at *Benares*. They mark the forehead with a transverse line of ashes, and smear the body with the same; they dress in various styles, but in travelling usually wear a cap of patch-work and garments dyed with red ochre. Some wear simply a *Dhoti*, or cloth round the loins.

The term *Jogi*, in popular acceptation, is of almost as general application as *Sanyási* and *Vairági;* and it is difficult to fix its import upon any individual class, besides the *Kánphata:* the vagrants so called, following usually the dictates of their own caprice as to worship and belief, and often, it may be conceived, employing the character as a mere plea for a lazy livelihood. The *Jogis* are, indeed, particularly distinguished amongst the different mendicant characters, by adding to their religious personification more of the mountebank than any others; most of the religious mendicants, it is true, deal in fortune-telling, interpretation of dreams, and palmistry; they are also often empirics, and profess to cure diseases with specific drugs, or with charms and spells: but besides these accomplishments, the *Jogi* is frequently musical, and plays and

* Solitary and independent living, however, appears to be improper, if the authority of the *Hatha Pradipa* is to be depended upon.

सुराज्ये धार्म्मिके देशे सुभिक्षे निरुपद्रवे ।
एकान्ते मठिकामध्ये स्थातव्यं हठ योगिना ॥

" In a well-governed and well-regulated country, fertile and prosperous, the *Hatha Yogi* (he who upholds the world in eternal continuity,) should reside in a solitary cell, within the precincts of a *Math*." " Other directions follow, applicable to most establishments of a similar nature. The cell should have a small door, be neither too lofty, nor too low, be well smeared with cow-dung, and should be kept clean and free from reptiles: the *Math* should have a temple, a mound or altar, and a well, adjoining, and be enclosed by a wall.

sings ; he also initiates animals into his business, and often travels about with a small bullock, a goat, or a monkey, whom he has taught to obey his commands, and to exhibit amusing gesticulations. The dress of this class of *Jogis* is generally a cap and coat, or frock of many colours: they profess to worship SIVA, and often carry the *Linga*, like the *Jangamas*, in the cap; all classes and sects assume the character, and *Musselman Jogis* are not uncommon. One class of the *Hindu Jogis* is called *Saringihar*, from their carrying a *Saringi*, or small fiddle or lute, with which they accompany their songs: these are usually *Bhásha* stanzas on religious or mythological topics, amongst which, stanzas ascribed to BHATRIHARI, and a *Pauranic* legend of the marriage of SIVA and PA'RVATI, are particularly celebrated. The *Saringihars* beg in the name of BHAIRAVA: another sect of them, also followers of that deity, are termed *Dúríhárs*, from their trafficking in small pedlary, especially the sale of thread and silk, to the housewives of the villages; another class adopt the name of *Matsyendris*, or *Macchendris*, from *Matsyendra*, whom they regard as their founder; and a fourth set are *Bhartriharis*, from a traditional reference to him as the institutor of this particular order. The varieties of this class of mendicants, however, cannot be specified: they are all errants; fixed residences, or *Maths*, of any *Jogis*, except the *Kánphatas*, rarely occurring: an observation that will apply to, perhaps, all the *Saiva* sects, of whom it yet remains to give an account.

JANGAMAS.

The worship of SIVA, under the type of the *Linga*, it has been observed, is almost the only form in which that deity is reverenced.*

* Its prevalence throughout the whole tract of the *Ganges*, as far as *Benares*, is sufficiently conspicuous. In Bengal, the temples are commonly erected in a range of six, eight, or twelve, on each side of a *Ghat*, leading to the river. At *Kalna* is a circular groupe of one hundred and eight temples, erected by the Raja of Bardwan. Each of the temples in Bengal, consists of a single chamber, of a square form, surmounted by a pyramidal centre; the area of each is very small, the *Linga*, of black or white marble, occupies the centre; the offerings are presented at the threshold. *Benares*, however, is the peculiar seat of this form of worship: the principal deity

It is also perhaps the most ancient object of homage adopted in India, subsequently to the ritual of the VEDAS, which was chiefly, if not wholly, addressed to the elements, and particularly to fire. How far the worship of the *Linga* is authorised by the VEDAS, is doubtful, but it is the main purport of several of the *Puranas*.* There can be no doubt of its universality at the period of the Mohammedan invasion of India. The idol destroyed by MAHMUD, of *Ghizni*, was nothing more than a *Linga*, being, according to MIRKHOND, a block of stone, of four or five cubits long, and proportionate thickness.† It was, in fact,

VISWESWARA, as observed already, is a *Linga*, and most of the chief objects of the pilgrimage are similar blocks of stone. Particular divisions of the pilgrimage direct visiting forty-seven *Lingas*, all of pre-eminent sanctity; but there are hundreds of inferior note still worshipped, and thousands whose fame and fashion have passed away. If we may believe SIVA, indeed, he counted a hundred *Parárrdhyas* in *Kasi*, of which, at the time he is supposed to tell this to DEVI, he adds sixty crore, or six hundred millions, were covered by the waters of the Ganges. A *Parárrdhya* is said, by the commentator on the *Kasi Khanda*, in which this dialogue occurs, to contain as many years of mortals as are equal to fifty of *Brahma's* years. Notwithstanding the acknowledged purport of this worship, it is but justice to state, that it is unattended in upper India by any indecent or indelicate ceremonies, and it requires a rather lively imagination to trace any resemblance in its symbols to the objects they are supposed to represent. The absence of all indecency from public worship and religious establishments in the Gangetic Provinces, was fully established by the Vindicator of the Hindus, the late General Stuart, and in every thing relating to actual practice, better authority cannot be desired. (Vindication, Part 1st, 99, and more particularly Part 2d, 135).

* The *Skanda Purana*, which contains the *Kasi Khanda*, particularly inculcates the worship of SIVA in this form; so do the *Siva*, *Brahmanda*, and *Linga Puranas*.

† The following is the passage from the *Rozet as Sefa*, alluded to:

وان خانه که سومنات درانجا بود طول وعرض تمام داشت
چنان که پنجاه وشش ستون وقایه مقف ان کرده بودند
وسومنات صنمي بود ازسنگ تراشیده طولش مقدار پنج گز
وعرض ان ظاهر و دو گز در زیر زمین مخفي ویمین الدوله
محمود ببتخانه درامده
باگرز گران سنگ سومنات را درهم شکست ومقداري ازان
سنگرا فرمود تابار کرده بغزنین میبردند ودر استانه مسجد
جائع بینداختند

one of the twelve great *Lingas*, then set up in various parts of India, several of which, besides *Someswara*, or *Somanath*, which was the

" The temple in which the Idol of *Somnath* stood, was of considerable extent, both in length and breadth, and the roof was supported by fifty-six pillars in rows. The Idol was of polished stone, its height was about five cubits, and its thickness in proportion: two cubits were below ground. MAHMUD having entered the temple, broke the stone *Somnath*, with a heavy mace: some of the fragments he ordered to be conveyed to *Ghizni*, and they were placed at the threshold of the great Mosque." Another authority, the *Tebkat Akbeeri*, a history of Akber's reign, with a preliminary Sketch of Indian History, has the following:

لشکر بجانب هندوستان بقصد سومنات کشیده واین سومنات
شهریست بزرگ برساحل دریا محیط معبد براهمنه است
وبتان در این بتخانه بسیار بودند وبت بزرگ را سومنات
نامند در تواریخ بنظر رسیده که درزمان ظهور حضرت ختمی
پناه مصطفی صلی الله علیه وسلم این بترا ازخانه کعبه
براورده بودند تا از این کتب سلف براهمنه معلوم میشود
ذکر چنین است از زمان کشن که چهار هزار سال میشد
معبود براهمنه است وبقول براهمنه کشن اینجا غیب نموده
— القصه چون سلطان بشهر نهرواله پتن رسید شهررا خالي
دید فرمود تاغلبه برداشتند وراه سومنات پیش گرفته چون
بسومنات رسیدند اهل انجا قلعه‌را برروی سلطان کشیدند
وبعد از جنگ وتردد بسیار قلعه مفتوح گشت لوازم بتاراج
وغارت بعمل آمد وخلق کثیر بقتل واسیر شد ببتخانها
شکسته از بیخ برکندند وسنگ سومنات را پارچه پارچه کرده پارا
را بغزنین برده بدر مسجد جامع گذاشته وسالها سنگ اینجا بود

" In the year 415 *(Hijera)* MAHMUD determined to lead an army against *Somnath*, a city on the sea-shore, with a temple appertaining to the followers of BRAHMA; the temple contained many idols, the principal of which was named *Somnath*. It is related in some histories that this idol was carried from the *Kaaba*, upon the coming of the Prophet, and transported to India. The Brahmanical records, however, refer it to the time of KRISHNA, or an antiquity of 4000 years. KRISHNA, himself, is said to have disappeared at this place.

name of the SIVA, demolished by MAHMUD, were destroyed by the early Mahommedan conquerors.* Most, if not all of them, also are named in works, of which the date cannot be much later than the

" When the Sultan arrived at *Neherwaleh,* (the capital of Guzerat) he found the city deserted, and carrying off such provisions as could be procured, he advanced to *Somnath:* the inhabitants of this place shut their gates against him, but it was soon carried by the irresistible valour of his troops, and a terrible slaughter of its defenders ensued. The temple was levelled with the ground: the idol *Somnath,* which was of stone, was broken to pieces, and in commemoration of the victory, a fragment was sent to *Ghizni,* where it was laid at the threshold of the principal mosque, and was there many years."

These statements shew that the idol was nothing more than a block of stone, of very moderate dimensions, like the common representation of the type of SIVA. FERISHTA, however, has converted it into something very different, or a colossal figure of the deity himself, and following Colonel Dow's version of that compiler, the historian of British India gives the following highly coloured account of a transaction which never took place. " Filled with indignation at sight of the gigantic idol, MAHMUD aimed a blow at its *head,* with his iron mace. The *nose* was struck off from its *face.* In vehement trepidation, the *Brahmans* crowded round and offered millions to spare the god. The *Omráhs,* dazzled with the ransom, ventured to counsel acceptance. MAHMUD crying out that he valued the title of Breaker not Seller of idols, gave orders to proceed with the work of destruction. At the next blow the *belly* of the *idol* burst open, and forth issued a vast treasure of diamonds, rubies and pearls, rewarding the holy perseverance of MAHMUD, and explaining the devout liberality of the *Brahmans!*" (Vol. 1. 491.)

* The twelve *Lingas* are particularised in the *Kedára Kalpa,* of the *Nandi Upapuràna,* where SIVA is made to say—" I am omnipresent, but I am especially in twelve forms and places." These he enumerates, and they are as follow:

1. *Somanatha,* in *Saurashtra,* i. e. *Surat,* in its most extensive sense, including part of *Guzerat,* where, indeed, *Patana Somnath,* or the city of *Somnath,* is still situated.

2. *Mallikárjuna,* or *Sri Saila,* described by Colonel Mackenzie, the late Surveyor General. Asiatic Researches, Vol. 5th.

3. *Mahákála,* in *Ougein.* This deity of stone was carried to *Dehli,* and broken there upon the capture of *Ougein,* by ALTUMSH. A. D. 1231,—Dow. According to the *Tebkat Akberi,* the shrine was then three hundred years old.

4. *Omkdra* is said to have been in *Ujayin,* but it is probably the shirne of MAHADEO, at *Omkára Mandatta,* on the *Nurmadá.*

5. *Amareswara* is also placed in *Ujayin:* an ancient temple of MAHADEO, on a hill near *Ujayin,* is noticed by Dr. Hunter, Asiatic Researches, Vol. 6th, but he does not give the name or form.

6. *Vaidyanáth,* at *Deogerh,* in Bengal; the temple is still in being, and is a celebrated place of pilgrimage.

7. *Ramésa,* at *Setubandha,* the island of *Ramisseram,* between Ceylon and the continent; this *Lingam* is fabled to have been set up by RAMA. The temple is still in tolerable repair, and is one of the most magnificent in India. The gateway is one hundred feet high. It has been repeatedly described, and is delineated in Daniel's Superb Plates of Indian Antiquities, from which it has been copied into Langle's Monuments de L'Hindoostan.

eighth or ninth century, and it is therefore, to be inferred, with as much certainty as any thing short of positive testimony can afford, that the worship of SIVA, under this type, prevailed throughout India at least as early as the fifth or sixth century of the Christian era. Considered as one great branch of the universal public worship, its prevalence, no doubt, dates much earlier; but the particular modifications under which the several types received their local designations, and became entitled to special reverence, are not in every case of remote antiquity.

One of the forms in which the *Linga* worship appears, is that of the *Lingayets*, *Lingawants*, or *Jangamas*, the essential characteristic of which is wearing the emblem on some part of the dress or person. The type is of a small size, made of copper or silver, and is commonly worn suspended in a case round the neck, or sometimes tied in the turban. In common with the *Saivas*, generally, the *Jangamas* smear their foreheads with *Vibhúti* or ashes, and wear necklaces, and carry rosaries, made of the *Rudráksha* seed. The clerical members of the sect usually stain their garments with red ochre. They are not numerous in upper India, and are rarely encountered, except as mendicants, leading about a bull, the living type of *Nandi*, the bull of SIVA, decorated with housings of various colours, and strings of cowri shells: the conductor carries a bell in his hand, and thus accompanied goes about from place to place, subsisting upon alms. In the south of India, the *Lingayets* are very numerous, and the officiating priests of the *Saiva* shrines, are commonly of this sect,* when they bear the designations of *Arádhya* and *Pandaram.*† The sect is also there known by the name of *Vira Saiva*. The following account of the restorer, if not the founder of the

8. *Bhimasankara*, in *Dákini*, which is, in all probability, the same with *Bhiméswara*, a *Linga* worshipped at *Dracharam*, in the *Rájamahendri* district, and there venerated as one of the principal twelve.

10. *Tryambaka*, on the banks of the *Gomati*; whether the temple still exists I have no knowledge.

11. *Gautamésa* is another of the twelve, whose original site and present fate are uncertain.

12. *Kedáresa*, or *Kedaranáth*, in the *Himalaya*, has been repeatedly visited by late travellers. The deity is represented by a shapeless mass of rock.

* They also officiate in this capacity at the temple of *Kedárnáth*, in *Benares*.

† This word seems to be properly *Pánduranga*, (पाण्डुरङ्गः) pale complexioned, from their smearing themselves with ashes. It is so used in *Hemachandra's* history of *Mahávira*, when speaking of the *Saiva Brahmans*.

faith, as well as a specimen of the legends by which it is maintained, are derived from the *Básava Purána.*

According to the followers of this faith, which prevails very extensively in the Dekhin, *Báswa, Básava, Báswana* or *Báswapa*, or *Básavappa*, different modes of writing his name, only restored this religion, and did not invent it. This person, it is said, was the son of *Mádiga Ráya*, a Brahman, and *Madevi* written also *Madala arasu* and *Mahámbá*, inhabitants of *Hinguleswar Parvati Agrahάram*, on the west of *Sri Saila*, and both devout worshippers of Siva. In recompense of their piety, *Nandi*, the bull of Siva, was born on earth as their son, becoming incarnate by command of Siva, on his learning from Na'reda, the decline of the *Saiva* faith, and prevalence of other less orthodox systems of religion. The child was denominated after the *Báswa* or *Básava*, the bull of the deity. On his arriving at the age of investiture, he refused to assume the thread ordinarily worn by Brahmans, or to acknowledge any *Guru*, except Iswara or Siva. He then departed to the town of *Kalyán*, the capital of *Bijala* or *Vijala Ráya*, and obtained in marriage *Gangámbá*, the daughter of the *Dandanáyak*, or minister of police. From thence he repaired to *Sangameswara*, where he received from *Sangameswara Swámí*, initiation in the tenets of the *Vira Saiva* faith. He was invited back from this place to succeed his father-in-law upon his decease, in the office he had held.

After his return to *Kalyán*, his sister, who was one of his first disciples, was delivered of a son, *Chenna Básava*, who is not unfrequently confounded with his uncle, and regarded, perhaps more correctly, as the founder of the sect.

After recording these events, the work enumerates various marvellous actions, performed by *Básava* and several of his disciples, such as converting grains of corn to pearls—discovering hidden treasures—feeding multitudes—healing the sick, and restoring the dead to life. The following are some of the anecdotes narrated in the *Purána*.

Básava having made himself remarkable for the profuse bounties he bestowed upon the *Jangamas*, helping himself from the Royal Treasury for that purpose, the other ministers reported his conduct to *Bijala*, who called upon him to account for the money in his charge. *Básava* smiled, and giving the keys of the treasury to the king, requested him to examine it, which being done, the amount was found wholly undiminished. *Bejala* thereupon caused it to be proclaimed, that whoever calumniated *Básava*, should have his tongue cut out.

A *Jangama*, who cohabited with a dancing girl, sent a slave for his allowance of rice to the house of *Básava*, where the messenger saw the wife of the latter, and on his return reported to the dancing girl the magnificence of her attire. The mistress of the *Jangama* was filled with a longing for a similar dress, and the *Jangama* having no other means of gratifying her, repaired to *Básava*, to beg of him his wife's garment. *Básava* immediately stripped *Gangámbá*, his wife, and other dresses springing from her body, he gave them all to the *Jangama*.

A person of the name of *Kanapa*, who regularly worshipped the image of EKA'MBESWARA, imagining the eyes of the deity were affected, plucked out his own, and placed them in the sockets of the figure. SIVA, pleased with his devotion, restored his worshipper his eyes.

A devout *Saiva* named *Mahadevala Macháya*, who engaged to wash for all the *Jangamas*, having killed a child, the Raja ordered *Básava* to have him secured and punished ; but *Básava* declined undertaking the duty, as it would be unavailing to offer any harm to the worshippers of SIVA. *Bijala* persisting, sent his servants to seize and tie him to the legs of an elephant, but *Machdya* caught the elephant by the trunk, and dashed him and his attendants to pieces. He then proceeded to attack the Raja, who being alarmed, applied to *Básava*, and by his advice, humbled himself before the offended *Jangama*. *Básava* also deprecated his wrath, and *Macháya* being appeased, forgave the king, and restored the elephant and the guards to life.

A poor *Jangam* having solicited alms of *Kinnaráya*, one of *Basava's* chief disciples, the latter touched the stones about them with his staff, and converting them into gold, told the *Jangam* to help himself.

The work is also in many places addressed to the *Jainas*, in the shape of a dialogue between some of the *Jangama* saints and the members of that faith, in which the former narrate to the latter instances of the superiority of the *Saiva* religion, and the falsehood of the *Jain* faith, which appears to have been that of *Bijala Ráya*, and the great part of the population of *Kalyána*. In order to convert them *Ekánta Ramáya*, one of *Básava's* disciples, cut off his head in their presence, and then marched five days in solemn procession, through and round the city, and on the fifth day replaced his head upon his shoulders. The *Jain* Pagodas were thereupon, it is said, destroyed by the *Jangamas*. It does not appear, however, that the king was made a convert, or that he approved of the principles and conduct of his minister. He seems, on the contrary, to have incurred his death by attempting to repress the extension of the *Vira Saiva* belief. Different authorities, although they disagree as to the manner in which *Bijala* was destroyed, concur in stating the fact: the following account of the transaction is from the present work.

"In the city of *Kalyána* were two devout worshippers of Siva, named *Allaya* and *Madhuvaya*. They fixed their faith firmly on the divinity they adored, and assiduously reverenced their spiritual preceptor, attending upon *Básava* whithersoever he went. The king, *Bijala*, well knew their merits, but closed his eyes to their superiority, and listening to the calumnious accusations of their enemies, commanded the eyes of *Allaya* and *Madhuvaya* to be plucked out. The disciples of *Básava*, as well as himself, were highly indignant at the cruel treatment of these holy men, and leaving to *Jagaddeva* the task of putting *Bijala* to death, and denouncing imprecations upon the city, they departed from *Kaláyna*—*Básava* fixed his residence at *Sangameswara*.

Macháya, *Bommidevaya*, *Kinnara*, *Kannatha*, *Bommadeva*, *Kakáyá*, *Masanaya*, *Kolakila Bommadeva*, *Kesirajaya*, *Mathirajaya*, and others, announced to the people, that the fortunes of *Bijala* had passed away, as indicated by portentous signs; and accordingly the crows crowed in the night, jackalls howled by day; the sun was eclipsed, storms of wind and rain came on, the earth shook, and darkness overspread the heavens. The inhabitants of *Kalyána* were filled with terror.

When *Jagaddeva* repaired home, his mother met him, and told him that when any injury had been done to a disciple of the *Saiva* faith, his fellow should avenge him or die. When *Daksha* treated Siva with contumely, Parvati threw herself into the flames, and so, under the wrong offered to the saints, he should not sit down contented: thus saying, she gave him food at the door of his mansion. Thither also came *Mallaya* and *Bommaya*, two others of the saints, and they partook of *Jagaddeva's* meal. Then smearing their bodies with holy ashes, they took up the spear, and sword, and shield, and marched together against *Bijala.* On their way a bull appeared, whom they knew to be a form of *Básava* come to their aid, and the bull went first, even to the court of the king, goring any one that came in their way, and opening a clear path for them. Thus they reached the court, and put *Bijala* to death in the midst of all his courtiers, and then they danced, and proclaimed the cause why they had put the king to death. *Jugaddeva* on his way back, recalling the words of his mother, stabbed himself. Then arose dissension in the city, and the people fought amongst themselves, and horses with horses, and elephants with elephants, until, agreeably to the curse denounced upon it by *Básava* and his disciples, *Kalyána* was utterly destroyed.

Básava continued to reside at *Sangameswara*, conversing with his disciples, and communing with the divine essence, and he expostulated with Siva, saying "By thy command have I, and thy attendant train, come upon earth, and thou hast promised to recall us to thy presence when our task was accomplished." Then Siva and Pa'rvati' came forth from the *Sangameswara Lingam*, and were visible to *Básava*, who fell on the ground before them. They raised him, and led him to the sanctuary, and all three disappeared in the presence of the disciples, and they praised their master, and flowers fell from the sky, and then the disciples spread themselves abroad, and made known the absorption of *Básava* into the emblem of Siva.—*Mackenzie Collection, Vol. 2nd. Hálakanara MSS.*

The date of the events here recorded is not particularised, but from various authorities, they may be placed with confidence in the early part of the eleventh century*.

The Mackenzie Collection, from which the above is taken, contains a number of works† of a similar description, in the ancient *Kanara* dialect. There are also several works of the same nature in *Telugu*, as the *Basaveswara Purana*, *Panditárádhya Cheritra*, and others. Although the

* Colonel Wilks gives the same date, (Mysore 1, 506,) but terms the founder *Chen Bas Ishwar*, intending clearly *Chenna* (little) *Básava*, the nephew of *Básava*, or *Basaveswara*. Buchanan has the name *Báswana*, (Mysore 1, 240,) but agrees nearly in the date, placing him about seven hundred years ago.

† As the *Báswana Purana*, *Chenna Básava Purana*, *Prabhulinga Lílá*, *Saranu Lilámrita*, *Viraktaru Kávyam*, and others, containing legends of a vast number of *Jangama* Saints and Teachers.—*Mackenzie Collection*, Vol. 2.

language of these compositions may now have become obscure or obsolete, it is not invariably so, and at any rate was once familiar. This circumstance, and the marvellous character of the legends they relate, specimens of which have been given in the above account of the founder of the sect, adapted them to the comprehension and taste of the people at large, and no doubt therefore exercised a proportionate influence. Accordingly, Wilks, Buchanan, and Dubois, represent the *Lingawants* as very numerous in the *Dekhin*, especially in *Mysore*, or those countries constituting ancient *Kanara*, and they are also common in *Telingana*. In Upper India there are no popular works current, and the only authority is a learned *Bháshya*, or Comment, by NILKANTHA, on the *Sútras* of VYA'SA, a work not often met with, and, being in Sanscrit, unintelligible to the multitude.*

PARAMAHANSA.

According to the introduction of the *Dwádasa Mahávákya*, by a *Dandi* author, VAIKUNTHE PURI, the *Sanyási* is of four kinds, the *Kutíchara*, *Bahudaka*, *Hansa*, and *Paramahansa:* the difference between whom, however, is only the graduated intensity of their self-mortification and profound abstraction. The *Paramahansa*† is the most eminent of these gradations, and is the ascetic who is solely occupied with the investiga-

* Besides the *Jangama* priests of *Kedárnáth*, an opulent establishment of them exists at *Benares:* its wealth arises from a number of houses, occupying a considerable space, called the *Jangam Bári:* the title to the property is said to be a grant to the *Jangamas*, regularly executed by MAN SINH, and preserved on a copper plate: the story with which the vulgar are deluded is, that it was granted by one of the Emperors of Hindustan, in consequence of a miracle performed by a *Jangama* devotee. In proof of the veracity of his doctrine, he proposed to fly: the Emperor promised to give him as much ground as he could traverse in that manner: not quite satisfied of the impossibility of the feat, he had a check string tied to the ascetic's legs, and held by one of the attendants: the *Jangama* mounted, and when he reached the limits of the present *Jangama Bári*, the Emperor thinking that extent of ground sufficiently liberal, had him constrained to fly back again.

† Moor, in his Hindu Pantheon, (page 352) asserts, upon, as he says, authentic information, that the *Paramahansas* eat human flesh, and that individuals of this sect

tion of BRAHMA, or spirit, and who is equally indifferent to pleasure or pain, insensible of heat or cold, and incapable of satiety or want.

Agreeably to this definition, individuals are sometimes met with who pretend to have attained such a degree of perfection: in proof of it they go naked in all weathers, never speak, and never indicate any natural want: what is brought to them as alms or food, by any person, is received by the attendants, whom their supposed sanctity or a confederation of interest attaches to them, and by these attendants they are fed and served on all occasions, as if they were as helpless as infants. It may be supposed that, not unfrequently, there is much knavery in this helplessness, but there are many Hindus whose simple enthusiasm induces them honestly to practice such self-denial, and there is little risk in the attempt, as the credulity of their countrymen, or rather country women, will, in most places, take care that their wants are amply supplied: these devotees are usually included amongst the *Saiva* ascetics; but it may be doubted whether the classification is correct.

AGHORIS.

The pretended insensibility of the *Paramahansa* being of a passive nature, is, at least, inoffensive, and even where it is mere pretence, the retired nature of the practice renders the deception little conspicuous or revolting. The same profession of worldly indifference characterises the *Aghori*, or *Aghorapanthi;* but he seeks occasions for its display, and demands alms as a reward for its exhibition.

The original *Aghori* worship seems to have been that of *Devi* in some of her terrific forms, and to have required even human victims for its

are not very unusually seen about *Benares*, floating down the river, and feeding upon a corpse: it is scarcely necessary to add that he is wholly wrong: the passage he cites from the Researches is quite correct, when it describes the *Paramanhansa* as an ascetic of the orthodox sects, in the last stage of exaltation; and the practice he describes, although far from usual, is sometimes heard of as a filthy exhibition, displayed for profit by individuals of a very different sect, those who occupy the ensuing portion of the present text—the *Aghoris*.

performance.* In imitation of the formidable aspect under which the goddess was worshipped, the appearance of her votary was rendered as hideous as possible, and his wand and water-pot were a staff set with bones and the upper half of a skull: the practices were of a similar nature, and flesh and spirituous liquors constituted, at will, the diet of the adept.

The regular worship of this sect has long since been suppressed, and the only traces of it now left are presented by a few disgusting wretches, who, whilst they profess to have adopted its tenets, make them a mere plea for extorting alms. In proof of their indifference to worldly objects, they eat and drink whatever is given to them, even ordure and carrion. They smear their bodies also with excrement, and carry it about with them in a wooden cup, or skull, either to swallow it, if by so doing they can get a few pice; or to throw it upon the persons, or into the houses of those who refuse to comply with their demands. They also, for the same purpose, inflict gashes on their limbs, that the crime of blood may rest upon the head of the recusant; and they have a variety of similar disgusting devices to extort money from the timid and credulous Hindu. They are, fortunately, not numerous, and are universally detested and feared.

URDDHABAHUS, AKAS MUKHIS, AND NAKHIS.

Personal privation and torture being of great efficacy in the creed of the Hindus, various individuals, some influenced by credulity, and some by knavery, have adopted modes of distorting their limbs, and forcing them out of their natural position, until they can no longer resume their ordinary direction.

* It may be credulity or calumny, but the *Bhils*, and other hill tribes, are constantly accused by Sanscrit writers of the eleventh and twelfth centuries, as addicted to this sanguinary worship. The *Vrihat Katha* is full of stories to this effect, the scene of which is chiefly in the *Vindhyá* range. Its covert existence in cities is inferable from the very dramatic situation in *Bhavabhuti's Drama*, *Málati* and *Mádhava*, where *Mádhava* rescues his mistress from the *Aghora Ghanta*, who is about to sacrifice *Málati* at the shrine of *Chamundá*.

The *Urddhabáhus** extend one or both arms above their heads, till they remain of themselves thus elevated. They also close the fist, and the nails being necessarily suffered to grow, make their way between the metacarpal bones, and completely perforate the hand. *The Urddahbáhus* are solitary mendicants, as are all of this description, and never have any fixed abode: they subsist upon alms; many of them go naked, but some wear a wrapper stained with ochre; they usually assume the *Saiva* marks, and twist their hair so as to project from the forehead, in imitation of the *Jata* of SIVA.

The *Akásmukhis*† hold up their faces to the sky, till the muscles of the back of the neck become contracted, and retain it in that position: they wear the *Jata*, and allow the beard and whiskers to grow, smearing the body with ashes: some wear coloured garments: they subsist upon alms.

The *Nakhis* are of a similar description with the two preceding, but their personal characteristic is of a less extravagant nature, being confined to the length of their finger nails, which they never cut: they also live by begging, and wear the *Saiva* marks.

GUDARAS.

The *Gúdaras* are so named from a pan of metal which they carry about with them, and in which they have a small fire, for the purpose of burning scented woods at the houses of the persons from whom they receive alms. These alms they do not solicit further than by repeating the word *Alakh*,‡ expressive of the indescribable nature of the deity. They have a peculiar garb, wearing a large round cap, and a long frock or coat, stained with ochery clay. Some also wear ear-rings, like the *Kánphata Jogis*, or a cylinder of wood passed through the lobe of the ear, which they term the *Khechari Mudrá*, the seal or symbol of the deity, of him who moves in the heavens.

* *Urddha*, above, and *Báhu*, the arm.

† *A'kás*, the sky, and *Mukha*, the face.

‡ *A, the* negative prefix, and *Lakshma*, a mark, a distinction.

RUKHARAS, SUKHARAS, AND UKHARAS.

The *Súkharas* are *Saiva* mendicants, distinguished by carrying a stick three spans in length: they dress in a cap and sort of petticoat stained with ochery earth, smear their bodies with ashes, and wear ear-rings of the *Rudráksha* seed. They also wear over the left shoulder a narrow piece of cloth dyed with ochre, and twisted, in place of the *Zenar*.

The *Rúkharas* are of similar habits and appearance, but they do not carry the stick, nor wear the *Ruddráksha* ear-rings, but in their place metallic ones: these two classes agree with the preceding in the watch-word, exclaiming *Alakh*, as they pass along; the term is, however, used by other classes of mendicants.

The *Ukharas* are said to be members of either of the preceding classes, who drink spirituous liquors, and eat meat: they appear to be the refuse of the three preceding mendicant classes, who, in general, are said to be of mild and inoffensive manners.

KARA LINGIS.

These are vagabonds of little credit, except sometimes amongst the most ignorant portions of the community: they are not often met with: they go naked, and to mark their triumph over sensual desires, affix an iron ring and chain on the male organ:* they are professedly worshippers of SIVA.

SANYASIS, BRAHMACHARIS, AND AVADHUTAS.

Although the terms *Sanyási* and *Vairági* are, in a great measure, restricted amongst the *Vaishnavas* to peculiar classes, the same limit

* These ascetics were the persons who attracted the notice of the earlier travellers, especially Bernier and Tavernier. They were more numerous then, probably, than they are at present, and this appears to be the case with most of the mendicants who practised on the superstitious admiration of the vulgar.

can scarcely be adopted with regard to the *Saivas*. All the sects, except the *Sanyogi Atíts*, are so far *Sanyási*, or excluded from the world, as not to admit of married teachers, a circumstance far from uncommon, as we have seen amongst the more refined followers of VISHNU. Most of the *Saiva* sects, indeed, are of a very inferior description to those of the *Vaishnavas*.

Besides the individuals who adopt the *Danda Grahana*, and are unconnected with the *Dasnámis*, there is a set of devotees who remain, through life, members of the condition of the *Bramachári*, or student :* these are also regarded as *Sanyásis*, and where the term is used in a definite sense, these twelve kinds, the *Dandis*, *Brahmacháris*, and ten *Dasnámi* orders are implied. In general, however, the term, as well as *Avadhúta*, or *Avdhauta*, and *Alakhnámí*, express all the *Saiva* classes of mendicants, except, perhaps, the *Jogis*.

NAGAS.

The *Siava Sanyásis* who go naked, are distinguished by this term. They smear their bodies with ashes, allow their hair, beards, and whiskers to grow, and wear the projecting braid of hair, called the *Jata* ; like the *Vairági Nágas*, they carry arms, and wander about in troops, soliciting alms, or levying contributions. The *Saiva Nágas* are chiefly the refuse of the *Dandí* and *Atít* orders, or men who have no inclination for a life of study or business : when weary of the vagrant and violent habits of the *Nága*, they re-enter the better disposed classes, which they had first quitted. The *Saiva Nágas* are very numerous in many parts of India, though less so in the Company's provinces than in any other : they were formerly in great numbers in *Bundelkand*,† and HIMMET

* The *Dirghakála Brahmacharyam*, or protracted period of studentship is, however, amongst the acts enumerated in various authorities of indisputable character, as those which are prohibited in the *Kali* age.

† A party of them attacked Colonel Goddard's troops in their march between *Dorawal* and *Herapur*, the assailants were no more than four or five hundred, but about two thousand hovered about the rear of the army: they are called *Pandarums* in the narrative, but were evidently *Saiva Nagas*. Pennant's Hindustan, 2, 192. The Vindicator of the Hindus, speaking of them, observes, that they often engage in

Bahadar was a pupil of one of their Mahants, Ra'jendra Gir, one of the lapsed *Dasnámi* ascetics. These *Nágas* are the particular opponents of the *Vairági Nágas*, and were, no doubt, the leading actors in the bloody fray at *Haridwar*,* which had excluded the *Vaishnavas* from the great fair there, from 1760, till the British acquired the country. The leader of the *Saiva* party was called Dhokal Gir, and he, as well as the spiritual guide of Himmet Bahadar, was, consequently of the *Dasnámí* order, which would thus seem to be addicted to violent and war-like habits. With respect to the sanguinary affray at *Haridwar*, in which we are told eighteen thousand *Vairágis* were left dead on the field, there is a different legend current of the origin of the conflict, from that given in the Researches, but neither of them is satisfactory, nor indeed is any particular cause necessary, as the opposite objects of worship, and the pride of strength and numbers, and consequent struggle for pre-eminence, are quite sufficient to account for the dispute.†

the rival contests of the Indian Chiefs, and, on a critical occasion some years ago, six thousand of them joined the forces of the Mahratta Chief Sindiah, and enabled him, with an equal number of his own troops, to discomfit an army of thirty thousand men, headed by one of his rebellious subjects.

* A. R. 11. 455. It may be observed, that a very accurate account is given in the same place of the general appearance and habits of the *Saiva Sanyásis* and *Jogis*, the *Vaishnava Vairágis*, and *Udásis* of *Nanckshah*. The term *Gosain*, as correlative to *Sanyási*, is agreeable to common usage, but, as has been elsewhere observed, is more strictly applicable to very different characters.

† The irregular practices of these and other mendicants, have attracted the lash of Ka'bir, in the following Remaini:

Remaini 69.

ऐसा योगी न देखा भाई ।

भूल फिरै लिये गफलाई, &c.

" I never beheld such a *Jogi*, Oh brother! forgetting his doctrine, he roves about in negligence. He follows, professedly, the faith of Maha'deva, and calls himself an eminent teacher; the scene of his abstraction is the fair or market. Ma'ya' is the mistress of the false saint. When did Dattatreya demolish a dwelling; when did Su'kadeva collect an armed host; when did Na'rada mount a matchlock; when did Vya'sadeva blow a trumpet. In making war, the creed is violated. Is he an *Atít*, who is armed with a quiver? Is he a *Viraktá*, who is filled with covetousness? His garb is put to shame by his gold ornaments; he has assembled horses and mares; is possessed of villages; is called a man of wealth; a beautiful woman was not amongst the embellishments of *Sánaká*, and his brethren; he who carries with him a vessel of ink, cannot avoid soiling his raiment.

SAKTAS.

The worshippers of the SAKTI, the power or energy of the divine nature in action, are exceedingly numerous amongst all classes of Hindus.* This active energy is, agreeably to the spirit of the mythological system, personified, and the form with which it is invested considered as the especial object of veneration, depends upon the bias entertained by the individuals towards the adoration of VISHNU or SIVA. In the former case, the personified *Sakti* is termed LAKSHMI', or MAHA' LAKSHMÍ, and in the latter, PA'RVATI, BHAVA'NI or DURGA'. Even SARASWATI' enjoys some portion of homage, much more than her lord, BRAHMA', whilst a vast variety of inferior beings of malevolent character, and formidable aspect, receive the worship of the multitude. The bride of SIVA, however, in one or other of her many and varied forms, is by far the most popular emblem in Bengal, and along the Ganges.

The worship of the female principle, as distinct from the divinity, appears to have originated in the literal interpretation of the metaphorical language of the *Vedas*, in which the *will* or *purpose to create* the universe, is represented as originating from the creator, and co-existent with him as his bride, and part of himself. Thus in the *Rig Veda*, it is said "That divine spirit breathed without afflation single, with *(Swadha)* her who is sustained within him; other than him nothing existed. First desire was formed in his mind, and that became the original productive seed,† and the *Sáma Veda*, speaking of the divine cause of creation, says, "He felt not delight, being alone. He wished another, and instantly became such. He caused his ownself to fall in twain, and thus became husband and wife. He approached her, and thus were human beings produced."‡ In these passages it is not unlikely that reference is made to the primitive tradition of the origin of mankind, but there is also a figurative representation of the first indication of *wish* or *will* in the Supreme Being. Being devoid of all qualities whatever, he was alone, until he permitted the wish to be multiplied, to be generated within himself. This wish being put into action, it is said, became united with its parent,

* It has been computed, that of the Hindus of Bengal, at least three-fourths are of this sect; of the remaining fourth, three parts are *Vaishnavas*, and one *Saivas*, &c.

† Asiatic Researches, VIII. 393.

‡ Asiatic Researches, VIII. 426.

and then created beings were produced. Thus this first manifestation of divine power is termed *Ichchhárúpaá*, personified, desire ; and the creator is designated as *Swechchamaya*,* united with his own will whilst in the *Vedanta* philosophy, and the popular sects, such as that of Kabir, and others, in which all created things are held to be illusory, the *Sakti*, or active will of the deity, is always designated and spoken of as *Mayá* or *Mahámayá*, original deceit or illusion.†

Another set of notions of some antiquity, which contributed to form the character of the *Sakti*, whether general or particular, were derived from the *Sánkhya* philosophy. In this system, Nature, *Prakriti*, or *Múla Prakriti*, is defined to be of eternal existence, and independent origin, distinct from the supreme spirit, productive though no production, and the plastic origin of all things, including even the gods. Hence *Prakriti* has come to be regarded as the mother of gods and men, whilst as one with matter, the source of error, it is again identified with *Mayá*, or delusion, and as co-existent with the Supreme as his *Sakti*, his personified energy, or his bride.‡

* Thus, in the *Brahma Vaivertta Purana*, which has a whole section dedicated to the manifestations of the female principle, or a *Prakriti Khanda*.

एवं रूपं विभ्रद्भगवानेक एव सः ।
दिग्भिश्च नभसा सार्द्धं शून्यंविश्वं ददर्शह ॥
आलोच्य मनसा सर्व्वं एकमेवा सहायवान्
स्वेच्छया स्रष्टुमारेभे सृष्टिंस्वेच्छामयः प्रभुः ॥

The Lord was alone invested with the Supreme form, and beheld the whole world, with the sky and regions of space, a void Having contemplated all things in his mind, he, without any assistant, began with the will, to create all things. He, the Lord, endowed with the wish for creation.

† So also in the authority last quoted.

साच ब्रह्मस्वरूपा मायानित्या सनातनी ।

She *(Prakriti,)* one with, *Brahma*, is *Mayá*, eternal, everlasting. And in the *Kalika Purana*.

अभिन्ना प्रकृति र्या सा जन्तून्सम्मोहति

Prakriti is termed Inherent *Mayá*, because she beguiles all beings.

‡ In the *Gita*, *Prakriti* is identified with all the elementary predicates of matter.

भूमिरापोनलोवायुः खंमनोबुद्धिरेवच ।
अहंकार इतीयं मेऽभिन्नाप्रकृतिरष्टधा ॥

These mythological fancies have been principally disseminated by the *Puranas*, in all which *Prakriti*, or *Mayá*, bears a prominent part. The aggregate of the whole is given in the *Brahma Vaivartta Purana*, one section of which, the *Prakriti Khanda*, is devoted to the subject, and in which the legends relating to the principal modifications of the female principle are narrated.

According to this authority, BRAHMA, or the Supreme Being, having determined to create the universe by his super-human power, became twofold, the right half becoming a male, the left half a female, which was *Prakriti*. She was of one nature with BRAHMA. She was illusion, eternal and without end: as is the soul, so is its active energy; as the faculty of burning is in fire.* In another passage it is said, that KRISHNA, who is in this work identified with the Supreme, being alone invested with the divine nature, beheld all one universal blank, and contemplating creation with his mental vision, he began to create all things by his own will, being united with his will, which became manifest as MU'LA PRAKRITI.† The original PRAKRITI first assumed five

" This, my *Prakriti*, is inherently eight-fold, or earth, water, fire, air, ether, mind, intellect, individuality."

So also the *Kúrma Purana* (Chapter, 12).

तस्य सर्व्वं जगन्मूर्त्तिः शक्तिर्मायेति विश्रुता।
तदेवं भ्रामयेदीशो मायावी पुरुषोत्तमः।
सैषामायात्मिकाशक्तिः सर्व्वाकारा सनातनी।
विश्वरूपं महेशस्य सर्व्वदा संप्रकाशयेत्॥

His Energy, being the universal form of all the world, is called *Mayá*, for so does the Lord the best of males and endowed will illusion cause it to revolve. That *Sakti* of which the essence is illusion, is omniform and eternal, and constantly displays the universal shape of *Mahésa*.

* योगेनात्मा सृष्टि विधौ द्विधा बभूव सः
पुमांश्च दक्षिणार्द्धाङ्गो वामाङ्गा प्रकृतिः स्मृता।

He, by the power of YOGA, became himself in the act of creation two-fold, the right half was the male, the left was called *Prakriti*.

† स्वेच्छामयस्येच्छयाच श्रीकृष्णस्यसिसृक्षया।
साविर्बभूवसहसा मूलप्रकृतिरीश्वरी॥

From the wish which was the creative impulse of *Sri Krishna*, endowed with his will, she, *Múla Prakriti*, the Supreme, became manifest.

forms*—DURGA' the bride, *Sakti*, and *Mayá*, of SIVA, LAKSHMI' the bride, *Sakti* and *Mayá* of VISHNU, SARASWATÍ the same of BRAHMA, or in the *Brahma Vaivartta Purana*, of HARI, whilst the next, SA'VITRI is the bride of BRAHMA'. The fifth division of the original *Prakriti*, was RA'DHA', the favourite of the youthful KRISHNA, and unquestionably a modern intruder into the Hindu Pantheon.

Besides these more important manifestations of the female principle, the whole body of goddesses and nymphs of every order, are said to have sprung from the same source, and indeed every creature, whether human or brutal, of the female sex, is referred to the same principle, whilst the origin of males is ascribed to the primitive *Purusha*, or male. In every creation of the universe, it is said the MU'LA PRAKRITI assumes the different gradations of *Ansarúpini*, *Kalárúpini* and *Kalánsarúpini*,† or manifests herself in portions, parts, and portions of parts, and further subdivisions. The chief *Ansas* are, besides the five already enumerated, GANGA', TULASI, MANASA' SASHTHI, or DEVASNA, MANGALA'CHANDIKA, and KA'LI'; the principal *Kalás* are SWA'HA', SWADHA, DAKSHINA, SWASTI, PUSHTI, TUSHTI, and others, most of which are allegorical personifications, as *Dhriti*, fortitude, *Pratishthá*, fame, and *Adharma*, Wickedness, the bride of *Mrityu*, or Death. ADITI, the mother of the gods, and DITI, the mother of the demons, are also *Kalás* of PRAKRITI. The list includes all the secondary goddesses. The *Kalánsas* and *Ansánsas*, or sub-divisions of the more important manifestations, are all womankind, who are distinguished as good, middling, or bad, according as they derive their being, from the parts of their great original, in which the *Satya*, *Rajas*, and *Tama Guna*, or property of goodness, passion, and vice predominates. At the same time as manifestations of the great Cause of all they are entitled to respect, and even to veneration: whoever, says the *Brahma Vaivartta Purana*, offends or insults a

* तदाज्ञया पञ्चविधा सृष्टि कर्म्मविभेदतः ।

And she (the *Múla Prakriti.*) became in the act of creation five-fold by the will of the Supreme.

† अंशरूपा कलारूपा कलांशांशस्यसम्भवा ।
प्रकृतेः प्रतिविश्वेषु देव्यश्च दिव्ययोगिनः ॥

In every creation of the universe the *Devi*, through divine *Yoga*, assumes different forms, and becomes *Ansarúpá*, *Kalárúpá*, and *Kalánsarúpá*, or *Ansánsarúpá*.

female, incurs the wrath of PRAKRITI, whilst he who propitiates a female, particularly the youthful daughter of a *Brahman*, with clothes, ornaments and perfumes, offers worship to PRAKRITI herself. It is in the spirit of this last doctrine that one of the principal rites of the *Sáktas*, is the actual worship of the daughter or wife of a *Brahman*, and leads with one branch of the sect at least to the introduction of gross impurities. But besides this derivation of PRAKRITI, or SAKTI, from the Supreme, and the secondary origin of all female nature from her, those who adopt her as their especial divinity, employ the language invariably addressed towards the preferential object of worship in every sect, and contemplate her as comprising all existence in her essence. Thus she is not only declared to be one with the male deity, of whose energy some one of her manifestations is the type, as DEVI with SIVA, and LAKSHMI with VISHNU; but it is said, that she is equally in all things, and that all things are in her, and that besides her, there is nothing.*

Although the adoration of PRAKRITI or SAKTI is, to a certain extent, authorised by the *Puránas*, particularly the *Brahma Vaivartta*, the *Skanda*, and the *Káliká*, yet the principal rites and formulæ are derived from an independent series of works, known by the collective term of *Tantras*. These are infinitely unmerous, and in some instances of great extent; they always assume the form of a dialogue between SIVA and his bride, in one of her many forms, but mostly as UMA' and PARVATI, in which the goddess questions the god as to the mode of performing various ceremonies, and the prayers and incantations to be used in them. These he explains at length, and under solemn cautions that

* Thus in the *Kasi Khanda*—

सर्व्वमन्त्रमयीत्वं ब्रह्माद्यास्त्वत्समुद्भवाः ।
चतुर्वर्गात्मकीत्वंवै चतुर्वर्गफलोदया ॥
त्वत्तः सर्व्वमिदंविश्वं त्वयिसर्व्वं जगन्निधे ।
यद्दृश्यं यददृश्यञ्च स्थूल सूक्ष्म स्वरूपतः ।
यत्तत्त्वं शक्तिरूपेण किञ्चिन्नत्वदृतेक्वचित्

Thou art predicated in every prayer—*Brahmá* and the rest are all born from thee. Thou art one with the four objects of life, and from thee they come to fruit. From thee this whole universe proceeds, and in thee, asylum of the world, all is, whether visible or invisible, gross or subtle in its nature: what is, thou art in the *Sakti* form, and except thee nothing has ever been.

they involve a great mystery, on no account whatever to be divulged to the profane.

The followers of the *Tantras* profess to consider them as a fifth *Veda*, and attribute to them equal antiquity, and superior authority.* The observances they prescribe have, indeed, in Bengal, almost superseded the original ritual. The question of there date is involved in considerable obscurity. From the practices described in some of the *Purάnas*, particularly that of the *Dikshά* or rite of initiation, in the *Agni Purάnas*, from the specification of formulæ, comprising the mystical monosyllables of the *Tantras* in that and other similar compilations, and from the citation of some of them by name in different *Paurάnic* works,† we must conclude that some of the *Tantras* are prior to those authorities. But the date of the *Purάnas* themselves is far from determined, and whilst some parts of them may be of considerable antiquity, other portions of most, if not of all, are undoubtedly subsequent to the tenth century of the Christian era. It is not unlikely, however, that several of the *Tan-*

* Thus, in the *Siva Tantra*, SIVA is made to say—

ममपञ्चखेभ्यश्चपञ्चाम्नायाविनिर्गताः ।
पुर्व्वश्च पश्चिमश्चैव दक्षिणश्चोत्तरस्तथा ॥
ऊर्द्धाम्नायश्च पञ्चैते मोक्षमार्गाः प्रकीर्त्तिताः ।
आम्नया वहवः सन्तिऊर्द्धाम्नायेन नोसमाः ॥

"The five Scriptures issued from my five mouths, and were the east, west, south, north, and upper. These five are known as the paths to final liberation. There are many Scriptures, but none are equal to the Upper Scripture." *Kullúka Bhatta*, commenting on the first verse of the second chapter of *Menu*, says, the *Sruti* is two-fold—*Vaidika* and *Tantrika;*

श्रुतिश्च द्विविधा वैदिकी तान्त्रिकी च ॥

† As in the *Kúrma Purána*, the *Kapála*, *Bhairava*, *Váma* and *Yámala*, and the *Pancharátrá* in the *Varáha;* we have also a number mentioned in the *Sankara Vijayas*, of both *Anandagiri* and *Mádhava* as the *Siva Gita*, *Siva Sanhitá*, *Rúdra Yámala*, and *Siva Rahasya*. It is also said in *Anandagiri's* work, that the *Brahmanas* were cursed by *Gáyatri*, to become *Tántrikas* in the *Kali* age.

वेदात्ता कर्म्महीनाश्च तान्त्रिकाचार तत्पराः ।
यूयं कलौ भवन्त्वेव मिति तानाङ्गसारुषा ॥

" She being angry said to them, in the *Kali* age, after abandoning the *Veda* ritual, become followers of the *Tantrika* observances.

tras are of earlier composition, especially as we find the system they inculcate, included by ANANDAGIRI, in his life of SANKARA'CHA'RYA, amongst the heterodoxies which that Legislator succeeded in confuting. On the other hand, there appears no indication of *Tantrika* notions in the *Mahábhárat*, and the name of *Tantra*, in the sense of a religious text book, does not occur in the vocabulary of AMERA SINHA. It may therefore be inferred, that the system originated at some period in the early centuries of Christianity, being founded on the previous worship of the female principle, and the practices of the *Yoga* with the *Mantras*, or mystical formulæ of the *Vedas*. It is equally certain that the observances of the *Tantras* have been carried to more exceptionable extremes in comparatively modern times, and that many of the works themselves are of recent composition. They appear also to have been written chiefly in Bengal and the Eastern districts, many of them being unknown in the West and South of India, and the rites they teach having there failed to set aside the ceremonies of the *Vedas*, although they are not without an important influence upon the belief and the practices of the people.

The *Tantras* are too numerous to admit in this place of their specification, but the principal are the *Syáma Rahusya, Rúdra Yámala, Mantra Mahodadhi, Sáreda Tileka,* and *Káliká Tantra*, whilst the *Kula-churámani, Kulárnava*, and similar works, are the chief authorities of one portion of the *Sáktas*, the sect being divided into two leading branches, the *Dakshináchari*s and *Vámácharis*, or followers of the right hand and left hand ritual.

DAKSHINAS, OR BHAKTAS.

When the worship of any goddess is performed in a public manner, and agreeably to the *Vaidik* or *Pauránik* ritual,* it does not comprehend

* The peculiarites of this sect are described in the *Dakshináchara Tantra Raja*, a modern summary of the system by *Kásináth* : according to this authority—

दक्षिणाचार तन्त्रोक्तं कर्म्मतच्छुद्धो वैदिकम्।

" The ritual declared in the *Tantras* of the *Dakshináchára*s, is pure, and conformable to the *Vedas*."

the impure practices which are attributed to a different division of the adorers of SAKTI, and which are particularly prescribed to the followers of this system. In this form it is termed the *Dakshina*, or right hand form of worship.* The only observance that can be supposed to form an exception to the general character of this mode is the *Bali*, an offering of blood, in which rite a number of helpless animals, usually kids, are annually decapitated. In some cases, life is offered without shedding blood, when the more barbarous practice is adopted of pummelling with the fists the poor animal to death: at other times blood only is offered without injury to life. These practices, however, are not considered as orthodox, and approach rather to the ritual of the *Vámácharis*,† the more pure *Bali*, consisting of edible grain, with milk and sugar. Animal victims are also offered to DEVI, in her terrific forms only, as KA'LI' or DURGA'. The worship is almost confined to a few districts; and, perhaps, is carried to no great extent.

* वामागमो मदुक्तोायं सर्व्वं शूद्रपरःप्रिये।
ब्राह्मणेा मदिरादाना द्ब्राह्मण्येन वियुज्यते॥
नकर्त्तव्यं न कर्त्तव्यं न कर्त्तव्यं कदाचन।
इदंतु साहसं देवि न कर्त्तव्यं कदाचन॥

The *Váma* ritual, although declared by me, was intended for *Súdras* only. A *Brahman*, from receiving spirituous liquor, forfeits his Brahmanical character—let it not be done—let it not ever be done. Goddess, it is brutality, never let it be practised.

† द्विविधवलिराख्यातेा राजसः सात्त्विको वुधैः।
राजसेा मांसरक्ताद्यं पलत्रय समन्वितः॥
मुद्ग पायस संयुक्तेा मधुरत्रय लेालितः।
ब्राह्मणेा नियतःशूद्धः सात्त्विकं वलिमाहरेत्॥

The *Bali* is of two kinds, *Rájasa* and *Sátwika*; the first consists of meat, and includes the three kinds of flesh; the second of pulse and rice-milk, with the three sweet articles, (ghee, honey, and sugar,) let the *Brahman*, always pure, offer only the *Sátwika Bali*.

The *Brahmavaivartta* also observes—"The animal sacrifices, it is true, gratify DURGA'; but they, at the same time, subject the sacrificer to the sin which attaches to the destroyer of animal life. It is declared by the *Vedas*, that he who slays an animal, is hereafter slain by the slain. "*Brahma Vaivartta Purana.*"

Although any of the goddesses may be objects of the *Sakta* worship, and the term *Sakti* comprehends them all, yet the homage of the *Saktas* is almost restricted to the wife of SIVA, and to SIVA himself, as identified with his consort.* The sect is, in fact, a ramification from the common *Saiva* stock, and is referred to SIVA himself as its institutor. In the *Tantras*, as has been noticed, he appears as its professor, expounding to PA'RVATI the mantras, tenets, and observances of the *Sakta* worship, whether of the right or left hand description.

The worship of DEVÍ, thus naturally resulting from the works on which the *Sakta* doctrines are founded, is one of considerable antiquity and popularity. Laying aside all uncertain and fabulous testimony, the adoration of *Vindhya Vásini*, near *Mirzapur*,† has existed for more than seven centuries, and that of *Jwálamukhí*, at *Nagarkot*, very early attracted Mohammedan persecution.‡ These places still retain their reputation, and are the objects of pilgrimage to devout Hindus. On the eighth of the dark fortnight of *Chaitra Kártik* in particular, a numerous assemblage of pilgrims takes place at them.

* शिवशक्ति मयंरुपं सम्पुज्यं साधकोत्तमैः ।
यस्तुसम्पुजयेच्छक्तिं शिवंनैव प्रपुजयेत् ।
सएव पातकीरोगी मान्त्रिको दुर्गतिर्भवेत् ।

"The joint form of SIVA and SAKTI is to be worshipped by the virtuous. Whoever adores SAKTI, and offers not adoration to SIVA, that *Mantrka* is diseased: he is a sinner, and hell will be his portion." For it appears that some of the *Saktas* elevate the SAKTI above the SAKTIMA'N, or deity: thus the *Vámis*, in the *Sankara Vijaya*, say:

शक्तिः शिवस्य वलकारिणी तयाविनातस्य तृणचलन क्रियायाम
समर्थत्वात् अवः शक्तिरेव शिवस्य कारणं ।

"SAKTI gives strength to SIVA, without her he could not stir a straw. She is, therefore, the cause of SIVA.

नित्यपदार्थयोर्मध्ये शक्तेरधिकत्वं

And again; of the two objects which are eternal, the greater is the SAKTI.

† It is frequently mentioned in the *Vrihat Kathá*, the age of which work is ascertained to be about seven centuries. *Nagarkot* was taken by FIROZ the 3d, in 1360, (Dow 2. 55,) at which time the goddess *Jwálamukhí* was then worshipped there.

‡ For a full account of both, the work of Mr. Ward may be advantageously consulted—II. 89 to 96, and 125 to 131.

The adoration of KA'LÍ, or DURGA', is, however, particularly prevalent in Bengal, and is cultivated with practices scarcely known in most other provinces. Her great festival, the *Dasahara*, is, in the West of India, marked by no particular honors, whilst its celebration in Bengal occupies ten days of prodigal expenditure. This festival, the *Durgá Pújá*, is now well known to Europeans, as is the extensive and popular establishment near Calcutta, the temple of KA'LÍ, at *Káli Ghát*. The rites observed in that place, and at the *Durgá Pújá*, however, almost place the *Bengali Saktas* amongst the *Vámácharis*, notwithstanding the rank assigned them in the *Dakshináchári Tantrarája*, which classes the *Gauras* with the *Keralas* and *Kashmirians*, as the three principal divisions of the purer worshippers of SAKTI.

VAMIS, OR VAMACHARIS.

The *Vámís* mean the left hand worshippers, or those who adopt a ritual contrary to that which is usual, and to what indeed they dare publicly avow.* They worship DEVÍ, the *Sakti* of SIVA, but all the goddesses, as LAKSHMÍ, SARASWATÍ, the *Mátris*, the *Náyikas*, the *Yoginis*, and even the fiend-like *Dákinis*, and *Sákinis*, are admitted to a share of homage. With them, as well as with the preceding sect, SIVA is also an object of veneration, especially in the form of BHAIRAVA, with which modification of the deity it is the object of the worshipper to identify himself.†

* The following verse is from the *Syáma Rahasya*—

अन्तश्शाक्ताः वहिश्शैवाः सभायां वैष्णवाः मताः ।
नानारूपधराः कौला विचरन्ति महीतले ॥

" Inwardly *Saktas*, outwordly *Saivas*, or in society nominally *Vaishnavas*, the *Kaulas* assuming various forms, traverse the earth."

† भैरवोह मितिज्ञात्वा सर्व्वज्ञोहंगुणान्वितः ।
इतिसञ्चिन्त्य योगिन्द्रः कुलपूजां समाचरेत् ॥

I am *Bhairava*, I am the omniscient, endowed with qualities. Having thus meditated, let the devotee proceed to the *Kula* worship.—*Syáma Rahasya*.

The worship of the *Vámácharis* is derived from a portion of the *Tantras:* it resolves itself into various subjects, apparently into different sects, of which that of the *Kaula*, or *Kulína*, is declared to be pre-eminent.* The object of the worship is, by the reverence of DEVI or SAKTI, who is one with SIVA, to obtain supernatural powers in this life, and to be identified after death with SIVA and SAKTI.

According to the immediate object of the worshipper, is the particular form of worship; but all the forms require the use of some or all of the five *Makáras*,† *Mansa, Matsya, Madya, Maithuna*, and *Mudrá*, flesh, fish, wine, women, and certain mystical gesticulations. Suitable *Mantras* are also indispensable, according to the end proposed, consisting of various unmeaning monosyllable combinations of letters of great imaginary efficacy.‡

* सर्व्वेभ्यश्चोत्तमावेदा वेदेभ्यो वैष्णवपरं ।
वैष्णवादुत्तमंशैवं शैवाद्दक्षिणमुत्तमं ॥
दक्षिणादुत्तमं वामं वामात्सिद्धान्त मत्तमं ।
सिद्धान्तादुत्तमं कौलं कौलात्परतरं नहि ॥

"The *Vedas* are pre-eminent over all works, the *Vaishnava* sect excels the *Vedas*, the *Saiva* sect is preferable to that of VISHNU, and the right hand SAKTA to that of SIVA—the left hand is better than the right hand division, and the *Siddhanta* is better still—the *Kaula* is better than the *Siddhanta*, and there is none better than it."—*Kulárnava.* The words *Kaula* and *Kulina* are both derivatives from *Kula*, family; and the latter is especially applied to imply of good, or high family: these terms have been adopted to signify, that those who follow this doctrine are not only of one, but of an exalted race.

† They are thus enumerated in the *Syáma Rahasya:*

मद्यंमांसञ्च मत्स्यञ्च मुद्रामैथुन मेवच ।
मकार पञ्चकञ्चैव महापातक नाशनम् ॥

Wine, flesh, fish, *Mudrá*, and *Maithuna*, are the five-fold *Makára*, which takes away all sin.

‡ Many specimens might be given, but one will be here sufficient. It is the combination H and S as ह्स, and is one of the very few to which any meaning is attempted to be given: it is called the *Prásáda Mantra*, and its virtues and import are thus described in the *Kulárnava*.

श्रीप्रासादपरामन्त्रमूर्ध्वाम्नाय प्रतिष्ठितं ।
आवयोः परमाकारं योवेत्तिसः शिवःस्वयं ॥

Where the object of the ceremony is to acquire an interview with and controul over impure spirits, a dead body is necessary. The adept is also to be alone, at midnight, in a cemetery or place where bodies are burnt or buried, or criminals executed: seated on the corpse, he is to perform the usual offerings, and if he does so without fear, the *Bhútas*, the *Yoginis*, and other male or female goblins, become his slaves.

In this, and many of the observances practised, solitude is enjoined; but all the principal ceremonies comprehend the worship of SAKTI, and require for that purpose the presence of a female, as the living representative and the type of the goddess. This worship is mostly celebrated in a mixed society, the men of which represent *Bhairavas* or *Viras*, and the women *Bhairavis* and *Náyikás*. The SAKTI is personated by a naked female, to whom meat and wine are offered, and then distributed amongst the assistants, the recitation of various *Mantras* and texts, and the performance of the *Mudrá*, or gesticulations with the fingers, accompanying the different stages of the ceremony, and it is terminated with the most scandalous orgies amongst the votaries.* The ceremony is entitled the *Sri Chakra*, or *Púrnábhisheka*, the Ring, or Full Initiation.

शिवादि क्रिमिपर्य्यन्तं प्राणिनां प्राण वर्त्तनां।
निश्वासोच्छ्वास रूपेण मन्त्रोयं वर्त्तते प्रिये॥

" He who knows the excellent *Prasáda Mantra*, that was promulgated by the fifth *Veda*, (the *Tantras*) and which is the supreme form of us both, he is himself SIVA: this *Mantra* is present in all beings that breathe from SIVA, to a worm, and exists in states of expiration and inspiration." The letter H is the expirated, and S the inspirated letter, and as these two acts constitute life, the *Mantra* they express is the same with life: the animated world would not have been formed without it, and exists but as long as it exists, and it is an integral part of the universe, without being distinct from it, as the fragrance of flowers, and sweetness of sugar, oil of Sesamum seed, and SAKTI of SIVA. He who knows it needs no other knowledge—he who repeats it need practice no other act of adoration. The authority quoted contains a great deal more to the same purpose.

* It might have been sufficient to have given this general statement, or even to have referred to the similar but fuller account of Mr. Ward: his information was, however, merely oral, and may therefore be regarded as unsatisfactory; and as it seems to be necessary to show that the charge is not altogether unfounded, I shall subjoin the leading rites of the *Sakti Sodhana*, or *Sri Chakra*, as they are prescribed in the *Devi Rahasya*, a section of the *Rudra Yámala*.

The occurrence of these impurities is certainly countenanced by the texts, which the sects regard as authorities, and by a very general belief of their occurrence. The members of the sect are enjoined secrecy,

SAKTI SODHANA.

The object of the ceremony should be either—

नटीकपालिनीवेश्यारजकीनापिताङ्गना ।
ब्राह्मणीशूद्रकन्याचतथागोपालकन्यका ॥
मालाकारस्यकन्यापि नवकन्याप्रकीर्त्तिताः ।
एतासुकाचिदानीयपूजयेत्कौलिकः

" A dancing girl, a female devotee, a harlot, a washerwoman, or barber's wife, a female of the *Brahmanical* or *Sudra* tribe, a flower girl, or a milk maid." It is to be performed at midnight, with a party of eight, nine, or eleven couple, as the *Bhairavas* and *Bhairavis*.

महानिशायामानीयनवकन्यासुभैरवान् ।
एकादशनवाष्टौवाकौलिकःकौलिकेश्वरि ।
शोधयेत्स्वभिर्मन्त्रैःपूजयेत्कौलिकोत्तमः ।

Appropriate Mantras are to be used, according to the description of the person selected for the *Sakti*, who is then to be worshipped, according to prescribed form; she is placed disrobed, but richly ornamented—on the left of a circle *(Chakra)* described for the purpose, with various *Mantras* and gesticulations, and is to be rendered pure by the repetition of different formulas.

तदीयंमन्त्रमालिख्यतस्मिन्तामेवपूजयेत्
श्रीचक्रेस्थापयेद्वामेकन्यांभैरववल्लभां ॥
मुक्तकेशांवीतलज्जां सर्व्वाभरणभूषितां ।
आनन्दलीनहृदयांसौन्दर्य्यातिमनोहरां ॥
शोधयेत्सुद्धिम न्त्रेणसुरानन्दामृताम्बुभिः ।

Being finally sprinkled over with wine, the act being sanctified by the peculiar *Mantra*.

मन्त्रेणानेनदेवेशिकामिनीमभिषिञ्चयेत्

The *Sakti* is now purified, but if not previously initiated, she is to be further made an adept by the communication of the radical *Mantra*, whispered thrice in her ear, when the object of the ceremony is complete.

which, indeed, it might be supposed they would observe on their own account, and, consequently, will not acknowledge their participation in such scenes. They will not, indeed, confess that they are of the *Sákta* sect, although their reserve in this respect is said, latterly, to be much relaxed. It is contrary, however, to all knowledge of the human character, to admit the possibility of these transactions in their fullest extent;

एवं शोधनमन्त्रास्तेवर्णिताः पृथक्मया।
योनौजपेत्कुमारीणां कौलिकःकरमालया॥
सञ्जप्यदद्यकर्णेच मूलमन्त्रं चिरञ्चरेत्
अदीक्षितापिदेवेशिदीक्षितैवभवेत्तदा॥
दीक्षितां शोधितोवीरोभवेत्सर्व्वार्थसिद्धये।

The finale is what might be anticipated, but accompanied throughout with *Mantras* and forms of meditation, suggesting notions very foreign to the scene.

अनन्दतर्पितां कान्तां वीरः स्वानन्दविग्रह।
एतेनतर्प्पयेत्तत्त्वश्रीचक्रेवीरसंसदि॥
पठन्प्रणवमुद्धृत्यमन्त्र राजं कुलेश्वरि।
धर्म्माधर्म्मंहवीर्दीप्तेस्वात्माग्नौमनसास्रुचा॥
सुषुम्णा वर्त्मनानित्यमक्षवृत्तीर्जुहोम्यहं।
स्वाहान्तं मन्त्रमुच्चार्य्यंजपमूलं स्मरन्परं॥
कुर्य्यान्निधुवनंमन्त्री मन्त्रसिद्धिमवाप्नुयात्।
एतान्तेसंजपेनन्मूलं पठेन्मन्त्रमिदंपुनः॥
तारद्वयान्तरगतं परमानन्दकारणं॥
ओं प्रकाशाकाशहस्ताभ्यामवलंब्योन्मनीस्रुचा।
धर्म्माधर्म्मकलास्नेहपूर्णंव वह्नौजुहोम्यऽहं।
स्वाहान्तेवायुमन्त्रेण शुक्रमादायपार्व्वति॥
श्रीचक्रेतर्प्पयेद्देवितत: सिद्धिमवाप्नुयात्।
सम्पूज्यकान्तां संतर्प्यस्तुत्वानत्वापरस्परं॥
संहार मुद्रयामन्त्रीशक्तिवीरान् विसर्ज्जयेत्।

and, although the worship of the SAKTI, according to the above outline, may be sometimes performed, yet there can be little doubt of its being practised but seldom, and then in solitude and secrecy. In truth, few of the ceremonies, there is reason to believe, are ever observed; and, although the *Chakra* is said to be not uncommon, and by some of the zealous *Saktas*, it is scarcely concealed, it is usually nothing more than a convival party, consisting of the members of a single family, or at which men only are assembled, and the company are glad to eat flesh and drink spirits,* under the pretence of a religious observance. In justice to the doctrines of the sect, it is to be observed, that these practices, if instituted merely for sensual gratification, are held to be as illicit and reprehensible, as in any other branch of the Hindu faith.†

* The zeal that is prescribed might suit some more civilized associations—

पीत्वापीत्वापुनःपीत्वायावल्लुठतिभूतले ।
उत्थायच पुनःपीत्वापुनर्जन्म न विद्यते

Let him pledge the wine cup again and again,
Till he measures his length on the ground.
Let him rise and once more the goblet drain,
And with freedom for aye, from a life of pain,
Shall the glorious feat be crowned.

† The *Kularnava* has the following and many similar passages: they occur constantly in other *Tantras*.

बह्व कौलिकंधर्म्मं मिथ्याज्ञान बिडम्बकाः ।
स्वबुद्ध्या कल्पयन्तीत्थं पारम्पर्य्यंविवर्ज्जिताः ॥
मद्यपानेन मनुजा यदिसिद्धिंलभन्तितत् ।
मद्यपानरताः सर्व्वेंसिद्धिंयान्तिसमीहितां ॥
मांसभक्षणमात्रेणयदि पुण्यगतिर्भवेत् ।
लोकेमांसाशिनः सर्व्वैंपुरायवन्तोभवन्तिकिम् ॥
स्त्रीसम्भोगेनदेवेशि यदि मोक्षं व्रजन्तितत् ।
सर्व्वेंपिजन्तवोलोके मुक्ताः स्यु स्त्रीनिषेवनात् ॥
कुलमार्गंपुतोदेविनमयानिन्दितः क्वचित् ।
आचाररहितायचनिन्दितास्तेनचेतरे ॥

The followers are considered as very numerous, especially amongst the Brahmanical tribe: all classes are however admissible, and are equal and alike at the ceremonies of the sect. In the world* they resume their characteristic distinctions, and wear the sectarial marks, and usually adopt the outward worship of any other division, whether orthodoxical or heretical. When they assume particular insignia, they are a semi-circular line or lines on the forehead, of red saunders or vermillion, or a red streak up the middle of the forehead, with a circular spot of red at the root of the nose. They use a rosary of *Rudráksha* seeds, or of coral beads, but of no greater length than may be concealed in the hand, or they keep it in a small purse, or a bag of red cloth. In worshipping, they wear a piece of red silk round the loins, and decorate themselves with garlands of crimson flowers.

कुलद्रव्याणिसेवन्तेयऽन्यदर्शनमाश्रिताः ।
तदङ्गरोमप्रमाणं पुनर्जन्मभविष्यति ॥

"Many false pretenders to knowledge, and who have not been duly initiated, pretend to practise the *Kaula* rites; but if perfection be obtained by drinking wine, independently of my commands, then every drunkard is a saint: if virtue consist in eating flesh, then every carnivorous animal in the world is virtuous; if eternal happiness be derived from sexual intercourse, then all beings will be entitled to it: a follower of the *Kula* doctrine is blameless in my sight, if he reproves those of other creeds who quit their established observances—those of other sects who use the articles of the *Kaula* worship, shall be condemned to repeated generations as numerous as the hairs of the body."—In fact, the texts of *Menu* are taken as authorities for the penance to be performed for the crimes of touching, smelling, looking at, or tasting the forbidden articles, except upon religious occasions, and when they are consecrated by the appropriate texts.

It is only to be added, that if the promulgators of these doctrines were sincere, which is far from impossible, they must have been filled with a strange phrenzy, and have been strangely ignorant of human nature.

* प्रवृत्तेभैरवीतन्त्रेसर्व्ववर्णा द्विजोत्तमाः ।
निवृत्तेभैरवीतन्त्रेसर्व्ववर्णाः पृथक्पृथक् ॥

"Whilst the *Bhairavi Tantra* is proceeding, all castes are *Brahmans*—when it is concluded, they are again distinct."—*Syáma Rahasya.* According to Ward, such of them as avow their creed, leading at the same time a mendicant life, are termed *Vyaktávadhutas*, or they who are openly free from restraints: those who conceal their creed and observe its practices in privacy, are termed Guptavadhútas, the liberated in secret. II. 296.

KANCHELIYAS.

This is a sect of which the existence may be questioned, nothwithstanding the assertion that it is not uncommon in the South of India; the worship is that of SAKTI, and the practices are similar to those of the *Kaulas*, or *Vámácharis*. It is said to be distinguished by one peculiar rite, the object of which is to confound all the ties of female alliance, and to enforce not only a community of women amongst the votaries, but disregard even to natural restraints. On occasions of worship, the female votaries are said to deposit their upper vests in a box in charge of the *Guru*. At the close of the usual rites, the male worshippers take each a vest from the box, and the female to whom the garment appertains, be she ever so nearly of kin to him, is the partner for the time of his licentious pleasures.*

KERARI.

The *Kerári* is the worshipper of DEVI, in her terrific forms, and is the representative of the *Aghora Ghanta* and *Kapálika*,† who, as

* This sect appears in the *Sankara Vijaya*, as the *Uchchishtha Ganapati*, or *Hairamba* sect, who declare that all men and all women are of one caste, and that their intercourse is free from fault.

पुरुषाणां सर्व्वजातिकानामेक जातिवदित्येकोधर्म्मः स्त्रीणाम्सर्व्व जातिकानामेकजातिवदित्येको धर्म्मः। तासाञ्चतेषाञ्चसंयोगे वियोगेच दोषाभावः।

The same sort of story is told, but apparently with great injustice of the Mohammedan *Byabaharis* or *Borahs*, and of a less known Mohammedan sect, the *Cheraghkesh*: something of the same kind was imputed to the early Christians by their adversaries.

† The following description of the *Kapálika*, is from the *Sankara Vijaya* of *Anandagiri*.

चितिभस्मपूर्णकलेवरः नरकपालमालावृतगलः फालदेशरचित कज्जलरेखः सकल केशरचितजटापाशिः व्याघ्रचर्म्मरचित कटिसूत्र

lately only as seven or eight centuries ago, there is reason to suppose sacrificed human victims to KA'LI', CHAMUNDA', CHHINNAMASTAKA', and other hideous personifications of the *Sakti* of SIVA. The attempt to offer human beings in the present day, is not only contrary to every known ritual, but it would be attended with too much peril to be practised, and, consequently, it cannot be believed that this sect is in existence: the only votaries, if any there be, consisting of the miscreants who, more for pay than devotion, inflict upon themselves bodily tortures, and pierce their flesh with hooks or spits, run sharp pointed instruments through their tongues and cheeks, recline upon beds of spikes, or gash themselves with knives, all which practices are occasionally met with throughout India, and have become familiar to Europeans from the excess to which they are carried in Bengal at the *Charak Pújá*, a festival which, as a public religious observance, is unknown any where else, and which is not directed nor countenanced by any of the authorities of the Hindus, not even by the *Tantras*.

MISCELLANEOUS SECTS.

The sects that have been described are those of the regular system, and particularly of what may be called Brahmanical Hinduism, emanating, more or less directly, from the doctrines of the original creed. Besides these, there are a number which it is not so easy to class, although they are mostly referable to a common source, and partake, in many respects, of the same notions, especially of those of a *Vaishnava* and *Vedanta* tendency. They exist in various degrees of popularity,

कौपीनः कपालशाभितवामकरः सहनाद घण्टाधृतदक्षिणकरः
सम्भो भैरव अहोकालीसइति मुहु मुहु र्जपन् ।

His body is smeared with ashes from a funeral pile, around his neck hangs a string of human skulls, his forehead is streaked with a black line, his hair is wove into the matted braid, his loins are clothed with a tiger's skin, a hollow skull is in his left hand, (for a cup) and in his right he carries a bell, which he rings incessantly, exclaiming aloud, Ho, *Sambhu Bhairava*—Ho, lord of *Kali*.

and date from various periods, and in most instances, owe their institution to enthusiastic or contemplative individuals, whose biography is yet preserved consistently enough by tradition.

This is not the case, however, with the first two on the list—the *Saurapátas* and *Ganapátas:* these are usually, indeed, ranked with the preceding divisions, and make, with the *Vaishnavas*, *Saivas*, and *Sáktas*, the five orthodox divisions of the Hindus: they are of limited extent and total insignificance.

SAURAPATAS, OR SAURAS.

The *Saurapátas* are those who worship SURYAPATI, the Sun-god only; there are a few of them, but very few, and they scarcely differ from the rest of the Hindus in their general observances. The *Tílaka*, or frontal mark, is made in a particular manner, with red sandal, and the necklace should be of crystal; these are their chief peculiarities: besides which they eat one meal without salt on every Sunday, and each *Sankránti*, or the sun's entrance into a sign of the Zodiac: they cannot eat either until they have beheld the sun, so that it is fortunate that they inhabit his native regions.

GANAPATYAS.

These are worshippers of GANESA, or GANAPATI, and can scarcely be considered as a distinct sect: all the Hindus, in fact, worship this deity, as the obviator of difficulties and impediments, and never commence any work, or set off on a journey, without invoking his protection. Some, however, pay him more particular devotion than the rest, and these are the only persons to whom the classification may be considered applicable. GANESA, however, it is believed, is never exclusively venerated, and the worship, when it is paid, is addressed to some of his forms, particularly those of *Baktratunda* and *Dhundhiráj*.

NANAK SHAHIS.

A sect of much greater importanee is that which originated with Na'nak Shah, and which, from bearing at first only a religious character, came, in time, to be a political and national distinction, through the influence of Mohammedan persecution and individual ambition. The enterprising policy of Govind Sinh, and the bigotry of Aurangzeb, converted the peaceful tenets of Na'nak into a military code, and his speculative disciples into the warlike nation of the *Sikhs*. It is not, however, in their political capacity that we are now to consider them, but as the professors of a peculiar form of faith, which branches into various sub-divisions, and is by no means restricted to the *Punjab*. At the same time it is unnecessary to detail the tenets and practices of the *Sikhs*, as that has been already performed in a full and satisfactory manner.

The *Sikhs*, or *Nának Shahis*, are classed under seven distinctions, all recognising *Nának* as their primitive instructor, and all professing to follow his doctrines, but separated from each other by variations of practice, or by a distinct and peculiar teacher. Of these the first is the sect of the *Udásís*.

UDASIS.

These may be regarded as the genuine disciples of *Nának*, professing, as the name denotes, indifference to worldly vicissitudes. They are purely religious characters, devoting themselves to prayer and meditation, and usually collected in *Sangats*, colleges or convents; they also travel about to places of pilgrimage, generally in parties of some strength. Individuals of them are to be met with in most of the chief cities of Hindustan, living under the patronage of some man of rank or property, but in all situations they profess poverty, although they never solicit alms; and although ascetics, they place no merit in wearing mean garments or dispensing altogether with clothes. On the contrary, they are, in general, well dressed, and, allowing the whiskers and beard to grow, are not unfrequently of a venerable and imposing appearance. Though usually practising celibacy, it does not appear to be a necessary condition amongst the *Sikhs* to be found in the Gangetic provinces: they are usually the ministrant priests; but their office consists chiefly in reading and expounding the writings of NA'NAK and GOVIND SINH, as collected in the *Adi Granth* and *Das Padshah kâ Granth*. The perusal is enlivened by the chaunting, occasionally, of Hindi *Padas* and *Rekhtas*, the compositions of KABI'R, MIRA BHAI, SUR DAS, and others. With that fondness for sensible objects of reverence which characterises the natives of India, the Book is also worshipped, and rupees, flowers, and fruits, are presented by the votaries, which become, of course, the property of the officiating *Udási*. In return, the *Udási* not uncommonly adopts the presentation of the *Prásáda*, and at the close of the ceremony, sweetmeats are distributed amongst the congregation. In some of the establishments at *Benares*, the service is held in the evening after sunset, and the singing and feasting continue through a great part of the night. Many of the *Udásis* are well read in *Sanscrit*, and are able expounders of the *Vedanta* philosophy, on which the tenets of NA'NAK are mainly founded.

The *Udási* sect was established by DHARMACHAND, the grandson of NA'NAK, through whom the line of the Sage was continued, and his descendants, known by the name of *Nának Putras*, are still found in the *Punjab*, where they are treated by the *Sikhs* with especial veneration.

The doctrine taught by NA'NAK, appears to have differed but little from that of KABI'R, and to have deviated, but inconsiderably, from the *Hindu* faith in general. The whole body of poetical and mythological fiction was retained, whilst the liberation of the spirit from the delusive deceits of *Máyá*, and its purification by acts of benevolence and self-denial, so as to make it identical even in life with its divine source, were the great objects of the devotee. Associated with these notions, was great chariness of animal life, whilst with NA'NAK, as well as with KABI'R, universal tolerance was a dogma of vital importance, and both laboured to persuade *Hindus* and *Mohammedans* that the only essential parts of their respective creeds, were common to both, and that they should discard the varieties of practical detail, or the corruptions of their teachers for the worship of one only Supreme, whether he was termed *Allah* or *Hari*. How far these doctrines are still professed by the *Nának Sháhis*, may be inferred from the translations in the eleventh volume of the Researches, to which the following may be added as part of the service solemnized at the *Sikh Sangat*, at *Benares*.

HYMN.

Thou art the Lord—to thee be praise.
All life is with thee.
Thou art my parents. I am thy child—
All happiness is derived from thy clemency.
No one knows thy end.
Highest Lord amongst the highest—
Of all that exists, Thou art the regulator.
And all that is from thee obeys thy will.
Thy movements—thy pleasure—thou only knowest.
Nának, thy slave, is a free-will offering unto thee.
The Priest then says—
Meditate on the *Saheb* of the Book, and exclaim *Wah Guru*.
The People accordingly repeat—
Wah Guru—Wah Guru kí fateh.
The Priest.
Meditating on *Rámachándra*, exclaim *Wah Guru*.
The People.
Wah Guru—Wah Guru kí fateh.

HYMN.

Love, and fix thy whole heart upon Him—
The world is bound to thee by prosperity—
No one is another's.
Whilst prosperity endures many will come,
And sit with thee and surround thee ;

But in adversity they will fly,
And not one will be near thee.
The woman of the house who loves thee,
And is ever in thy bosom ;
When the spirit quits the body,
Will fly with alarm from the dead.
Such is the way of the world,
With all on which we place affection ;
Do thou, *Nának*, at thy last hour,
Rely alone upon *Hari*.

Priest as before.

Meditating on the Saheb of the Book, &c.

People as before.

Wah Guru, &c.

HYMN.

My holy teacher is he who teaches clemency—
The heart is awake within : who seeks may find.
Wonderful is that rosary, every bead of which is the breath.
Lying apart in its arbour, it knows what cometh to pass—
The Sage is he who is merciful ;—the merciless is a butcher.
Thou wieldest the knife and regardlessly exclaimest—
What is a goat, what is a cow, what are animals ?
But the *Saheb* declares that the blood of all is the same.
Saints, Prophets, and Seers, have all passed in death.
Nánack, destroy not life for the preservation of the body.
That desire of life which is in the heart, do thou, brother, repress.
Nánack, calling aloud, says—take refuge with *Hari*.

Priest as before.

Meditating on the *Saheb*, &c.

People as before.

Wah Guru—Wah Guru kí fateh.

GANJ BAKHSHIS.

Of this division of the *Sikhs*, no particulars, except the name, have been ascertained. This is said to have been derived from that of the founder. They are not numerous nor of any note.

RAMRAYIS.

These derive their appellation from that of RA'MA RA'YA, the son or grandson of HARI RA'YA, and their distinction from the other *Sikhs* is more of a political than religious complexion. RA'MA RA'YA disputed the succession to the Pontificate with HARI KRISHNA, the son of HARI RA'YA, and was unsuccessful. His followers, however, maintain the superiority of his pretensions, and record many miracles wrought by him in proof of his sanctity. He flourished about A. D. 1660. The *Rámráyis* are not common in Hindustan.

SUTHREH SHAHIS.

These are more often met with than either of the two preceding, and the priests are recognisable by distinguishing marks. They make a perpendicular black streak down the forehead, and carry two small black sticks about half a yard in length, which they clash together when they solicit alms. They lead a vagabond life, begging and singing songs in the *Punjabi* and other dialects, mostly of a moral or mystic tendency.

They are held in great disrepute, however, and are not unfrequently gamblers, drunkards, and thieves. They look up to TEGH BAHADER, the father of GURU GOVIND, as their founder.

GOVIND SINHIS.

These form the most important division of the *Sikh* community, being, in fact, the political association to which the name is applied, or to the *Sikh* nation generally.* Although professing to derive their national faith from *Nának*, and holding his memory in veneration, the faith they follow is widely different from the quietism of that reformer, and is wholly of a worldly and warlike spirit. GURU GOVIND devoted his followers to steel, and hence the worship of the sword, as well as its employment against both Mohammedans and Hindus. He also ordered his adherents to allow their hair and beards to grow, and to wear blue garments: he permitted them to eat all kinds of flesh, except that of kine, and he threw open his faith and cause to all castes, to whomsoever chose to abandon the institutes of *Hinduism*, or belief in the mission of Mohammed, for a fraternity of arms and life of predatory daring. It was then only that the *Sikhs* became a people, and were separated from their *Indian* countrymen in political constitution, as well as religious tenets—at the same time the *Sikhs* are still, to a certain extent, *Hindus:* they worship the deities of the *Hindus*, and celebrate all their festivals: they derive their legends and literature from the same sources, and pay great veneration to the *Brahmanas*. The impress of their origin is still, therefore, strongly retained, notwithstanding their rejection of caste, and their substituting the *Das Padshah ki granth*,† the compilation of GURU GOVIND, for the *Vedas*, and *Puranas*.

* Described by Sir John Malcolm, in the eleventh volume of the Asiatic Researches. The *Sikh* priest to whom he alludes (page 198) as one of his authorities, was afterwards well known to me, and was an individual every way worthy of confidence. His name was *Atmá Ram*, and although advanced in years, he was full of energy and intelligence, combining with them extreme simplicity and kindliness of disposition. The old man was a most favourable and interesting specimen of the *Punjabi* nation and disciples of *Nának*. He died a few years ago in Calcutta.

† From the succession of Chiefs, GOVIND was tenth teacher in succession from *Nának*, who flourished at the close of the 17th and beginning of the 18th century.

The other standard authority of the Sikhs, the *Adi Granth*, is a compilation chiefly of the works of *Nának*, and his immediate successors, made by *Arjunmal*, a *Sikh* teacher, in the end of the 16th century. As it is usually met with, however, it comprehends the writings of many other individuals, many of whom are *Vaishnavas*. At a *Sikh Sangat*, or Chapel, in Benares, the Book, a large folio, there denominated the *Sambhu Granth*, was said to contain the contributions of the following writers:—

NIRMALAS.

These differ but little from the *Udásis*, and are, perhaps, still closer adherents to the doctrines of the founder, as the name imports: they profess to be free from all worldly soil or stain, and, consequently, lead a wholly religious life. They observe celibacy, and disregard their personal appearance, often going nearly naked. They are not like the *Udásis*, assembled in colleges, nor do they hold any particular form of divine service, but confine their devotion to speculative meditation on the perusal of the writings of NA'NAK, KA'BIR, and other unitarian teachers. They are always solitary, supported by their disciples or opulent individuals, and are often known as able expounders of the *Vedanta* philosophy, in which *Brahmans* do not disdain to become their scholars. They are not very numerous; but a few are almost always to be found at the principal seats of *Hindu* wealth and learning, and particularly at *Benares*.*

NAGAS.

The naked mendicants of the *Sikhs* are said to differ from those of the *Vaishnava* and *Saiva* sects, by abstaining from the use of arms, and following a retired and religious life. Except in going without clothes, they are not distinguishable from the *Nirmalas*.

Nának, Nam Doe, Kábir, Sheikh Feridaddin, Dhana, Rámánand, Pipa, Sena, Jayadeva, Phandak, Sudáma, Prahlád, Dhuru, Raidas, Vibhishana, Mira Bái, Kermu Bái.

* An interesting account of the religious service of the *Sikhs*, in their college at *Patna*, was published by Mr. Wilkins, in the first volume of the Asiatic Researches. I witnessed a similar ceremony at a *Sikh* establishment at Benares, and partook of the *Prasáda* or sweetmeats, distributed to the assistants. Both Mr. Wilkins and Sir John Malcolm notice this eating in common, as if it were peculiar to the *Sikh* faith; but this, as elsewhere observed, is not the case. It prevails with most of the *Vaishnava* sects; but it should be remembered that it is always restricted to articles which have been previously consecrated by presentation to the object of worship, to the Idol, the sarcophagus, the sculptured foot-marks, or the book.

JAINS.

A satisfactory account of the religion of the *Jains* would require a distinct dissertation, and cannot be comprised within the limits necessarily assigned to this general sketch of the *Hindu* sects. The subject is of considerable interest, as affecting a very large proportion of the population of India, and involving many important considerations connected with the history of the *Hindu* faith: an extended inquiry must, however, be left to some further opportunity; and in the meantime our attention will be confined to a few observations on the peculiar tenets and practices of the *Jain* religion, its past history, and actual condition.

Previously, however, to entering upon these subjects, it may be advisable to advert briefly to what has been already done towards their elucidation, and to the materials which exist in the original languages for a complete view. The latter are of the most extensive description, whilst the labours of European writers are by no means wanting to an accurate estimate of the leading doctrines of the *Jain* faith, or to an appreciation of the state in which it exists in various parts of *Hindustan*.

The first authentic notices of the *Jains* occur in the ninth volume of the Asiatic Researches, from the pens of the late Colonel Mackenzie, Dr. Buchanan, and Mr. Colebrooke. The two first described the *Jains* from personal acquaintance, and from their accounts, it appeared, that they existed, in considerable numbers and respectability, in Southern India, particularly in *Mysore*, and on the *Canara Coast;* that they laid claim to high antiquity, and enumerated a long series of religious teachers, and that they differed in many of their tenets and practices from the orthodox Hindus, by whom they were regarded with aversion and contempt. A further illustration of their doctrines, and a particular account of their deified teachers, was derived by Mr. Colebrooke from some of their standard authorities, then first made known to Europeans.

Little more was published on the subject of the *Jains* until very lately, with exception of numerous but brief and scattered notices of the sect in the *Peninsula*, in Buchanan's Travels in Mysore. Some account of them also occurs in Colonel Wilks' Historical Sketch of the South of India, and in the work of the Abbè Du Bois. Mr. Ward has an article dedicated to the *Jains*, in his account of the Hindus; and Mr. Erskine has briefly adverted to some of their peculiarities in his observations on the Caves of *Elephanta*, and the remains of the *Bauddhas* in India, in the Proceedings of the *Bombay Literary Society*. It is, however, to the Transactions of the *Royal Asiatic Society* that we are indebted for the latest and most detailed accounts, and the papers of Mr. Colebrooke, Major Delamaine, Dr. Hamilton, Colonel Franklin and Major Tod,* furnish many interesting particulars relative to the doctrines and past or present condition of the *Jains*. Some valuable illustrations of the latter subject is to be found in the Calcutta Quarterly Magazine ;† some historical notices obtained from the inscriptions at *Abu*, occur in the last volume of our Researches, whilst a novel and rather comprehensive view of *Jain* literature is contained in the Catalogue of Manuscripts collected by the late Colonel Mackenzie.‡

From this latter authority, we learn that the literature peculiar to *Jainas*, comprises a number of works peculiar to the sect, the composition of their own writers, and on a variety of subjects.§ They have a series of works called *Puranas*, as the *Adi* and *Uttara Puranas*, *Chámunda Ráya Purana*, and *Chaturvinsati Purana* ;‖ but these are not to be

* On the Philosophy of the Hindus, part IV. by Mr. Colebrooke, vol. I. On the *Sráwaks*, or *Jains*, by Major Delamaine, vol. 1, 418. On Inscriptions in Jain Temples, in Behar, by Mr. Colebrooke, Dr. Hamilton, and Colonel Franklin, vol. 1, 520. On the *Sráwaks*, or *Jains*, by Dr. Hamilton, vol. I, 531. On the Religious Establishments in Mewar, by Major Tod, vol. 2.

† Particularly in the Journal of a Native Traveller from Calcutta, and back again through Behar. The traveller was a learned *Jain*, in the service of Colonel Mackenzie. There is also an interesting account of a visit to the temple of PA'RSWANA'TH, at *Samet Sikhar*.

‡ Vol. 1, page 144, &c.

§ The List comprises 44 Works—

Puranas, ...	7
Cheritras and Legends, ...	10
Ritual, Prayers, &c.	18
Medicine, ...	1
Grammar, ...	2
Arithmetic, ...	2
Miscellaneous, ...	4

‖ Hamilton says, the *Digambaras* have twenty-four *Puranas*, twenty-three giving an account of each *Tirthankara*, and the twenty-fourth, of the whole; but this seems to be erroneous. The actions of the twenty-four *Tirthankaras*, are described in a single *Purana*, but the section devoted to each is called after him, severally as the *Purana* of each, as *Rishabha Deva Purana*, one section of the *Chámunda Ráya Purana*. In the *Adi* and *Uttara Puranas*, forming, in fact, but one work, the *Adi*, or first part, is appropriated to the first *Tirthankara*, whilst the *Uttara*, or last portion, confounded with the *Puranas* of the *Hindus ;* as, although they occasionally insert legends borrowed from the latter, their especial object is the legendary history of the *Tirthakaras,* or deified teachers, peculiar to the sect. The chief *Puranas* are attributed to JINA SENA SCHA'RYA, whom some accounts make contemporary with VIKRAMA'DITYA ; but the greater number, and most consistent of the traditions of the South, describe him as the spiritual preceptor of AMOGHAVERSHA, king of *Kánchi*, at the end of the ninth century of the Christian era. Analogous to the *Jain Puranas*, are works denominated *Cheritras,* their subject being, in general, the marvellous history of some *Tirthankara,* or some holy personage, after whom they are denominated ; as the *Jinadatta Ráya Cheritra, Pújyapáda Cheritra,* and others. They have a number of works explanatory of their philosophical notions and religious tenets of the sect, as well as rituals of practice, and a grammatical system founded on the rules of SA'KATA'YANA, is illustrated by glosses and commentaries. The *Jains* have also their own writers on astronomy and astrology, on medicine, or the mathematical sciences, and the form and disposition of the universe.

This general view of *Jain* literature is afforded by the Mackenzie Collection, but the list there given is very far from including the whole of *Jain* literature, or even a considerable proportion. The works there alluded to, are, in fact, confined to Southern India, and are written in *Sanscrit,* or the dialects of the *Peninsula ;* but every province of Hindustan can produce *Jain* compositions, either in Sanscrit or its vernacular idiom, whilst many of the books, and especially those which may be regarded as their scriptural authorities, are written in the *Prákrit* or *Mágadhi,* a dialect which, with the *Jains,* as well as the *Bauddhas,* is considered to be the appropriate vehicle of their sacred literature.

The course of time, and the multiplication of writings, have probably rendered it almost impossible to reduce what may be considered as the sacred literature of the *Jains* to a regular system. They are said to have a number of works entitled *Siddhántas* and *Agamas,** which are to

contains the accounts of all the other deified Sages. There are several collections, comprehending what may be termed twenty-four *Puranas ;* but it does not appear that there are twenty-four distinct works so denominated.

* Hamilton enumerates eight works, as the *Agamas* of the *Digambara* sect, the *Trailokya Sara,* the *Gomatisara, Pungjiraj, Trailokya Dipika, Kshepanásara, Tri-*

them what the *Vedas* are to the Brahmanical Hindus, and this appears to be the case, although the enumeration which is sometimes made of them is of a loose and popular character, and scarcely reconcilable with that to be derived from written authoritity.*

bhangisara, and *Shatpawar*, attributed to the pupils of *Mahavira*. He states also, that the *Swetambaras* have forty-five, or as some allege, eighty-four *Siddhántas*, amongst which he specifies the *Thánángi Sútra*, *Gnyánanti Sútra*, *Sugorangi Sútra*, *Upasakadesa*, *Mahapandanna*, *Nandi Sútra*, *Rayapseni*, *Jirabhigam*, *Jambudwipa-pannati*, *Surapannatti*, *Chandrasagarapannatti*, *Kalpa Sútra*, *Katantravibhrama Sutra*, *Shakti Sútra*, and *Sangrahani Sútra*. Some of these are incorrectly named, and others inaccurately classed, as will be seen from what follows in the text.

* The following Works are either in my possession or in the library of the Sanscrit College of Calcutta:—Compositions descriptive of the tenets or practices of the *Jain* religion. *Bhagavatyangam*. This is one of the eleven primary works, and is entitled also in *Prakrit*, *Viváha Pannatti*, in *Sanscrit*, *Vivdha*, or *Vivádhá Prajnapti*. Instruction in the various sources of worldly pain, or in the paths of virtue. It consists of lessons given to GAUTAMA by MAHA'VI'RA, and is in *Prákrit*. It contains 36,000 stanzas. *Bhagavtyanga Vritti*, a *Sanscrit* Commentary on the preceding (defective.) *Thánánga Sútra*,—also one of the eleven *Angas*. *Kalpa Sútra*, the precepts of the *Jain* faith—these are originally 1250; but they are interspersed with legends of the *Tirthánkaras*, and especially of MAHA'VI'RA, at the pleasure of the writer, and the several copies of the work therefore differ. *Prákrit*

Kalpa Sútra Bálabodha, a sort of abridgment of the preceding. Prakrit.
Kalpa Sútra Siddhanta, the essence of the *Kalpa Sútra* Prakrit.
Dasavaikalika Sútra. Prakrit.
Ditto. Tika.
Rayaprasna Sútra Siddhánta. Tika.
Gautamaproshtha. Prakrit.
Sangrahini Sútra. Prakrit.
Laghu Sangrahini Sútra.
Nava Tatwa Sútra. Prakrit.
Nava Tatwa Prakarana. Prakrit.
Nava Tatwa Bálabodha. Prakrit.
Karma Grantha.
Jiva Vichara. Sanscrit.
Jiva Vinaya.
Smarana Sútra. Prakrit.
Vriddhatichara. Prakrit.
Sindúraprakara Tika. Sanscrit.
Ekavinsati Sthana, Bhasha.
Dasakshapanavratavidhi. Bhasha.
Upadesa Mala Prakrit.
Pratikramana Vidhi. Prakrit.
Pratikramana Sútra. Bhasha.
Chaturdasa Gunasthana. Bhasha.
Chaturdasa Gunanamani.
Pakshi Sútra. Bhasha.
Shattrinsat Kermakatha. Bhasha.
Dhermabuddhi Chatushpadi. Bhasha.
Balavibodha. Bhasha
Upadhanavidhi. Prakrit.
Ashtahnikamahotsava. Prakrit.
Ashtahnikavyakhyana.
Mahamuni Swadhyaya.
Pragnasúkta Muktavali.
Aradhana Prakara.
Parswanatha Gita.
Uttaradhyayana Gita.
Sadhusamachari.
Sravakaradhana.
Jnyanapúja
Dikshamahotsava.
Barah Vrata.
Saptavinsati Sadhu Lakshana.
Ratribhojana Nishedha.
Sadhwapashana Vidhi.
Dwisashti Vakya.
Kshetrasamasa Sútra.
Samyaktwadhyayana.
Prishnottara Retnamala.
Navakárúnta Bálabodha.
Asahyana Vidhi.
Santaraka Vidhi.
Atmánusásana. Bhasa.
Panchástikáya, according to the *Digambara* faith.
Jinapratima Sthapana Vidhi.
Jalakshalana Vidhi.
Sudopakara Muktavali.
Moksha Marga.
Nitisangraha.
Vicharamanjari.
Parswanatha Dasabhavavisaha.
Sataviasbhava.
Anandasravaka Sandhi.
Rohinitapa.

The author of the *Abhidháha Cyintámani*, a useful vocabulary, HEMACHANDRA, is well known as a zealous and able propagator of the *Jain* doctrines in the twelfth century. He was no doubt well versed in the peculiarity of the system which he taught, and may be regarded as a safe guide. In his vocabulary he specifies what appear to be the *Jaina* scriptures, at least in the estimation of the *Swetámbara* sect, to which he belonged, and in a valuable Commentary on his own work he has further particularised the works named in his text. From this it appears that the principal authorities of a sacred character were termed *Angas*, and were eleven in number, or with a supplementary division, twelve. They are thus enumerated and described; *Acháránga*, a book teaching sacred observances after the practice of *Vasishtha* and other saints.

Siddhdchala Pújá.
Pújápaddhati. Bhasha.
Sílopadesa Mala.
Snana Vidhi.
Navapattatupa Vidhi.
Amritashtamitapa.
Dévapúja.
Baranbhavanasandhi. Bhasha.
Panegyrics of the *Jain* teachers, &c. which are not unfrequently repeated in the temples.
Sánti Jina Stava. Bhasha.
Vrihat Sánti Stava. Sanscrit.
Mahavira Stava. Bhasha.
Laghu Santi Stava.
Rishabha Stava.
Parswanath Stava.
Parswanath Stuti. Prakrit.
Neminatha Stava.
Ashanta Stava. Prakrit.
Ajitasánti Stava.
Bhaktamaya Stotra.
Kalyána Mandira Stotra Sanscrit.
Chaturvinsati dandakastava.
Sádhubandana.
Satrunjaya Stava.
Párswanath Namaskára.
Champaka Stavana.
Upasergahara Stotra.
Guru Stava.
Karmma Stava.

LEGENDARY TALES AND HISTORIES.

Padma Purana. Bhasha.
Maháwira Cheritra, which is called by others a portion of the *Trisashti Salátka Purusha Cheritra*, or Legend of the sixty-three personages, most eminent in *Jain* Tradition. Sanscrit.
Nemirájarshi Cheritra.
Salabhadra Cheritra. Bhasha.
Chitrasena Cheritra. Prakrit.
Gajasukumara Cheritra. Bhasha.
Chandraraja Cheritra. Bhasha.
Bhaktamara.
Sripala Cheritra. Bhasha.
Kalikacharya Katha.
Samyaktwa Kaumudi.
Vastradana Katha.
Meghadutapada Samasya.
Avantisakumara Cheritra.
Retanchuropakhyana.
Mrigavati Cheritra.
Retnachura Muni; Chaupai. Bhasha.
Mrigavati Chaupai. Bhasha.
Sadhu Charitra.
Satrunjaya Mahatmya.
Gajasinha Charitra.
Dasadrishtanta Katha.

MISCELLANEOUS.

Vriddhayavana, Astronomy. Sanscrit.
Chaturdasaswapanavichara.
Trailokya Dipika.
Setunjoddhar.
Pathanarambhapithika.
Hastarekhavivarana. Prakrit.
Namavali.
Patavali.
Many of these are of small extent, but others are exceedingly voluminous, as the *Bhagavatyanga*, *Padma Purana*, *Satrunjaya Mahatmya*, and others.

Sútrakritángam, a work on acts imposed by positive precepts. *Sthánángam*—On the organs in which life abides, or the ten acts essential to purity. *Samavayángam*—On the hundred *Padárthas or* categories. *Bhagavatyangam*—On the ritual, or rules for worship. *Jnyátadhermakathá*—An account of the acquisition of knowledge by holy personages. *Upásakadasá*—Rules for the conduct of *Sráwakas*, or secular *Jains*, apparently in ten lectures. *Antakriddasa*—On the actions of the *Tirthakaras*, in ten lectures. *Anuttaropapatikadara*—On the principal or final births of the *Tirthakaras*, in ten lectures. *Prasnavyakaranam*—Grammar of questions, probably on the Code of the *Jains*. *Vipákasrutam*—On the fruits or consequences of actions.

With these are connected inferior *Angas* or *Upángas*, the names of which are not specified—whilst the *Drishtabáda*, the twelfth *Anga*, which seems to be a supplementary authority, is divided into five portions, entitled; *Parikermma*—On moral acts; *Sútra*—Precepts for conduct and life; *Púrvánuyoga*—On the doctrines and practice of the *Tirthakaras* before attaining perfection; *Púrvagata*—On the same after perfection! *Chúliká*—On doctrines and practice not comprised in the two preceding.

These different works profess to be derived from the oral instructions of MAHA'VI'RA himself to his disciple, especially to GAUTAMA; but besides these a class of works is enumerated by HEMACHANDRA, entitled *Púrvas*, because they were drawn up by the *Ganadharas* before the *Angas*.* There are fourteen of them treating of the chief tenets of the sect, apparently sometimes controversially, as the *Astipraváda*, the doctrine of existence and non-existence. *Jnyánapraváda*, the doctrine of holy knowledge—*Satyapraváda*, discussion of truth—*Atmapraváda*, investigation of spirit—*Prándváya*, nature of corporeal life—*Kriyávisála*, consequences of acts, and others.† They are held to be the works of MAHAVÍRAS *Ganas*, or of that *Tirthakára* and his predecessors, or to have emanated from them originally, although committed to writing by other hands. Some of them still exist, it appears,‡ although in

* सूत्रितानिगणधरैरङ्गेभ्यः पूर्व्वमेवयत् ।
पूर्व्वाणीत्यभिधीयंतेतेनैतानिचतुर्दश ॥ *Máha Cher.* Section 5.

† A similar enumeration of these Works occurs in the *Máhavira Cheritra*.

‡ Thus the *Thánángisútra* and *Upasakadesa*, of Hamilton, are no doubt the *Sthananga* and *Upasakadasa*, of *Hemachandra's* text, and the *Bhagavatyanga* is in the *Sanscrit* College Library.

general their places have been assumed by a list of more recent compositions.

From this brief statement it will be evident that there is no want of original authorities with regard to the belief, the practices, or the legends of the *Jaina* sect. There is indeed more than a sufficiency, and the vast extent of the materials is rather prejudicial to the enquiry, it being impossible to consult any extensive proportion of what has been written, and it being equally impossible without so doing to know that the best guides have been selected. For such accounts as are here given, the Vocabulary of HEMACHANDRA, with his own Commentary, the *Mahávira Cheritra* of the same author, the *Kalpa Sútra*, the *Avasyakavrihad Vritta*, the *Bhagavatyanga Vritta, Nava Tatwabodha*, and *Jiva Vìchára* have chiefly been consulted.

The leading tenets of the *Jains*, and those which chiefly distinguish them from the rest of the *Hindus*, are well known—they are, first, the denial of the divine origin and infallible authority of the *Vedas;* secondly, the reverence of certain holy mortals who acquired, by practices of self-denial and mortification, a station superior to that of the gods; and thirdly, extreme and even ludicrous tenderness for animal life.

The disregard of the authority of the *Vedas* is common to the *Jains* and the *Bauddhas*, and involves a neglect of the rites which they prescribe: in fact, it is in a great degree from those rites that an inference unfavourable to the sanctity of the *Vedas* is drawn, and not to speak of the sacrifices of animals which the *Vedas* occasionally enjoin; the *Homa*, or burnt offering, which forms a part of every ceremonial in those works, is an abomination; as insects crawling amongst the fuel, bred by the fermented butter, or falling into the flame, cannot fail to be destroyed by every oblation. As far, however, as the doctrines they teach are conformable to *Jain* tenets, the *Vedas* are admitted and quoted as authority.

The veneration and worship of mortals is also common to the *Jains* and *Bauddhas*, but the former have expanded and methodised the notions of the latter. The *Bauddhas*, although they admit an endless number of earthly *Buddhas* to have existed, and specify more than a century of names,* confine their reverence to a comparatively small number—to seven. The *Jainas* extend this number to twenty-four for

* Asiatic Researches, vol. XVI. pages 446 to 449.

a given period, and enumerate, by name, the twenty-four of their past age, or *Avasarpini*, the twenty-four of the present, and the twenty-four of the age to come. The statues of these, either all or in part, are assembled in their temples, sometimes of colossal dimensions, and usually of black or white marble. The objects held in highest esteem in *Hindustan* are PA'RSWANA'TH and MAHA'VIRA, the twenty-third and twenty-fourth *Jinas* of the present era, who seem to have superseded all their predecessors.

The generic names of a *Jaina* saint express the ideas entertained of his character by his votaries. He is *Jagatprabhu*, lord of the world; *Kshinakermmá*, free from bodily or ceremonial acts; *Sarvajna*, omniscient; *Adhiswara*, supreme lord; *Devádideva*, god of gods; and similar epithets of obvious purport; whilst others are of a more specific character, as *Tirthakára*, or *Tirthankara*, *Kevali*, *Arhat*, and *Jina*. The first implies one who has crossed over, *(Tiryate anena,)* that is, the world, compared to the ocean; *Kevali*, is the possessor of *Kevala*, or spiritual nature, free from its investing sources of error: *Arhat* is one entitled to the homage of gods and men, and *Jina* is the victor over all human passions and infirmities.*

Besides these epithets, founded on attributes of a generic character, there are other characteristics common to all the *Jinas* of a more specific nature. These are termed *Atisayas*, or super-human attributes, and are altogether thirty-six; four of them, or rather four classes, regard the person of a *Jina*, such as the beauty of his form, the fragrance of his body, the white colour of his blood, the curling of his hair, its non-increase, and that of the beard and nails, his exemption from all natural impurities, from hunger and thirst, from infirmity and decay: these properties are considered to be born with him. He can collect around him millions of beings, gods, men, and animals, in a comparatively small space, his voice is audible to a great distance, and his language, which is *Arddha Mágadhi*, is intelligible to animals, men and gods, the back of

* तीर्य्यंतेसंसारसमुद्रोऽनेनेतितीर्थं तत्करोतितीर्थंकरः। सर्व्वं थावरणविलयेचेतनस्वरूपा विर्भावःकेवलं तदस्यास्तिकेवलिन् सुरें द्रादिकृतापूजामर्हंत्यर्हंन्जयतिरागद्वेषमोहानितिजिनः॥
These Etymologies are from *Hemachandra's* Commentary.

his head is surrounded with a halo of light, brighter than the disk of the sun, and for an immense interval around him, wherever he moves, there is neither sickness nor enmity, storm nor dearth, neither plague portents, nor war. Eleven *Atisayas* of this kind are ascribed to him. The remaining nineteen are of celestial origin, as the raining of flowers and perfumes, the sound of heavenly drums, and the menial offices rendered by *Indra* and the gods.

Notwithstanding the sameness of the general character and identity of generic attributes, the twenty-four *Jinas* are distinguished from each other in colour, stature, and longevity. Two of them are red, two white, two blue, two black, the rest are of a golden hue, or a yellowish brown. The other two peculiarities are regulated with very systematic precision, and observe a series of decrement from *Rishabha,* the first *Jina,* who was five hundred poles in stature, and lived 8,400,000 great years to *Mahávira,* the 24th, who had degenerated to the size of man, and was not more than forty years on earth. These peculiarities have been detailed by Mr. Colebrooke, in the ninth volume of the Researches, and he draws a probable inference from the return to reason in the stature and years of the two last *Jinas,* that they alone are to be considered as historical personages. The rest are the creatures of fiction. The notion of decreasing longevity, like that of the existence of human beings, superior to the gods, is common to the *Bauddhas.**

There is also great similarity in the general tenor of the legends related of each of the *Jinas.* They are all born a number of times, and in a variety of characters, before they arrive at the state of a *Tirthankara :* after which, as their attainment of divine knowledge is the work of self-denial and ascetic meditation, we need not expect much varied

* A comparison of the *Jain* and *Bauddha* series suggests strong confirmation of the opinion, that the *Jain* legends are only *Bauddha* notions exaggerated. The ages of the seven *Buddhas* run thus—

Vipaswi, ...	80,000 years.
Sikhi, ...	70,000 ditto.
Viswabhú, ...	60,000 ditto.
Krakuchchanda, ...	40,000 ditto.
Kanaka, ...	30,000 ditto.
Kasyapa, ...	20,000 ditto.
Sákya, ...	100 ditto.

A. R. vol. XVI. p. 453. The last *Jina* but one, or *Parswanath,* lived like *Sákya,* 100 years.

incident in their adventures, a sketch of the life of MAHA'VI'RA, from the *Mahávira Cheritra*, will convey some notion of their ordinary history, whilst further illustration may be derived from an abstract of the *Párswanáth Cheritra*, or life of PA'RSWANA'TH, in the Royal Asiatic Society's Transactions.

LIFE OF MAHAVIRA.

The twenty-fourth *Tirthankara* MAHA'VI'RA's first birth, which occurred at a period indefinitely remote, was as NAYASA'RA, head man of a village, in the country of *Vijaya*, subject to SATRUMERDDANA. His piety and humanity elevated him next to the heaven called *Saudherma*, where he enjoyed happiness for some oceans of years. He was next born as MARICHI, the grandson of the first *Tirthankara* RISHABHA, then transferred to the *Brahmaloka*, whence he returned to earth as a worldly-minded and sensual *Brahman*, the consequence of which was his repeated births in the same caste, each birth being separated by an interval passed in one of the *Jain* heavens, and each period of life extending to many *lakhs* of years. He then became VISWABHU'TA, prince of *Rajagriha*, and next a *Vásudeva*, named TRI'PRI'SHTHA, from having three back bones: his uncle and foe in a former life, *Visabhanandi*, was born as his *Protagonist*, or *Prativásudevá*, named ASWAGRIVA or HAYAGRIVA, and was, in the course of events, destroyed by the *Vásudeva*, a palpable adaptation of the *Pauranic* legend of VISHNU and HAYAGRIVA. TRI'PRI'SHTHA having put his chamberlain cruelly to death, was condemned to hell, and again born as a lion: he migrated through various forms, until he became the *Chakravertti* PRIYAMITRA, in the division of the world, *Mahavideha*. After a victorious reign of eighty-four *lakhs* of years, he became an ascetic for a further period of a hundred *lakhs*, and was then translated to one of the higher heavens. Thence he returned to earth in the *Bharata* division, as NANDANA, the son of JITASATRU, he adopted a life of devotion, and diligently adored the *Jinas*. After an existence of twenty-five *lakhs* of years, he was raised to the dignity of king of the gods in the *Pushpottara* heaven, in which capacity he preserved his ancient faith, offering flowers to, and bathing daily the one hundred and eight images of the *Arhats*. Such exalted piety was now to meet with its reward, and the pains of existence to be terminated in the person of the *Tirthankara*, MA'HA'VI'RA, or VERDDHAMA'NA.

On the return of the spirit of NANDANA to earth, it first animated the womb of the wife of a *Brahman*, but MAHENDRA disapproving of the receptacle as of low caste, transferred it to the womb of TRISALA', wife of SIDDHA'RTHA, of the family of *Ikshwaku*, and prince of *Pavana*, in *Bharatakshetra*. MAHA'VI'RA was born on the thirteenth of the light fortnight of *Chaitra:* the fifty-six nymphs of the universe assisted at his birth, and his consecration was performed by SAKRA, and the other sixty three *Indras*. The name given by his father was VERDDHAMA'NA, as causing increase of riches and prosperity, but SAKRA gave him also the appellation of MAHA'VI'RA, as significant of his power and supremacy over men and gods.

When arrived at maturity, MAHA'VI'RA was prevailed upon by his parents to marry YASODA', daughter of the prince SAMARAVI'RA. By her he had a daughter, PRIYADERSANA', who was married to JAMA'LI, a prince, one of the saint's pupils, and founder of a schism. SIDDHA'RTHA and his wife died when their son was twenty-eight years old, on which MAHA'VI'RA adopted an ascetic life, the government devolving on his elder brother NANDIVERDDHANA. After two years of abstinence and self-denial at home, he commenced an erratic life, and the attainment of the degree of a *Jina*.

During the first six years of his peregrination, MAHA'VI'RA observed frequent fasts of several months duration, during each of which he kept his eyes fixed upon the tip of his nose, and maintained perpetual silence. He was invisibly attended by a *Yaksha*, named SIDDHA'RTHA, who, at the command of INDRA, watched over his personal security, and where speech was necessary acted as spokesman. At *Nálándá*, a village near *Rájagriha*, MAHA'VI'RA acquired a follower named GOSA'LA, so called from his birth in a cow-house, a man of low caste and vulgar propensities, and who acts as a sort of buffoon.* He is involved in repeated difficulties,

* Some curious and unintelligible things are related of this individual, which suggest a suspicion that the author had in view some of the oriental legends relating to *Mani* or *Manes*. The birth of GOSA'LA, in a cow-house, may or may not refer to

and not unfrequently receives a beating, but when free from fault, the *Yakshas*, who attend on SIDDHA'RTHA, come to his aid, and destroy with fire the houses and property of his assailants. Amongst other enemies he provokes the followers of VERDDHANA SU'RI, the disciple of CHANDRA-A'CHA'RYA, a teacher of the *Jain* faith, according to the doctrines of PA'RSWANA'TH. In the course of the dispute it appears that the followers of PA'RSWANA'TH wore clothes, whilst MAHA'VI'RA was indifferent to vesture, and the latter consequently belonged to the division of the *Jains* called *Digambaras*, or those who go naked, whilst PA'RSWANA'TH's disciples were *Swetámbaras*, dressed in garments.* During the six years expended in this manner, MAHA'VI'RA visits a number of places, most of which appear to be in *Behar* and the adjacent provinces, as *Rájagriha*, *Srávasti* near *Oude*, *Vatsálí*, which is identified with the capital of *Behar*, and others.

Proceeding on his peregrinations, MAHA'VI'RA voluntarily exposed himself to be maltreated by the *Mlechha* tribes of *Vajrabhúmi Suddhibhúmi*, and *Lát*, or *Lár* the countries apparently of the *Gonds*, who abused and beat him, and shot at him with arrows, and baited him with dogs, to all which he offered no resistance, and indeed rejoiced in his sufferings, for, however necessary to personal purification, it is not the duty of a *Jain* ascetic to inflict tortures upon himself—his course of penance is one of

Christianity; but it is also observed that his father and mother carried about a *Chitra Pattika*, a painted cloth or picture, which GOSA'LA stole from them, and that when he adopted the service of MAHA'VI'RA, he abandoned the heresy of the picture, चित्रफलक पाषण्डं विहाय

* They reply to GOSA'LA's enquiry: निर्ग्रन्थाः पार्श्वशिष्याः वयं "We are the pupils of PA'RSWA, free from restrain"—to which he rejoins कथन्तुयूयंनिर्ग्रन्था वस्त्रादिग्रन्थधारिणः। केवलं जीविकाहेतो रियं पाषण्डकल्पना॥ वस्त्रादि संगरहितो निरपेक्षोवपुष्यपि। धर्म्माचार्य्योहि यादृग्मेनिर्ग्रन्था तादृशा खलु॥ "How can you be free from restraint encumbered with clothes and the like, these heretical practices are adopted merely for a livelihood: wholly unfettered by clothes and such things, and disregarding the body, the followers of such a teacher as mine is, are the only persons exempt from restraint." Further confirmation of MAHA'VI'RA and his followers being *Digambaras*, occurs in various places, especially in a passage where GOSA'LA gets beaten, and almost killed by the women of a village in *Magadha*, because he is a naked *Sramana*, or mendicant.

self-denial, fasting and silence, and pain however meritorious its endurance, must be inflicted by others, not himself. At the end of the ninth year, Maha'vi'ra relinquished his silence in answer to a question put by Gosa'la, but continued engaged in the practice of mortification and in an erratic life. His squire having acquired from him the possession of the *Téjalesya*, or power of ejecting flame, and having learned from certain of the disciples of Pa'rswana'th, what is technically termed the *Mahánimitta* of the eight *Angas*, intending probably their scriptural doctrines, set up for himself as a *Jina*, and quitted his master.

Indra having declared that Maha'vi'ra's meditations could not be disturbed by men or gods, one of the inferior spirits of heaven, indignant at the assertion, assailed the Sage with a variety of horrors and temptations, but in vain. Maha'vi'ra's pious abstraction was unbroken. He then wandered about and visited *Kausámbi*, the capital of *Satánika*, where he was received with great veneration, and where his period of self-denial ended in perfect exemption from human infirmities. The whole of the time expended by him in these preparatory exercises was twelve years and six months, and of this he had fasted nearly eleven years. His various fasts are particularised with great minuteness, as one of six months, nine of four months each, twelve of one month, and seventy-two of half a month each, making altogether ten years and three hundred and forty-nine days.

The bonds of action were snapped like an old rope, and the *Kevala*, or *only knowledge* attained by Maha'vi'ra on the north bank of the *Rijupáliká*, under a *Sál* tree, on the tenth of the light fortnight of *Vaisákha*, in the fourth watch of the day, whilst the moon was in the asterism *Hasta*. Indra instantly hastened to the spot, attended by thousands of deities, who all did homage to the saint, and attended him on his progress to *Apápápuri*, in *Behar*, where he commenced his instructions on a stage erected for the purpose by the deities, a model of which is not uncommonly represented in *Jain* temples. The following is the introductory lecture ascribed to Maha'vi'ra by his biographer.

" The world is without bounds, like a formidable ocean ; its cause is action *(Karma,)* which is as the seed of the tree. The being *(Jiva)* invested with body, but devoid of judgment, goes like a well-sinker, ever downwards, by the acts it performs, whilst the embodied being which has attained purity, goes ever upwards, by its own acts, like the builder of a palace. Let not any one injure life, whilst bound in the bonds of action; but be as assiduous in cherishing the life of another as his own. Never let any one speak falsehood, but always speak the truth. Let every one who has a bodily form avoid giving pain to others as much as to himself. Let no one take property not given to him, for wealth is like the external life of men, and he who takes away such wealth commits as it were murder. Associate not with women, for it is the destruction of life: let the wise observe continence, which binds them to the Supreme. Be not incumbered with a family, for by the anxiety it involves, the person separated from it falls like an ox too heavily laden. If it be not in their power to shun these more subtle destroyers of life, let those who desire so to do, avoid at least the commission of all gross offences."

When MAHA'VI'RA's fame began to be widely diffused, it attracted the notice of the *Brahmans* of *Magadhá*, and several of their most eminent teachers undertook to refute his doctrines. Instead of effecting their purpose, however, they became converts, and constituted his *Ganadharas*, heads of schools, the disciples of MAHA'VI'RA and teachers of his doctrines, both orally and scripturally. It is of some interest to notice them in detail, as the epithets given to them are liable to be misunderstood, and to lead to erroneous notions respecting their character and history.

This is particularly the case with the first INDRABHU'TI, or GAUTAMA, who has been considered as the same with the GAUTAMA of the *Bauddhas*, the son of MA'YA'DEVI, and author of the Indian metaphysics.* That any connexion exists between the *Jain* and the *Brahmana* Sage is, at least, very doubtful; but the GAUTAMA of the *Bauddhas*, the son of SUDHODANA and MA'YA', was a *Kshetriya*, a prince of the royal or warrior caste. All the *Jain* traditions make their GAUTAMA a *Brahman*, originally of the *Gotra*, or tribe of GOTAMA *Rishi*, a division of the *Brahmans* well known, and still existing in the South of India. These two persons therefore cannot be identified, whether they be historical or fictitious personages.

INDRABHU'TI, AGNIBHU'TI, and VA'YUBHU'TI, are described as the sons of VASUBHU'TI, a *Brahman* of the *Gotama* tribe, residing at *Govara*, a village in *Magadha*: from their race, HEMACHANDRA, in the commentary on the vocabulary, observes, they are all called GAUTAMAS. VYAKTA and

* R. A. S. Transactions, vol. I. p. 538.

SUDHERMA were the sons of DHANAMITRA and DHAMMILLA, two *Brahmans* of *Kollaka,* the former of the *Bharadwája,* and the latter of the *Agnivaisya* tribe. MANDITA and MAURYA PUTRA were half-brothers, the sons of VIJAYADEVI′ by DHANA DEVA and MAURYA, two *Brahmans* of the *Vásishtha* and *Kásyapa* races, but cousins by the mother's side, and consequently, according to the custom of the country, it is stated, the one took the other's widow to wife upon his decease. AKAMPITA was the son of a *Maithili Brahman,* of the *Gautama* tribe. ACHALABHRA′TA′, of a *Brahman* of Oude, of the *Hárita* family. METARYA was a *Brahman* of *Vatsa,* of the *Kaundilya* tribe; and PRABHA′SA, a *Brahman* of the same race, but a native of *Rájagriha* in Behar. These are the eleven *Ganadharas,* or *Ganádhipas,* holders or masters of *Jain* schools, although, before their conversion, learned in the four *Vedas,* and teaching the doctrines contained in them,

These converts to *Jain* principles are mostly made in the same manner: each comes to the Saint, prepared to overwhelm him with shame when he salutes them mildly by name, tells them the subject that excites their unuttered doubts, and solves the difficulty, not always very satisfactorily or distinctly it must be admitted; but the whole is an epitome of the *Jain* notions on those subjects which chiefly engage the attention of the Hindu philosophers.

INDRABHU′TI doubts whether there be life *(Jiva)* or not—MAHA′VI′RA says there is, and that it is the vessel of virtue and vice, or where would be the use of acts of virtue or piety.

AGNIBHU′TI questions if there be acts *(Kerma)* or not, to which MAHA′VI′RA replies in the affirmative, and that from them proceed all bodily pleasure and pain, and the various migrations of the living principle through different forms.

VA′YUBHU′TI doubts if life be not body, which the Sage denies, as the objects of the senses may be remembered after the senses cease to act, even after death, that is, in a succeeding state of existence occasionally.

VYAKTA questions the reality of elementary matter, referring it with the *Vedántis* to illusion; the Sage replies that the doctrine of vacuity is false, illustrating his position rather obscurely, by asking if there are no other worlds than the *Gandharba,* cities of dreams, or castles in the air.

SUDHERMA imagines that the same kind of bodies which are worn in one life will be assumed in another, or that a human being must be born again amongst mankind; for as the tree is always of the same nature as the seed, so must the consequences of acts, in a peculiar capacity, lead to results adapted to a similar condition. This MAHA'VI'RA contradicts, and says that causes and effects are not necessarily of the same nature as horn, and similar materials are convertible into arrow barbs, and the like.

MANDITA has not made up his mind on the subjects of bondage and liberation, *(Bandha* and *Moksha)*; the *Jina* explains the former to be connexion with and dependence on worldly acts, whilst the latter is total detachment from them, and independence of them effected by knowledge.

MAURYAPUTRA doubts of the existence of gods, to which MAHA'VI'RA opposes the fact of the presence of INDRA, and the rest around his throne. They cannot bear the odour of mere mortality, he adds; but they never fail to attend at the birth, inauguration, and other passages of the life of a *Jina*.

AKAMPITA is disposed to disbelieve the existence of the spirits of hell, because he cannot see them; but the Sage says that they are visible to those possessing certain knowledge, of whom *he* is one.

ACHALABHRA'TA' is sceptical as to the distinction between vice and virtue, for which MAHA'VI'RA rebukes him, and desires him to judge of them by their fruits: length of days, honorable birth, health, beauty and prosperity, being the rewards in this life of virtue; and the reverse of these the punishments of vice.

META'RYA questions a future existence, because life having no certain form must depend on elementary form, and consequently perish with it; but MAHA'VI'RA replies, that life is severally present in various elementary aggregates to give them consciousness, and existing independent of them, may go elsewhere often they are dissolved. He adds, in confirmation of the doctrine, that the *Srutis* and *Smritis*, that is, the scriptural writings of the *Brahmanas*, assert the existence of other worlds.

The last of the list is PRABHA'SA, who doubts if there be such a thing as *Nirván*, that state of nonentity which it is the object of a *Jaina* saint to attain. The solution is not very explicit. *Nirván* is declared to be the same with *Moksha*, liberation, and *Kermakshaya*, abrogation of acts, and that this is real is proved by the authority of the *Veda*, and is visibly manifested in those who acquire true knowledge.

According to this view of the *Jain* system, therefore, we find the vital principle recognised as a real existence, animating in distinct portions, distinct bodies, and condemned to suffer the consequence of its actions by migrations through various forms. The reality of elementary matter is also asserted, as well as of gods, demons, heaven, and hell. The final state of the vital and sentient principle is left rather obscure, but as its actual and visible exemption from human acts is taught, it follows that it is exempt from their consequences, or repeated births in various shapes, and therefore ceases to be in any sensible or suffering form. It is unnecessary to dwell longer on the subject here, as we shall have occasion to recur to it.

After the conversion of these *Brahmans* and their disciples, MAHA'VI'RA instructed them further in his doctrines, and they again taught them to others, becoming the heads of separate schools. AKAMPITA and ACHALABHRA'TA, however, and META'RYA and PRABHA'SA taught in common, so that the eleven *Ganadhipas* established but nine *Ganas* or classes.

Having thus attained the object of his penance and silence, MAHA'VI'RA, attended by his disciples, wandered about to different places, disseminating the *Jain* belief, and making numerous converts. The scene of his labours is mostly along the Ganges, in the modern districts of *Behar* and *Allahabad*, and principally at the cities of *Kausámbi* and *Rájagriha*, under the kings SATA'NI'KA and SRENI'KA, both of whom are *Jains*. The occurrences described relate more to the disciples of the Saint than to himself, and there are some curious matters of an apparently historical character. There is also a prophetic account of HEMACHANDRA himself, and his patron KUMA'RA PA'LA of *Guzerat*, put into the mouth of MAHA'VI'RA; but these are foreign to our present purpose, which is confined to the progress of the *Jain* sage.

MAHA'VI'RA having completed the period of his earthly career, returned to *Apápapuri*, whither he was attended by a numerous concourse of followers of various designations. However fanciful the enumeration, the list is not uninstructive, as it displays the use of various terms to signify different orders of one sect, and not, as has been sometimes erroneously supposed, the sect itself. *Sramanas*, *Sadhs* and *Srávaks*, may be *Jains*, but they are not necessarily so, nor do they singly designate all the individuals of that persuasion. *Virá's* train consists of *Sádhus*, holy men, fourteen thousand; *Sádhwi's* holy women, thirty-six thousand; *Sramanas* or ascetics, versed in the fourteen *Purvas*, three hundred; *Avadhíjnánis* those knowing the limits or laws, one thousand and three hundred; *Kevalis*, or detached from acts, seven hundred; *Manovits*, possessors of intellectual wisdom, five hundred; *Bádis*, controversialists, four hundred; *Srávakas*, the male laity, one lack and fifty-nine thousand; and *Srávikas*, female hearers of the word, double that number, or three lacks and eighteen thousand. The only *Ganadharas* present, were GAUTAMA and SUDHERMA, the other nine having attained felicity, or having died before their master.

The period of his liberation having arrived, MAHA'VI'RA resigned his breath, and his body was burned by SAKRA and other deities, who divided amongst them such parts as were not destroyed by the flames, as the teeth and bones, which they preserved as reliques; the ashes of the pile were distributed amongst the assistants: the gods erected a splendid monument on the spot, and then returned to their respective heavens. These events occurred on the day of new moon, in the month *Kártik*, when MAHA'VI'RA was seventy-two years of age, thirty of which were spent in social duties, and the rest in religious avocations, and he died two hundred and fifty years after the preceding *Jina*, PA'RSWANA'TH: no other date is given, but in the passage in the prophetic strain above alluded to, it is mentioned that KUMA'RA, PA'LA will found *Anahilla Patan*, and become the disciple of HEMACHANDRA, one thousand six hundred and sixty-nine years after the death of MAHA'VI'RA.

The conversion of KUMA'RA PA'LA occurred about A. D. 1174, and consequently the last *Jina* expired about five hundred years before the Christian era. According to other authorities, the date assigned to this event, is commonly about a century and a half earlier, or before Christ six hundred and sixty-three,* but HEMACHANDRA is a preferable guide, although, in point of actual chronology, his date is probably not more to be depended upon than those derived from other sources.

The doctrines of the *Jains*, which constitute the philosophy of their system, it is not part of the present plan to discuss: but a few of the leading tenets, as derived from original authorities, may be here briefly

* Colonel Mackenzie, on the information of the *Belligolu Jains*, says *Verddhamána* attained beatitude 2464 years before the year 1801, which is 663 years before Christ. Mr. Colebrooke observes, that the *Jains* of Bengal reckon *Verddhamána* to have lived 580 years before *Vikramaditya*, which is A. C. 636.

adverted to. It is the more necessary to dwell on the subject as the chief opinions of the sect of *Jina*, as described elsewhere, have, for the most part, been taken from verbal communication, or the controversial writings of the *Brahmans*.

An eternal and presiding first cause forms no part of the *Jain* creed, nor do the *Jains* admit of soul or spirit as distinct from the living principle. All existence is divisible into two heads—*Life (Jiva)* or the living and sentient principle; and *Inertia* or *Ajiva*, the various modifications of inanimate matter. Both these are uncreated and imperishable. Their forms and conditions may change, but they are never destroyed; and with the exception of the unusual cases in which a peculiar living principle ceases to be subject to bodily acts, both life and matter proceed in a certain course, and at stated periods the same forms, the same characters, and the same events, are repeated.

To proceed, however, according to the original authorities, all objects sensible or abstract, are arranged under nine categories, termed *Tatwas*, truths or existences, which we shall proceed to notice in some detail.

I. *Jiva*, Life, or the living and sentient principle, as existing in various forms, but especially reducible to two classes, those with and those without mobility. The first comprises animals, men, demons, and gods—the second, all combinations of the four elements, earth, water, fire, air, as minerals, vapours, meteors, and tempests—and all the products of the vegetable kingdom. They are again arranged in five classes, according to their possession of as many *Indriyas*, or sensible properties. The wholly unconscious bodies to ordinary apprehension, but which have a subtle vitality perceptible to saintly and super-human beings, have the property of form: such are minerals, and the like. Snails, worms, and insects, in general, have two properties—form and face. Lice, fleas, and the like, have three properties, or form, face, and the organ of smell. Bees, gnats, and the rest have, in addition to these, vision; whilst animals, men, demons, and gods, have form, vision, hearing, smell, and taste. To these five predicates of vital beings, two others are sometimes added, and they are said to be *Sanjnina* and *Asnajnina*, or, born by procreation, or spontaneously generated. Again, these seven orders are distinguished as complete or incomplete, making altogether fourteen classes of living things. According to the acts done or suffered in each condition, the vital principle migrates to an inferior or superior grade, until it is emancipated from bodily acts altogether. It is a peculiarity of the *Jain* notions of life, that it is always adapted to the body it animates, and diminishes with the gnat, and expands to the elephant, a notion that is treated with just ridicule by the *Brahmans*. Generically, it is defined to be without beginning or end, endowed with attributes of its own agent and enjoyer, conscious, subtle, proportionate to the body it animates; through sin, it passes into animals, or goes to hell; through virtue and vice combined, it passes into men, and through virtue alone, ascends to heaven; through the annihilation of both vice and virtue, it obtains emancipation.

II. *Ajiva*, the second predicate of existence, comprises objects or properties devoid of consciousness and life. These seem to be vaguely and variously classed, and to be in general incapable of interpretation; but the enumeration is commonly fourteen, like the modification of vitality. They are *Dhermástikaya*, *Adhermástikaya*, and *Akásástikaya*, each comprehending three varieties. *Kála*, or time, is the tenth; and *Pudgala*, or elementary matter, in four modifications, completes the series.

It is not very easy to understand these technicalities, for the etymology of the words is of little avail. *Astikaya* indicates the existence of body, "*Body is*;" whilst *Dherma* signifies virtue, and *Adherma*, vice; but *Dherma* means also peculiar function or office, in which sense it seems to be here intended, thus—*Dhermástikaya* is defined to be that which facilitates the motion of animate or inanimate bodies, as water for fish. *Adhermástikaya* is that which impedes or stops their motion. *Akásástikaya* is the principle of repulsion, that which keeps bodies separate, or space: the varieties of these are only in degree, of little, more, and complete. Time is sufficiently intelligible, but the *Jains* indulge in modifications of it infinitely more extravagant than those for which the Hindus are reproached; thus after enumerating days, weeks, months, and years, we have the *Palya*, or *Palyopama*, a period measured by the time in which a vast well, one hundred *Yojans* every way, filled with minute hairs so closely packed that a river might be hurried over them without penetrating the interstices, could be emptied at the rate of one hair in a century. A *Sagaropama* is one hundred million millions of *Palyas*, and an *Avasarpini* and *Utserpini*, which make up a great age, consist each of one hundred million millions of *Sagaras*. *Pudgala* is atomic matter, distinguished like the first three categories, by being combined in three degrees—

little, much, and most, whilst it adds a fourth state, or that of *Paramanu*, primitive, subtle, indivisible, and uncombined.

III. The third *Tatwa* is *Punya, Good*, or whatever is the cause of happiness to living beings: the sub-divisions of this category are forty-two, it will be sufficient here to enumerate a few of the principal.

1. *Uchchairgotra*, high birth, rank, or the respect of mankind.

2. *Manushyagati*, the state of man, either as obtained from some other form of being or continuance in it.

3. *Suragati*, the state of divinity, Godhead.

4. *Panchendriya*, the state of superior vitality, or possession of five organs of sense.

5. *Panchadeha*, the possession of body, or form of one of five kinds.

Audárika, elementary—that arising from the aggregation of elements, as the bodies of men and beasts.

Vaikriya, transmigrated—that assumed in consequence of acts, as the forms of spirits and gods.

Ahárakam, adventitious, one assumed, such as that of the *Purvadharas*, of one cubit in stature, when they went to see the *Tirthankaras* in *Mahávidehakshetra*.

Taijasa, the form obtained by suppressing mortal wants, in which state fire can be ejected from the body.

Kármanam, the form which is the necessary consequence of acts. These two last are necessarily connected from all time, and can only be disunited by final liberation, or *Moksha*.

Other varieties of '*Good*', are colour, odour, flavour, touch, warmth, coolness, and the like.

IV. *Pápa*, or '*Ill*,' in contradistinction to the preceding, and implying that which is the cause of unhappiness to mankind; there are eighty-two kinds;

As the five *Avaranas*, or difficulties in acquiring as many gradations of holy or divine wisdom. Five *Antaráyas*, disappointments, or impediments, as not obtaining what is about to be presented, not being able to enjoy an object of fruition when in possession of it, and want of vigour though in bodily health. Four *Dersanavasánas*, obstruction, or impediment to information derivable from the senses, or the understanding; or to the acquirement of divine knowledge. Five states of sleep, inferior birth, pain, as a condition of existence, as when condemned to purgatory, belief in false gods, defect of size or shape, and all the human passions and infirmities—as anger, pride, covetousness, &c., including, amongst the ills of life, laughter and love.

V. *Asrava* is that source from which the evil acts of living beings proceed. The varieties are the five *Indriyas*, or organs of sense; the four *Kasháyas*, or passions, as wrath, pride, covetousness, and deceit; the five *Avratas*, non-observance of positive commands, as lying, stealing, &c. and three *Yogas*, addiction or attachment of the mind, speech, and body to any act; *Kraiyas*, or acts, of which twenty-six varieties are specified as those performed with any part of the body, or with the instrumentality of a weapon, or the like—those prompted by feelings of hate or wrath—those which are inceptive, progressive, or conclusive—those performed by oneself, or through another creature—those which are suggested by impiety, or unbelief in the doctrine of the *Trithankáras*.

VI. The sixth *Tatwa* is termed *Samvara*, and is that by which acts are collected or impeded. There are fifty-seven varieties classed under six heads.

1. *Samiti*, keeping the attention properly alive, so as to see immediately if an insect is in the way, to refrain from uttering what should not be said, to distinguish any of the forty-two defects in food given as alms, taking or relinquishing any thing indifferently, and avoiding or abandoning unfit things.

2. *Gupti*, secrecy, or reserve of three kinds, or in mind, speech and person.

3. *Parishahá*, endurance or patience, as when a person has taken a vow of abstemiousness he must bear hunger and thirst; so he must endure heat and cold, when he practices the immoveable posture of *Jain* abstraction; if he is disappointed in what he has laboured or begged for, he must not murmur; and if he is reviled or even beaten, he must patiently submit.

4. *Yatidherma*, the duties of an ascetic, these are ten in number, patience, gentleness, integrity, and disinterestedness, abstraction, mortification, truth, purity, poverty, and continence.

5. *Bhávaná*, conviction or conclusion, such as that worldly existences are not eternal, that there is no refuge after death, that life is perpetually migrating through the eighty-four lakhs of living forms, that life is

one or many : it also includes perception of the source whence evil acts proceed, and the like.

The sixth division of this class is *Cheritra*, practice or observance, of five sorts. *Sámáyika*, conventional, or the practice and avoidance of such actions as are permitted or prescribed. *Chhedopasthápaniya*, prevention of evil, as of the destruction of animal life. *Parihâravisuddhi*, purification by such mortification and penance as are enjoined by the example of ancient saints and sages. *Sulkshmasamparáya*, the practises of those pious men who have attained a certain degree of eminence; and *Yathakhyátam*, the same after all the impediments and impurities of human nature are overcome or destroyed.

VII. *Nírjará*, the seventh *Tatwa*, is the religious practice that destroys mortal impurities, or, in other words, penance : it is of two kinds, external and internal ; the first comprehends fasting, continence, silence, and bodily suffering ; the second, repentance, piety, protection of the virtuous, study, meditation, and disregard, or rejection of both virtue and vice.

VIII. *Bandha* is the integral association of life with acts, as of milk with water, fire with a red hot iron ball : it is of four kinds—*Prakriti*, the natural disposition or nature of a thing—*Sthiti*, duration, or measure of time, through which life continues—*Anubhága*, feeling, or sensible quality—*Pradesa*, atomic individuality. The characters of this principle are illustrated by a *confection*. 1. According to its natural properties it cures phlegm, bile, &c.; 2, it remains efficient but for a given period ; 3, it is sweet, bitter, sour, &c. ; and 4, it is divisible into large or small proportions, retaining each the properties of the whole mass.

IX. The last of the nine principles is *Moksha*, or liberation of the vital spirit from the bonds of action : it is of nine sorts.

Satpadaprarúpana. The determination of the real nature of things, the consequence of a finite course of progress through different stages of being and purification. It is attainable only by living creatures of the highest order, or those having the five organs of sense ; by those possessed of the *Trasakáya*, or a body endowed with consciousness and mobility ; by those beings which are engendered, not self-produced ; by those which have reached the fifth *Charita*, or exemption from human infirmity ; by those which are in the *Kshayika Samyaktwa*, or that state of perfection in which elementary or material existence is destroyed ; by those no longer requiring material existence; by those who have acquired the *Kevalajnána*, the only knowledge, and the *Kevala Dersana*, or only vision.

2. *Dravyapramána*, as regulated by the fitness of the things or persons to be emancipated.

3. *Kshetrapramána*, depending on the essentiality of certain holy places at which only it can be obtained.

4. *Spersana*, contact, or identity of the individuated living principle with that of the universe, or any part of it.

5. *Kála*, the times or ages at which emancipation is attainable; or the periods spent in various transmigrations.

6. *Antaram*, the difference of temperaments or dispositions.

7. *Bhága*, the existence of the imperishable part of all living bodies in which the purified essences or *Siddhas* reside.

8. *Bháva*, the nature or property of that pure existence which has attained the *Kevalajnána*, and other perfections essential to final liberation.

9. *Alpabahutwa*, the degree or ratio in which different classes of beings obtain emancipation.*

From the details of these nine *Tatwas* the sum of the whole *Jain* system may be collected, but they form only the text on which further subtilties are founded, and they leave the end and scope of all the doctrine or the attainment of ultimate liberation singularly indistinct.

The *Moksha* of the *Jains* is exemption from the incidents of life, and above all from the necessity of being born again; but in what state the living principle subsists after it is so exempted, does not very satisfactorily appear. In one state indeed the bodily individuality remains, or that of *Jivanmukti*, liberation during life, whilst from most of the subdivisions of *Moksha*, it follows that the *Siddahs*, the pure existences, correspond with our notions of spiritual beings, having an impassive and inappreciable form, variable at will, capable of infinite contraction or dilation, and wholly void of feeling or passion. This is not incompatible with their enjoyment of *Nirván*, another term for *Moksha*, and which, as Mr. Colebrooke observes, meaning literally, extinct or gone out as a

* Although termed मोचभेदाः in the original authorities, these varieties are rather in the requisite conditions for attaining *Moksha*, than in the kind or sort of emancipation attained.

fire, set, as a heavenly luminary, defunct as a saint who has passed away, implies profound calm. "It is not annihilation," he concludes, "but unceasing apathy which they, 'the *Jains* and *Buddhas*,' understand to be the extinction of their saints, and which they esteem to be supreme felicity worthy to be sought by practice of mortification as well as by acquisition of knowledge."

Besides the notions exhibited in the detail of the nine *Tatwas*, the *Jains* are known in controversial writings by the title *Saptabádis*, or *Saptabhangis*, the *disputers* or *refuters* of seven positions: more correctly speaking, they are reconcilers, or could be so of seven contradictory assertions, evincing a sceptical character which justifies another epithet which they acknowledge, of *Syádbádis*, or assertors of possibilities: the seven positions are the following:

1, a thing is: 2—It is not: 3—It is and it is not: 4—It is not definable: 5—It *is*, but is not definable: 6—It is not, neither is it definable: 7—It is and it is not, and is not definable—Now these positions imply the doctrines of the different schools, the *Sánkhya, Vedánta*, and others, with regard to the world, to life, and to spirit, and are met in every case by the *Jains* with the reply, *Syádbá, It may be so sometimes*: that is, whatever of these dogmas is advanced will be true in some respects, and not in others; correct under some circumstances, and not under others; and they are therefore not entitled to implicit trust, nor are they irreconcilable. There is one inference to be drawn from this attempt to reconcile the leading doctrines of the principal schools, of some importance to the history of the *Jain* doctrines, and it renders it probable that they were posterior to all the rest. As this reasoning however has been opposed by RAMANUJA, it dates earlier than the twelfth century.

Liberation during life, and as a necessary consequence, exemption after it from future birth, implies the abandonment of eight classes of *Karmas*, or acts, four of which are noxious and four innoxious—they are all included under the *Tatwa, Pápa*, ILL, as above noticed, but are also more especially detailed. To the first order belong the following:

Jyanávarani, disregard of the various stages of knowledge, from simple comprehension to the only true wisdom, as so many steps to final liberation.

Dersanávarani, disbelief in the doctrines of the *Jain* Saints.

Mohani, hesitation in obeying the injunctions of the *Jain* code, or doubt as to their importance and the consequences of their neglect.

Antaráya, impeding or vexing those engaged in seeking liberation.

The second class comprises—

Vedaníya, self-consciousness or sufficiency.

Náma, pride of name—*Gotra*, pride of birth—and *Ayushka*, attachment to bodily existence.

These essential principles of the faith are common to all classes of *Jains*, but some differences occur in their *Duties* as they are divided into religious or lay orders, *Yatis* and *Srávakas*. Implicit belief in the doctrines and actions of the *Tirthankaras* is, of course, obligatory on both ; but the former are expected to follow a life of abstinence, taciturnity, and continence, whilst the latter add to their moral and religious code, the practical worship of the *Tirthankaras*, and profound reverence for their more pious brethren. The moral code of the *Jains* is expressed in five *MaháVratas*, or great duties—Refraining from injury to life, truth, honesty, chastity, and freedom from worldly desires. There are four *Dhermas*, or merits—liberality, gentleness, piety, and penance ; and three sorts of restraint—government of the mind, the tongue, and the person. To these are superadded a number of minor instructions or prohibitions, sometimes of a beneficial and sometimes of a trivial, or even ludicrous tendency, such as to abstain, at certain seasons, from salt, flowers, green fruit, and roots, honey, grapes, and tobacco ; to drink water thrice strained ; never to leave a liquid uncovered, lest an insect should be drowned in it ; not to deal in soap, natron, indigo, and iron ; and never to eat in the dark lest a fly should be swallowed. Religious characters wear a piece of cloth over their mouths to prevent insects from flying into them, and carry a brush under their arms to sweep the place on which they are about to sit, to remove any ants or other living creatures out of the way of danger. Upon the whole, the doctrine of the *Jainas* is a system of quietism, calculated to render those who follow it perfectly innoxious, but to inspire them with apathetic indifference towards both this world and the next.

The ritual of the *Jains* is as simple as their moral code. The *Yati*, or devotee, dispenses with acts of worship at his pleasure, and the lay votary is only bound to visit daily a temple where some of the images of the *Tirthankaras* are erected, walk round it three times, make an obeisance to the images, with an offering of some trifle, usually fruit or flowers, and pronounce some such *Mantra*, or prayer, as the following—" *Namo Arihantánam, Namo Siddhánam, Namo Aryanám, Namo Upájyánám, Namo Löe Sabba Sahúnam*—Salutation to the *Arhats*, to the Pure Existences, to the Sages, to the Teachers, to all the Devout in the world." A morning prayer is also repeated—*Ichchhami Khama Samano bandiyon, jo man jáye nisiáye; mathena bandámi*—I beg forgiveness, oh Lord, for your slave, for whatever evil thoughts the night may have produced—I bow with my head." The worshipper then perhaps remains to hear read, part of the *Kalpasútra* or *Bhaktámara*, or some narrative of one or other of the *Tirthankars*, and the devotion of their followers, and proceeds to his daily occupations.

The reader in a *Jain* temple is a *Yati*, or religious character; but the ministrant priest, the attendant on the images, the receiver of offerings, and conductor of all usual ceremonies, is a *Brahman*. It is a curious peculiarity in the *Jain* system, that they should have no priests of their own, but it is the natural consequence of the doctrine and example of the *Tirthankars*, who performed no rites, either vicariously or for themselves, and gave no instruction as to their observance. It shews also the true character of this form of faith, that it was a departure from established practices, the observance of which was held by the *Jain* teachers to be matter of indifference, and which none of any credit would consent to regulate: the laity were, therefore, left to their former priesthood, as far as outward ceremonies were concerned.

The objects of worship are properly only the *Tirthankaras*, but the *Jains* do not deny the existence of the Hindu gods, and admit such of them as they have chosen to connect with the adventures of their saints, according to a classification of their own, to a share in the worship offered to their human superiors.

According to the Mythology which they have adopted and modified, the *Jains* reckon four classes of divine beings, whom they name *Bhuvanapatis, Vyantaras, Jyotishkas*, and *Vaimánikas:* the first comprises ten orders: the progeny of the *Asuras*, Serpents, *Garura, Dikpálas*, Fire, Air, the Ocean, Thunder and Lightning—who are supposed to reside in the several hells or regions below the Earth. The second has eight orders, the *Pisáchas, Bhútas, Kinnaras, Gaudherbas*, and other monstrous or terrestrial divinities, inhabiting mountains, woods, and forests, as well as the lower regions, or air. The third has five orders—the Sun, Moon, Planets, Asterisms, and other heavenly bodies. The fourth, includes the Gods of present and past *Kalpas*. Of the first kind are those born in the Heavens, *Saudherma, Isána, Máhendra, Bráhma, Sanatkumára, Sukra,* and others to the number of twelve, or in the *Kalpas,* when Sudherma and the rest were severally presiding Deities. The last class reside in two divisions of five and of nine heavens—the five termed *Vijaya, Vaijayanti,* &c.; the second termed *Anúttara,* because there are none beyond them, as they crown the triple construction of the universe. In the sovereignty of the hosts of heaven, a great number of *Indras* are recognised, but of these two are always specified as the chief, Sukra and Isa'na, one regent of the north, the other of the south heaven: the former alone has eighty-four thousand fellow gods, each of whom has myriads of associates and attendants.

Above all these rank in dignity, and as objects of worship, the twenty-four *Tirthankaras,* or with those of the past and of the future periods, seventy-two. Allusion is made by Hemachandra in his life of Maha'vi'ra, to a hundred and one, and the same work specifies four *Sáswat* or eternal *Jinas,* Rishabha'nana, Chandra'nana, Va'risena, and Verddhama'na—what is meant by them is not explained, and they are not recognised by all *Jains.*

The presence of Brahman ministrants, or the lapse of time and the tendency of the native mind to multiply objects of veneration, seems to have introduced different innovations into the worship of the *Jainas* in different parts of Hindustan; and in upper India the ritual in use is often intermixed with formulæ derived from the *Tantras,* and belonging more properly to the *Saiva* and *Sákta* worship. Images of the *Bhairavas* and *Bhairavis,* the fierce attendants on Siva and Ka'li, take their place in *Jain* temples, and at suitable seasons the *Jains* equally with the Hindus address their adoration to Saraswati' and Devi.*

* Thus, in a *Pújapaddhati,* procured at *Mainpuri,* where a *Jain* temple of considerable size stands, the *Tirthankaras,* as they are severally presented with offerings, are addressed; *Om Sri Rishabháya Swasti—Om Hrim hum:* and *Om Hrim Sri Sudhermácharya, Adigurubhyo Nama—Om Hrim Hram, Samajinachaityalayebhyo Sri Jinendrabhyo Nama.* There are also observances for regular Hindu festivals, as the *Sripanchami, Akshayatritiyá,* &c., when Saraswati and other goddesses are invoked. Rules are given for the *Ghata Sthápana,* when Sakti or Devi is supposed to be present in a water jar, erected as her receptacle and emblem, and the

In the South of India, from the account given by Colonel Mackenzie, it appears that the *Jains* observe all the Brahminical *Sanskáras*, or essential ceremonies. This is not the case in upper India, and the only rites followed are the Initiation of the infant, twelve days after birth, by repeating a *Mantra* over it, and making a circular mark with the sandal and perfumes on the top of the head: Marriage and Cremation, which are much the same as those of the Brahmans, omitting the *Mantras* of the *Vedas*. *Sráddhas*, obsequial ceremonies at stated periods, are not performed by the *Jains* in upper Hindustan.

The festivals of the *Jains* are peculiar to themselves, and occur especially on days consecrated by the birth or death of some of the principal *Tirthankars*, especially the two last *Párswanáth* and *Verddhamána*: the places where these events occurred are also objects of pilgrimage, and very numerous assemblages of devout pilgrims occur at them at different seasons—thus in Behar, a very celebrated place of resort is the scene of *Parasnáth's* liberation; the mountain *Samet Sikhara*, or *Parasnáth*, near *Pachete*;* and another of equal sanctity, the scene of *Verddhamána's* departure from earth, is at *Pápapuri*,† in the same province. Pilgrims come from all parts of India to these places at all seasons, but the principal *Melas* are held at the former in *Mágh*, and in *Kártika*, at the latter. On the western side of India, the mountains of *Abu*,‡ and *Girinar*, are the great scenes of pilgrimage, being covered with *Jain* temples and remains. Rishabha Deva and Nemina'th seem to be the favourite divinities in that quarter.

Besides these particular festivals, the *Jains* observe several that are common to the Hindus, as the *Vasantayátrá*, or spring festival, the *Sripanchami*, and others; they also hold in veneration certain of the Lunar days, as the 2d, 5th, 8th, 11th, and 12th; on these no new work should be undertaken, no journey commenced, and fasting, or abstinence at least, and continence should be observed.

Sorasa Karana Pújá ends with a *Lakshmi Stotra*, or Hymn, addressed to the Goddess of Prosperity.

* Described very fully, as previously noticed, in the Quarterly Magazine for December, 1827.

† It is also written *Apapapuri*, and *Pávapuri*, under which latter name, it and other celebrated *Jaina* shrines in Behar, are described by a Native traveller, a *Jain*, in the service of Colonel Mackenzie, in the Calcutta Magazine for June, 1823.

‡ See Asiatic Researches, vol. XVI. *Jain* Inscriptions at Abu.

The origin of the *Jain* faith is immersed in the obscurity which invests all remote history amongst the Hindus. That it is the most recent of all the systems pursued in Hindustan is rendered highly probable by the extravagances in which it deals, by the doctrine it opposes to those of all other schools, and by the comparatively recent date of many *Jain* authors of celebrity, and of numerous monumental reliques; but at what period it actually took its rise it is not easy to determine.* Mr. Colebrooke has suggested the probability of the *Jain* religion being the work of PA'RSWANA'TH, in the account of whom there is a nearer approach to sober history and credible chronology than in the narratives of his predecessors—this would throw back the origin of the *Jain* faith to the ninth century before the Christian era, admitting the *Jain* chronology of VERDDHAMA'NA's existence, but it is difficult to concur in the accuracy of so remote a date, and whatever indirect evidence on the subject is procurable, is opposed to such a belief.

It has been supposed that we have notices of the *Jaina* sect as far back as the time of the Macedonian invasion of India, or at least at the period at which MEGASTHENES was sent ambassador to SANDRACOPTUS, and that these notices are recorded by STRABO and ARRIAN—the nature of the expressions which those and other writers have employed has been canvassed by Mr. Colebrooke, and shewn satisfactorily to establish the existence at that time of the regular Brahmans, as well as of other sects: what those sects were, however, it was no part of his object to enquire, and he has left it still to be ascertained how far it can be concluded that the *Jainas* were intended.

* Major Delamaine observes, "the usual idea of the *Jains* being a modern sect may not be erroneous: the doctrines originating with *Rishabha*, and continued by *Arhanta*, dividing at periods of schism into more distinct classes, of which the *Jains* or *Sráwacs*, as now established from one, and the modern *Buddhas*, as in *Burma*, *Siam*, *Ceylon*, *Tibet*, &c. another.—*Major Delamaine*, *T. R. A. S.* 1. 427. "Were I disposed to speculate on the origin of the *Jains*, from the striking coincidences of doctrine and religious usages between them and the *Bouddhists*, I should be led to conjecture that they were originally a sect of Bouddhists."—*Mr Erskine*, *Bombay Trans.* 3. 502. "It is certainly probable, as remarked by Dr. Hamilton and Major Delamaine, that the *Gautama* of the *Jainas* and of the *Bauddhas*, is the same personage, and this leads to the further surmise that both these sects are branches of one stock.—Both have adopted the Hindu Pantheon, or assemblage of subordinate deities—both disclaim the authority of the *Vedas*, and both elevate their pre-eminent saints to divine supremacy—*Mr. Colebrooke*, *Trans. R. A. S.* I. 521.

Much perplexity in the Greek accounts of the Brahmans and Gymnosophists has, no doubt, occurred from their not having been acquainted with the subdivision of the priestly caste into the four orders of student, householder, hermit, and mendicant, and therefore they describe the Brahman sometimes as living in towns, sometimes in woods, sometimes observing celibacy, and sometimes married, sometimes as wearing clothes, and sometimes as going naked; contradictions which, though apparently irreconcilable if the same individuals, or classes, be meant, were appreciated by the shrewdness of Bayle more justly than he was himself aware of,* and are all explained by the *Achâras*, or institutes of the Hindus, as affecting the various periods of life and corresponding practices of Brahmanical devotion.

As far, therefore, as the customs or observances of the Gymnosophists are described, we have no reason to conclude that any but the followers of the *Vedas* are intended, and the only part of the account applicable to any other sect is the term *Germanes*, or *Sermanes*, or *Samanæans*, applied to one division of the Sophists or Sages. This name, as Mr. Colebrooke observes, seems to bear some affinity to the *Sramanas*, or asceticks of the *Jains* or *Bauddhas*, but we can derive no positive conclusion from a resemblance, which may possibly be rather imaginary than real, and the object of which, after all, is far from being the individual property of any sect, but is equally applicable to the ascetic of every religious system. As distinct from the Brahmans, the *Sarmanes* will be equally distinct from the *Jains*; for the Brahmans, it is said by PORPHYRY, are of one race; and the *Samanæans* are selected from all the tribes, and consist of persons choosing to prosecute divine studies, precisely the independent *Sanyási* or *Gosain*, of modern times, few persons of which description belong to the order of the *Brahmans*, or are united with the rest by any community of origin or peculiarity of faith.

Again, another *word* has been adduced in corroboration of the existence of the *Jains*, and it may be admitted, that this is a better proof than the preceding, as the *Pramnæ* are declared to be the opposers of the

* "It may be that they 'the Brachmans did not follow the same institute in all ages, and that with a distinction of time one might reconcile some of the variations of the authors who have spoken of them."—Article Brachmans, Note. C. Harris, (I.454) also has rightly estimated the real character of the Germanes, and concluded that they were nothing but Gioghis, from Pietro della Valle's description of the latter.

Brahmans, which is no where mentioned of the *Sarmanes*. This expression is said to designate the *Jains*, but this is far from certain : the term is probably derived from *Pramána*, proof, evidence, and is especially the right of the followers of the logical school, who are usually termed *Prámánikas* : it is applicable, however, to any sect which advocates positive or occular proof in opposition to written dogmas, or belief in scriptural authority, and is in that sense more correctly an epithet of the *Bauddha* sectaries than of the *Jains*, who admit the legends and worship the deities of the *Puránas*, and who hold it the height of impiety to question the written doctrines of their own teachers. The proofs from classical writers, therefore, are wholly inadequate to the decision of the antiquity of the *Jains*, and we are still entirely left to sources of a less satisfactory description.

All writers on the *Jains*, entitled to our attention, agree in admitting an intimate connexion between them and the *Bauddhas* ; the chief analogies have been above adverted to, and the inference of later origin is justly founded on the extravagant exaggerations of the system adopted by the *Jains*. Their identity of origin rests chiefly upon the name of GAUTAMA, which appears as that of VERDDHAMA'NA's chief pupil, and as the legislator of the *Bauddha* nations in the east. The dates also assigned to both are not far removed ; the apotheosis of the *Buddha*, GAUTAMA, occurring five hundred and forty-three years before Christ, and the death of MAHA'VI'RA, the preceptor of the *Jain* GAUTAMA, about the same time. That there is some connexion may be conceded, but for reasons already assigned, it is not likely that the persons are the same ; the *Jains* have not improbably derived their GAUTAMA from that of their predecessors.

No argument for the antiquity of the *Jains* is derivable from the account given of RISHABHA in the *Bhágavat Purána*. He was not a seceder from the true faith, although the mistaken imitation of his practices is said to have led others into errors, evidently intending the *Jain* heresy. He is scarcely identifiable, in consequence, with the *Jain* RISHABHA, the first of the *Tirthankaras ;* but even if that were the case, no confidence could be placed in the authority, as the work is a modern compilation, not exceeding, at the most, twelve centuries of antiquity. The refutation of *Jain* doctrines in the *Brahma Sútras*, is a less questionable testimony of their early existence; but the date of that work is to be yet ascertained. Sankara Acharya, the commentator on the texts of Vya'sa, affords a more definite approximation; but he will not carry us back above ten centuries. It is also to be observed, that the objects of the attacks of the *Sútras* and of Sankara are philosophical and speculative tenets, and these may have been current long before they formed part of a distinct practical system of faith, as promulgated by a class of *Bauddhas,* the germ of the *Jains.*

However we may admit from these authorities the existence of the *Jains* as a distinct sect, above ten or twelve centuries ago; we have reason to question their being of any note or importance much earlier. The *Bauddhas,* we know from Clemens of Alexandria, existed in India in the second century of the Christian era, and we find them not only the principal objects of Hindu confutation and anathema, but they are mentioned in works of lighter literature, referable to that period, in which the *Jains* are not noticed, nor alluded to: the omission is the more worthy of notice, because, since the *Bauddhas* disappeared from India, and the *Jains* only have been known, it will be found that the Hindu writers, whenever they speak of *Bauddhas,* shew, by the phraseology and practices ascribed to them, that they really mean *Jains:* the older writers do not make the same mistake, and the usages and expressions which they give to *Bauddha* personages are not *Jain,* but *Bauddha;* with the one they were familiar, the other were yet unknown.

The literature of the *Jains* themselves is unfavourable to the notion of high antiquity. Hemachandra, one of their greatest writers, flourished in the end of the twelfth century, and the compiler of the *Jain Puránas* of the *Dekhin,* is said to have written at the end of the ninth. The *Kalpa Sútra* professes to have been composed nine hundred and eighty years after the death of Maha'vi'ra, or fifteen centuries ago; but from internal evidence, it could not have been composed earlier than the twelfth or thirteenth century. Various eminent *Jain* authors were cotemporary also with Munja and Bhoja, princes of *Dhár,* in the ninth and tenth century, and a number of works seem to have been compiled in the sixteenth century, during the tolerant reign of Akber.

Of the progress of the *Jain* faith in the Gangetic provinces of upper India, we have no very satisfactory traces. It may be doubted if they ever extended themselves in Bengal. Behar, according to their own traditions, was the birth place of VERDDHAMA'NA, and Benares of PA'RSWANA'TH; and temples and monuments of their teachers are common in both, particularly the former; but all those now existing are of very recent dates* and there are no vestiges referable to an intermediate period between the last *Tirthankara*, and the eighteenth century. At Benares, its princes professed the faith of *Bauddha* as late as the eleventh century, whilst during the same period, as is proved by inscriptions and the historical work of CHNDRAKAVI, the sovereigns of Kanoj and Delhi were of the orthodox persuasion. It is very doubtful, therefore, if the *Jains* ever formed a leading sect in this part of Hindustan. They were more successful in the west and south.

In western Marwar, and the whole of the territory subject to the *Chaulukya* princes of Guzerat, the *Jain* faith became that of the ruling dynasty; but this occurred at no very remote period. The Mohammedan Geographer, EDRISI, states that the king of *Nehrwala*, the capital of Guzerat, worshipped BUDDHA; and we know from the writings of HEMACHANDRA, that he was the apostle of the *Jain* faith in that kingdom—converting KUMA'RA PALA, the monarch of Guzerat, to his creed. This is also an occurrence of the twelfth century, or about 1174. The consequences of this conversion are still apparent in the abundant reliques of the *Jain* faith, and the numbers by whom it is professed in Marwar, Guzerat, and the upper part of the Malabar Coast.

On the Coromandel side of the Peninsula, the *Jains* were introduced upon the downfall of the *Bauddhas*, in the reign of AMOGHAVERSHA, king of *Tonda Mandalam*, in the ninth century, or according to some traditions, in the eighth. Farther south, in Madura, the date of their introduction is not known, but they were in power in the eleventh century under KUNA PA'NDYA. In this, and in the twelfth, they seem to have reached their highest prosperity, and from that period to have declined. KUNA PA'NDYA became a *Saiva*—VISHNU VERDDHANA, raja

* As late even as the eighteenth and nineteenth centuries.—These dates are sometimes said to indicate the periods at which the temples were repaired, but the intelligent author of the 'Visit to Mount *Parswanath*' observes, "only in one instance is there reason to suspect that the buildings are much older than the inscriptions announce." The most ancient Mundir at that place, is reckoned to be but fifty years old —*Calcutta Magazine, December*, 1827.

of Mysore, was converted from the *Jain* to the *Vaishnava* faith in the twelfth century, and about the same time the *Lingavant Saivas* deposed and murdered VIJALA, the *Jain* king of *Kalyán*. The sect, however, continued to meet with partial countenance from the kings of *Vijayanagar*, until a comparatively modern date.

The conclusions founded on traditionary or historical records are fully supported by the testimony of monuments and inscriptions—the latter of which are exceedingly numerous in the south and west of India. Most of these are very modern—none are earlier than the ninth century. An exception is said to exist in an inscription on a rock at *Belligola*, recording a grant of land by *Chámunda Raya* to the shrine of GOMATISWARA, in the year 600 of the *Kali* age, meaning the *Kali* of the *Jains*, which began three years after the death of VERDDHAMANA. This inscription, therefore, if it exists, was written about fifty or sixty years before the Christian era—but it is not clear that any such record is in existence, the fact resting on the oral testimony of the head Pontiff at *Belligola*: even, if it be legible on the face of the rock, it is of questionable authenticity, as it is perfectly solitary, and no other document of like antiquity has been met with.

The Mackenzie collection contains many hundred *Jain* inscriptions. Of these, the oldest record grants made by the princes of *Homchi*, a petty state in *Mysur*. None of them are older than the end of the ninth century. Similar grants, extending through the eleventh and twelfth centuries, by the VELALA sovereigns of *Mysur*, are also numerous, whilst they continue with equal frequency to the sixteenth and seventeenth centuries, during the existence of the sovereignty of *Vijayanagar*. Again, at *Abu*, under the patronage of the Guzerat princes, we have a number of *Jain* inscriptions, but the oldest of them bears date *Samvat* 1245, (A. D. 1189);* they multiply in the thirteenth and fourteenth centuries, and are found as late as the middle of the eighteenth—and, finally, in *Magadha*, the scene of VERDDHAMANA's birth and apotheosis, the oldest inscriptions found, date no further back than the beginning of the sixteenth century.†

* Asatic Researches, Vol. XVI. Page 317.

† Dr. Hamilton's description of Jain Temples in Behar.—*Trans. R. A. S.* I. 525. To these may be added the inscriptions at *Parswanath*, and a number of inscriptions at *Gwalior*, copies of which were sent to Mr. Fraser, and which are all dated in the middle of the 15th century.

From all credible testimony, therefore, it is impossible to avoid the inference that the *Jains* are a sect of comparatively recent institution, who first came into power and patronage about the eighth and ninth century: they probably existed before that date as a division of the *Bauddhas*, and owed their elevation to the suppression of that form of faith to which they contributed. This is positively asserted by the traditions of the south in several instances: the *Bauddhas* of *Kánchi* were confuted by AKALANKA, a *Jain* priest, and thereupon expelled the country. VARA PANDYA, of *Madura*, on becoming a *Jain*, is said to have persecuted the *Bauddhas*, subjecting them to personal tortures, and banishing them from the country. In *Guzerat*, *Bauddha* princes were succeeded by the *Jains*. There is every reason to be satisfied, therefore, that the total disappearance of the *Bauddhas* in India proper is connected with the influence of the *Jains*, which may have commenced in the sixth or seventh centuries, and continued till the twelfth.

The inveteracy prevalent between kindred schisms is a sufficient reason for any enmity felt by the *Jains* towards the *Bauddhas*, rather than towards the Brahmanical Hindus. There is, indeed, a political leaning to the latter, observable in their recognition of the orthodox Pantheon, in the deference paid to the *Vedas*, and to the rites derivable from them, to the institution of castes, and to the employment of Brahmans as ministrant priests. They appear also to have adapted themselves to the prevailing form of Hinduism in different places: thus at *Abu*, several *Jain* inscriptions commence with invocations of SIVA,* and in the *Dekhin*, an edict promulgated by BUKKA RA'YA, of *Vijayanagar*, declares there is no real difference between the *Jains* and *Vaishnavas*.† In some places the same temples are resorted to by *Jains* and *Rámánujiya Vaishnavas*, and as observed by Mr. Colebrooke, a *Jain* on renouncing the heretical doctrines of his sect, takes his place amongst the orthodox Hindus as a *Kshetriya* or *Vaisya*, which would not be the case with a convert, who has not already caste as a Hindu.‡ In the South of India, indeed, the *Jains* preserve the distinction of castes; in upper India, they profess to be one caste, or *Vaisyas*. It is very clear,

* Major Delamaine notices that the mountain *Girnar*, is equally sacred to *Hindus* as to *Jains*, and that an ancient temple of MAHADEVA is erected there.

† Asiatic Researches, Vol. IX. Page 270.

‡ Transactions Royal Asiatic Society, 1. 549.

however, that admission to the *Jain* communion was originally independent of caste,* and the partial adoption of it or pretension to it, is either a spontaneous or politic conformity to the strong feeling on the subject which prevails amongst all Hindus.

These are the great outlines of the rise and progress of the sect, as derivable from sources entitled to credit; but the *Jains* have amongst themselves records of sectarial value, detailing the succession of different teachers, and the origin of various heresies. Some extracts from one of these attached to a copy of the *Kalpa Sútra,* may be acceptable.

The succession of teachers is always deduced from MAHA'VI'RA, through his disciple SUDHERMA. Of the rest; all but GAUTAMA died before their master, as has been observed above, and GAUTAMA survived him but a month, which he spent in penance and fasting. SUDHERMA, therefore, was the only one who remained competent to impart instruction. His pupil was JAMBUSWA'MI', the last of the *Kévalis,* or possessors of true wisdom: six teachers follow, termed *Srúta Kévalis,* or hearers of the first masters, and then seven others, *Dasapúrvis,* from having been taught the works so named.† These are common to all the lists when correct. In the *Belligola* list they are omitted, and the successor of JAMBUSWA'MI' is there named VERASI'NA, who may have been, as Mr. Colebrooke remarks, a hundred degrees removed. The lists, subsequently, vary according to the particular line of descent to which they belong.

Of these persons, the second *Srutakevalí* is reputed to be the author of the *Dasavaikaliká,* one of the standard works of the sect. SUHASTI, the second *Dasapúrvi,* was the preceptor of SAMPRATI RAJA, and the

* MAHA'VI'RA himself was the son of a king, and should therefore be a *Kshetriya.* His chief disciples, INDRABHUTI, and the rest, were *Brahmans.* His especial attendant, GOSA'LA, was an outcast, and his followers, of both sexes, were of every caste.

† The following are the names of the individuals alluded to in the text:

SRUTAKEVALIS.	DASAPU'RVI'S.
Prabhava Swámi.	*Arya Maháigiri Súri.*
Sayyambhadra Súri.	*Arya Suhasti Súri.*
Yasobhadra Súri.	*Arya Susthita Súri.*
Sambhuta Vijaya Súri.	*Indradinna Súri.*
Bhadrabáhu Súri.	*Dinna Súri.*
Sthúlabhadra Súri.	*Sinhagiri Súri.*
	Vajraswámi Súri.

fourth SUSTHITA, founded the *Kote gachcha*, or tribe. VAJRASWA'MI' the last, established a particular division called the *Vájra Sákhá.*

Of the succeeding teachers, or *Súris*, the title borne by the spiritual preceptors of the *Jains*, CHANDRASU'RI the second, is the founder of the family of that name, eight hundred and nine years, it is said, after the emancipation of MAHA'VI'RA. In his time, it is stated, the *Digambaras* arose; but we have seen that they were at least cotemporary with MAHA'VI'RA.

The 38th on the list, from MAHA'VI'RA inclusive, UDYOTANA SU'RI first classed the *Jains* under eighty-nine Gachchas. The 40th JINESWARI' who lived A. D. 1024, founded the *Khertara* family.* With the 44th JINADATTA originated the *Oswal* family, and the *Madhyakhertara* branch; he was a teacher of great celebrity, and impressions of his feet in plaster or on stone are preserved in some temples, as at *Bhelupur* in Benares; he lived in 1148. Other divisions, either of a religious or civil nature, are attributed to various teachers, as the *Chitrabala Gachcha* to JINAPATI *Súri*, in A. D. 1149; the *Anchalika* doctrine to JINESWARA in 1160; the *Laghu Khertara* family to JINACHANDRA in 1265; another JINACHANDRA, the 61st in the list, was cotemporary with AKBER. The list closes with the 70th *Jina*, HERSHA SU'RI, with whom, or his pupils, several works originated in the end of the seventeenth century.†

Admitting this record to have been carefully preserved, we have seventy-one persons from MAHA'VI'RA, to whom a period of less than fourteen centuries can scarcely be assigned, and whose series would, therefore, have begun in the third century. It is not at all unlikely that such was the case, but no positive conclusion can be drawn from a single document of this nature: a comparison with other lists is necessary, to determine the weight to be attached to it as an authority.

The *Jains* are divided into two principal divisions, *Digambaras* and *Swetambáras;* the former of which appears to have the best pretensions

* Major Tod gives a somewhat different account of the origin of this tribe. *Khartra*, he says, means true, an epithet of distinction which was bestowed by that great supporter of the *Buddhists* or *Jains*, SIDRAJ, King of *Anhulwara Paten*, on one of the branches *Gachcha*, in a grand religious disputation at the capital, in the eleventh century. The accounts are by no means incompatible, and my authority represents *Jineswari* victorious in a controversy.

† HEMACHANDRA, at the end of the *Mahávira Cheritra*, after stating that VAJRA'SWA'MI founded the VAJRASA'KHA', which was established in the *Chandra Gachcha*, gives the teachers of that family down to himself, YASOBHADRA, PRADYUMNA, VISWASENA, DEVACHANDRA, and HEMACHANDRA.

to antiquity, and to have been most widely diffused.* The discriminating difference is implied in these terms, the former meaning the *Sky-clad*, that is, naked, and the latter the white-robed, the teachers being so dressed. In the present day, however, the *Digambara* ascetics do not go naked, but wear coloured garments; they confine the disuse of clothes to the period of their meals, throwing aside their wrapper when they receive the food given them by their disciples: the points of difference between the two sects are far from restricted to that of dress, and comprehend a list of no fewer than seven hundred, of which eighty-four are regarded as of infinite importance: a few of these may be here noticed.

The *Swetámbaras* decorate the images of the *Tírthankaras* with earrings, necklaces, armlets, and tiaras of gold and jewels: the *Digambaras* leave their images without the foreign aid of ornament.

The *Swetámbaras* assert that there are twelve heavens, and sixty-four *Indras*: the *Digambaras* maintain that there are sixteen heavens, and one hundred Olympian monarchs.

The *Swetámbaras* permit their *Gurus* to eat out of vessels: the *Digambaras* receive the food in their open hands from their disciples.

The *Swetámbaras* consider the accompaniments of the brush, water-pot, &c., as essential to the character of an ascetic: the *Digambaras* deny their importance.

The *Swetámbaras* assert that the *Angas*, or scriptures, are the work of the immediate disciples of the *Tirthankaras*: the *Digambaras*, with more reason, maintain that the leading authorities of the *Jain* religion are the composition of subsequent teachers or *Achâryas*.

The advantage gained by the *Digambaras*, in the last debateable matter, they lose, it is to be apprehended, in the next, when they assert that no woman can obtain *Nirván*, in opposition to the more gallant doctrine of their rivals, which admits the fair sex to the enjoyment of final annihilation.

These will be sufficient specimens of the causes of disagreement that divide the *Jainas* into two leading branches, whose mutual animosity is, as usual, of an intensity, very disproportionate to the sources from whence it springs.

* All the *Dekhini Jains* appear to belong to the *Digambara* division. So it is said do the majority of the *Jains* in Western India. In the early philosophical writings of the Hindus, the *Jains* are usually termed *Digambaras*, or *Nagnas*, naked. The term *Jain* rarely occurs, and *Swetambara* still more rarely if ever, as observed in the text; also VERDHAMA'NA, practically at least, was a *Digambara*.

Besides these two great divisions, several minor sects are particularised as existing amongst the *Jains*. They appear, however, to be of no importance, as it has been found impossible to obtain any satisfactory account of the heresies they have adopted, or of their origin and present condition. Schism was contemporary even with MAHA'VI'RA, and his son-in-law, JA'MA'LI, founded a dissentient order. His follower, GOSA'LA, was also the institutor of a sect, and an impostor into the bargain, pretending to be the twenty-fourth *Tirthankara*. BAJRABANDA, the pupil of a very celebrated *Digambara* teacher, KUNDA KUND A'CHA'RYA, founded the *Drávír* sect, according to some in the fifth, and to the others, in the seventh century. VAJRASWA'MI' instituted the *Mahánisítha* sect, and JINENDRA SU'RI founded the *Lampaka* sect, by which images were discarded. The sects now most often heard of, although little known, are the *Múla Sanghis*, who use brushes of peacock's feathers, wear red garments, and receive alms in their hands: the *Káshta Sanghis*, who make their images of wood and employ brushes of the tail of the *Yak*: the *Tera Panthis* and *Bis Panthis*, or followers of ten and of twenty, said sometimes to refer to the number of objects which are most essential to salvation, and at others, explained by a legend of the foundation of the heresy by a number of persons, such as the denomination implies. Both these are said to deny the supremacy of a *Guru*, to dispense with the ministration of a *Brahman*, and to present no perfumes, flowers, nor fruits to the images of the *Tirthankaras*.* The *Bhíshana Panthis* carry their aversion to external emblems still farther, and discard the use of images altogether. The *Dundiyas* and *Samvégis* are religious orders: the former affect rigorous adherence to the moral code, but disregard all set forms of prayer or praise, and all modes of external worship: the *Somvégis* follow the usual practices, but subsist upon alms, accepting no more than is indispensable for present wants.

The whole of the *Jains* are again distinguished into clerical and lay, or into *Yatis* and *Srávakas:* the former lead a religious life, subsisting upon the alms supplied by the latter. According to the greater or less degree of sanctity to which they pretend, are their seeming purity and outward precision, shewn especially in their care of animal life: they carry a brush to sweep the ground before they tread upon it; never eat

* The *Bis Panthis* are said to be, in fact, the orthodox *Digambaras*, of whom the *Tera Panthis* are a dissenting branch.

nor drink in the dark, lest they should inadvertently swallow an insect, and sometimes wear a thin cloth over their mouths lest their breath should demolish some of the atomic ephemera that frolic in the sun-beams; they wear their hair cut short, strictly they should pluck it out by the roots; they profess continence and poverty, and pretend to observe frequent fasts and exercise profound abstraction. Some of them may be simple enthusiasts; many of them, however, are knaves, and the reputation which they enjoy all over India, as skilful magicians, is not very favourable to their general character: they are, in fact, not unfrequently *Charlatans*, pretending to skill in palmistry and necromancy, dealing in emperical therapeutics, and dabbling in chemical, or rather alchemical manipulations. Some of them are less disreputably engaged in traffic, and they are often the proprietors of *Maths* and temples, and derive a very comfortable support from the offerings presented by the secular votaries of *Jina*. The *Yatis*, as above remarked, never officiate as priests in the temples, the ceremonies being conducted by a member of the orthodox priesthood, a *Brahman*, duly trained for the purpose. The *Yatis* are sometimes collected in *Maths*, called by them *Posálas* and even when abroad in the world, they acknowledge a sort of obedience to the head of the *Posála* of which they were once members.

The secular members of the *Jaina* religion, or *Srávakas*, follow the usual practices of the other Hindus, but give alms only to the *Yatis*, and present offerings and pay homage only to the *Tirthankaras*; the present worship, indeed, is almost restricted to the two last of these personages, to PA'RSWANATH, as commonly named *Parisnath*, the twenty-third, and to VERDDHAMA'NA OR MAHVI'RA SWAMI, the twenty-fourth *Tirthankara* of the present age. The temples of these divinities are, in general, much handsomer buildings than those of the orthodox Hindus: they consist of a square or oblong room, large enough to admit a tolerably numerous assemblage, surrounded by an open portico: on one side is a sort of altar-piece of several stages; on the centre of the upper tier sits the chief deity of the temple, supported by two other *Arhats*, whilst the rest, or a portion of them, are ranged upon the inferior tiers: the steeple is also distinguishable from that of other temples, being formed of departments, which are intended, apparently, to represent leaves, and surmounted by a pole resembling a flag staff, terminating in a gilt knob: there are several of these temples in the chief cities along the Ganges, and no fewer than a dozen in *Murshedabad*, to which the circumstance of the *Set* family, being of *Jaina* persuasion, attracted a number of fellow worshippers. In Calcutta there are four temples, two belonging to each sect. In Behar are the temples of PA'RISNA'TH and the *Pádukas*, or feet of VERDDHA'MANA, and VA'SUPU'JYA. Benares possesses several temples, one of which, in the suburb, called *Belupura*, is honoured as the birth-place of PA'RSWANA'TH. The shrine comprises two temples, one belonging to the *Swetámbaras*, and one to the *Digambaras*. A temple of some size and celebrity occurs at *Mainpuri*, in the Doab, and most of the towns in that direction present *Jain* spires. The chief temples, however, are to the westward, and especially at *Jaypur*. The whole of *Mewar* and *Márwar* is strewed with remains of the sacred edifices of this sect.

The *Jains* of the South of India, as has been observed, are divided into castes: this is not the case in upper Hindustan, where they are all of one caste, or, which is the same thing, of none. They are nevertheless equally tenacious of similar distinctions, and not only refuse to mix with other classes, but recognise a number of orders amongst themselves, between which no intermarriages can take place, and many of whom cannot eat together. This classification is the *Gachcha* or *Got*, the family or race, which has been substituted for the *Verna*, the *Játi*, or caste. Of these *Gachchas*, or family divisions, they admit eighty-four,* and these again appear to comprehend a variety of subdivisions:

* The following are the appellations of the eighty-four *Gachchas*:

Khandewál.	*Natila.*	*Dhaktha.*	*Bikriya.*
Porwál.	*Mothiya.*	*Vaisya.*	*Bidyabya.*
Agarwál.	*Tattora.*	*Nágdhár*	*Bersári.*
Jaiswál.	*Bágerwál.*	*Por.*	*Astaki.*
Barihiya.	*Harsola.*	*Surendra.*	*Ashtadhár.*
Golál.	*Sriguru.*	*Kadaya.*	*Pawarábhi.*
Gajapúrbi.	*Jolura*	*Kúhari.*	*Dhakkachúla.*
Srimál.	*Gahakhanduja.*	*Soniya.*	*Bogosri.*
Banswál, or Oswál.	*Chowdiya.*	*Sorathiya.*	*Naraya.*
Porwar.	*Bhungeriwál.*	*Rájiya.*	*Korghúriya.*
Palliwál.	*Brahmatá.*	*Maya.*	*Bamúriya.*
Danderwál	*Beduja.*	*Kammeha.*	*Séksantánya.*
Himmárgujeráti.	*Búhariya.*	*Bhangela.*	*Anándi.*
Baramora.	*Goguwál.*	*Gangarda.*	*Nágóra.*
Kharawa.	*Andaluja.*	*Márkeya.*	*Tattora.*
Labechu.	*Gogayya.*	*Motwál.*	*Púkhastya.*
Khandoya.	*Mandaluja.*	*Swetwál.*	*Sacchora.*
Kathnora.	*Pancham.*	*Chakkichap.*	*Jannora.*
Kabliya.	*Somabansibogar.*	*Khandarya*	*Nemilára.*
Kapola.	*Chatúrtha.*	*Narischya.*	*Gandoriya.*
Nadila.	*Hardar.*	*Bimongai*	*Dhuwaljóti.*

some of the *Gachchas* comprehend a portion of *Sri Vaishnavas*, between which sect and the *Jains* in upper India, a singular alliance seems sometimes to prevail.

The condition of *Jaina* worship may be inferred from the above notices of its temples. Its professors are to be found in every province of Hindustan, collected chiefly in towns, where, as merchants and bankers, they usually form a very opulent portion of the community. In Calcutta there are said to be five hundred families; but they are much more numerous at *Murshedabad*. In *Behar* they have been estimated at between three and four hundred families. They are in some numbers in *Benares*, but become more numerous ascending the *Doab*. It is, however, to the westward that they abound: the provinces of *Mewar* and *Márwar* being apparently the cradle of the sect.* They are also numerous in *Guzerat*, in the upper part of the Malabar coast, and are scattered throughout the Peninsula. They form, in fact, a very large, and from their wealth and influence, a most important division of the population of India.

BABA LALIS.

The followers of Baba Lal are sometimes included amongst the *Vaishnava* sects, and the classification is warranted by the outward seeming of these sectaries, who streak the forehead with *Gopichandana*, and profess a veneration for Rama: in reality, however, they adore but one God, dispensing with all forms of worship, and directing their devotion by rules and objects derived from a medly of *Vedánta* and *Sufi* tenets.

Some of these are well known, but many of the others are never met with. The list was furnished by a respectable *Yati*—but how far it is throughout genuine, I cannot pretend to say. It omits several *Gachchas* of celebrity, particularly the *Chandra* and *Khertara*.

* According to Major Tod, the Pontiff of the *Khartra Gachcha* has eleven thousand clerical disciples scattered over India, and the single community of *Oswal* number one hundred thousand families. In the West of India, the officers of the state and revenue, the bankers, the civil magistrates, and the heads of corporations, are mostly *Jains.—Trans. R. As. Soc. vol.* II. *p.* I. 263.

BA'BA LA'L was a *Khetriya*, born in *Malwa*, about the reign of JEHANGIR: he early adopted a religious life under the tuition of CHETANA SWA'MI', whose fitness as a teacher had been miraculously proved. This person soliciting alms of BA'BA LA'L, received some raw grain, and wood to dress it with: lighting the wood, he confined the fire between his feet, and supported the vessel in which he boiled the grain upon his insteps, BA'BA LA'L immediately prostrated himself before him as his *Guru*, and receiving from him a grain of the boiled rice to eat, the system of the universe became immediately unfolded to his comprehension. He followed CHETANA to *Lahore*, whence being dispatched to *Dwáraká* by his *Guru*, to procure some of the earth called *Gopichandana*, he effected his mission in less than an hour: this miraculous rapidity, the distance being some hundred miles, attesting his proficiency, he was dismissed by his *Guru*, in order to become a teacher. He settled at *Dehanpur*, near *Serhind*, where he erected a *Math*, comprehending a handsome temple, and where he initiated a number of persons in the articles of his faith.

Amongst the individuals attracted by the doctrines of BA'BA LA'L, was the liberal-minded and unfortunate DARA SHEKOH: he summoned the sage to his presence to be instructed in his tenets, and the result of seven interviews was committed to writing, in the form of a dialogue between the Prince and the *Pir*, by two literary Hindus, attached to the Prince's train, one YADU DA's, a *Khettriya*, and the other RAICHAND *Brahman*, the latter the *Mirmunshi*; the interview took place in the garden of JAFFER KHAN SADUH, in the 21st year of SHAH JEHAN's reign, or 1649: the work is entitled *Nádir unnikát*, and is written, as the name implies, in the Persian language. Some miscellaneous extracts from it may not be unacceptable, as they may not only explain the tenets of BA'BA LA'L, and something of the *Vedánta* and *Sufi* doctrines, but may illustrate better than any description the notions generally prevailing of the duties of a religious and mendicant life. The interrogator is the Prince, BA'BA LA'L himself the respondent.

What is the passion of a Fakir?—Knowledge of God.

What is the power of an Ascetic?—Impotence.

What is Wisdom?—Devotion of the heart to the Heart's Lord.

How are the hands of a Fakir employed?—To cover his ears.

Where are his feet?—Hidden, but not hampered by his garments.

What best becomes him?—Vigilance, night and day.

In what should he be unapt ?—Immoderate diet.

In what should he repose ?—In a corner ; seclusion from mankind, and meditation on the only True.

What is his dwelling ?—God's creatures.

His Kingdom ?—God.

What are the lights of his mansion ?—The Sun and Moon.

What is his couch ?—The Earth.

What is his indispensable observance ?—praise and glorification of the Cherisher of all things, and the needer of none.

What is suitable for a Fakir ?—*Lá*, none ; as *Lá Allah*, &c. there is no God but God.

How passes the existence of a Fakir ?—Without desire, without restraint, without property.

What are the duties of a Fakir ?—Poverty and faith.

Which is the best religion ?—Verse, " The Creed of the lover differs from other Creeds. God is the faith and creed of those who love him, but to do good is best for the follower of every faith." Again, as HAFIZ says—

The object of all religions is alike,
All men seek their beloved,
What is the difference between prudent and wild,
All the world is love's dwelling,
Why talk of a Mosque or a Church.

With whom should the Fakir cultivate intimacy ?—With the Lord of loveliness.

To whom should he be a stranger ?—To covetousness, anger, envy, falsehood, and malice.

Should he wear garments or go naked ?—The loins should be covered by those who are in their senses—nudity is excusable in those who are insane. The love of God does not depend upon a cap or a coat.

How should a *Fakir* conduct himself ?—He should perform what he promises, and not promise what he cannot perform.

Should evil be done to evil doers ?—The *Fakir* is to do evil to none, he is to consider good and ill alike, so HAFIZ says—" The repose of the two worlds depends upon two rules, kindness to friends, and gentle, ness to foes."

What is the nature of the *Takia* (the pillow or abbacy ?)—To commence with a seat upon it is improper, and at all times an erratic life is preferable; when the body is weakened by age or sickness, the *Fakir* may then repose upon his pillow: so situated, he should welcome every *Fakir* as his guest, and consider nothing but God to be his own.

Is it necessary for a *Fakir*, to withdraw from the world ?—It is prudent, but not necessary: the man in society who fixes his heart on God is a *Fakir*, and the *Fakir* who takes an interest in the concerns of men is a man of the world, so MAULANA RUM observes—"What is the world? forgetfulness of God, not clothes, nor wealth, nor wife, nor offspring."

What is the difference between nature and created things ?—Some compare them to the seed and the tree. The seed and the tree are equivalent though related; although the same in substance, they are not necessarily co-existent nor co-relative. They may be also compared to the waves and the sea; the first cannot be without the second, but the sea may be without waves, wind is necessary to their product: so, although nature and created things are of one essence, yet the evolution of the latter from the former requires the interference of an evolving cause, or the interposition of a Creator.

Are the soul, life, and body merely shadows ?—The soul is of the same nature as God, and one of the many properties of universal life; like the sea, and a drop of water; when the latter joins the former, it also is sea.

How do the *Paramátmá* (supreme soul) and *Jivátmá* (living soul) differ ?—They do not differ, and pleasure and pain ascribable to the latter, arises from its imprisonment in the body—the water of the Ganges is the same whether it run in the river's bed or be shut up in a decanter.

What difference should that occasion ?—Great—a drop of wine added to the water in the decanter will impart its flavor to the whole, but it would be lost in the river. The *Paramátmá*, therefore, is beyond accident, but the *Jivátmá* is afflicted by sense and passion. Water cast loosely on a fire will extinguish the fire; put that water over the fire in a boiler, and the fire will evaporise the water, so the body being the confining caldron, and passion the fire, the soul, which is compared to the water, is dispersed abroad;—the one great supreme soul is incapable of these properties, and happiness is therefore only obtained in reunion with it, when the dispersed and individualized portions combine again with it, as the drops of water with the parent stream; hence, although God needs not the service of his slave, yet the slave should remember that he is separated from God by the body alone, and may exclaim perpetually, Blessed be the moment when I shall lift the veil from off that face. The veil of the face of my beloved is the dust of my body.

What are the feelings of the perfect *Fakir?*—They have not been, they are not to be, described, as it is said—a person asked me what are the sensations of a lover? I replied, when you are a lover, you will know.

PRAN NATHIS.

These are also called *Dhámis:* they owe their origin to Pra'n Na'th, a *Khetriya*, who being versed in Mohammedan learning, as well as in his own, attempted to reconcile the two religions: with this view, he composed a work called the *Mahitáriyal*, in which texts from the *Koran*, and the *Vedas* are brought together, and shewn not to be essentially different. Pra'n Na'th flourished about the latter part of Aurungzeb's reign, and is said to have acquired great influence with Chattrasa'l, *Raja* of *Bundelkand*, by effecting the discovery of a diamond mine. *Bundelkand* is the chief seat of his followers, and in *Punna* is a building consecrated to the use of the sect, in one apartment of which, on a table covered with gold cloth, lies the volume of the founder.

As a test of the disciple's consent to the real identity of the essence of the Hindu and Mohammedan creeds, the ceremony of initiation, consists of eating in the society of members of both communions: with this exception, and the admission of the general principle, it does not appear that the two classes confound their civil or even religious distinctions: they continue to observe the practices and ritual of their forefathers, whether Musselman or Hindu, and the union, beyond that of community of eating, is no more than any rational individual of either sect is fully prepared for, or the admission, that the God of both, and of all religions, is one and the same.

SADHS

A full account of this sect of Hindu Unitarians, by the Reverend Mr. Fisher, was published in the Missionary Intelligencer some years ago, and some further notice of them is inserted in the Transactions of the Royal Asiatic Society, by Mr. Trant. They are distinguished from other Hindus, by professing the adoration of one Creator, and by personal and moral observances which entitle them, in their own estimation, to the appellation of *Sáds, Sádhus*, Pure or Puritans.

The *Sádhs* are found chiefly in the upper part of the *Doab*, from *Farakhabad* to beyond *Delhi*. In the former, they occupy a suburb called *Sádhwára*, and are more numerous there than in any other town, their numbers are estimated at two thousand. There are said to be some at *Mirzapore*, and a few more to the South; their numbers, however, are limited, and they are chiefly from the lower classes.

The sect originated in the year of VIKRAMA'DITYA, 1714, (A. D. 1658) according to Mr. Trant, with a person named BIRBHA'N, who received a miraculous communication from one UDAYA DA'S, and in consequence taught the *Sádh* doctrines. Mr. Fisher calls BIRBHA'N the disciple of JOGI DAS, who commanding a body of troops in the service of the *Raja* of *Dholpur*, was left as slain on the field of battle, but restored to life by a stranger in the guise of a mendicant, who carried him to a mountain, taught him the tenets of the faith, and having bestowed upon him the power of working miracles, sent him to disseminate his doctrines. These circumstances are rather obscurely alluded to in the original authorities consulted on the present occasion, but they agree with the above in considering BIRBHA'N an inhabitant of *Brijhasir*, near *Narnoul*, in the province of *Delhi*, as the founder of the sect, at the date above mentioned. BIRBHA'N received his knowledge from the SAT GURU, the pure teacher, also called *Udaka Dás*, the servant of the one

God, and particularly described as the *Málekka Hukem*, the order of the Creator, the personified word of God.

The doctrines taught by the super-human instructor of Birbha'n were communicated in *Sabdas* and *Sákhis*, detached Hindi stanzas like those of Kabir. They are collected into manuals, and read at the religious meetings of the *Sádhs*: their substance is collected into a tract entitled *Adi Upadés*, first precepts, in which the whole code is arranged under the following twelve *Hukems*, or Commandments.

1. Acknowledge but one God who made and can destroy you, to whom there is none superior, and to whom alone therefore is worship due, not to earth, nor stone, nor metal, nor wood, nor trees, nor any created thing. There is but one Lord, and the word of the Lord. He who meditates on falsehoods, practices falsehood, and commits sin, and he who commits sin falls into Hell.

2. Be modest and humble, set not your affections on the world, adhere faithfully to your creed, and avoid intercourse with all not of the same faith, eat not of a stranger's bread.

3. Never lie nor speak ill at any time to, or of any thing, of earth or water, of trees or animals. Let the tongue be employed in the praise of God. Never steal, nor wealth, nor land, nor beasts, nor pasture: distinguish your own from another's property, and be content with what you possess. Never imagine evil. Let not your eyes rest on improper objects, nor men, nor women, nor dances, nor shows.

4. Listen not to evil discourse, nor to any thing but the praises of the Creator, nor to tales, nor gossip, nor calumny, nor music, nor singing, except hymns; but then the only musical accompaniment must be in the mind.

5. Never covet any thing, either of body or wealth: take not of another. God is the giver of all things, as your trust is in him so shall you receive.

6. When asked what you are, declare yourself a *Sádh*, speak not of caste, engage not in controversy, hold firm your faith, put not your hope in men.

7. Wear white garments, use no pigments, nor collyrium, nor dentifrice, nor *Mehndi*, nor mark your person, nor your forehead with sectarial distinctions, nor wear chaplets, or rosaries, or jewels.

8. Never eat nor drink intoxicating substances, nor chew *pán*, nor smell perfumes, nor smoke tobacco, nor chew nor smell opium, hold not up your hands, bow not down your head in the presence of idols or of men.

9. Take no life away, nor offer personal violence, nor give damnatory evidence, nor seize any thing by force.

10. Let a man wed one wife and a woman one husband, let not a man eat of a woman's leavings, but a woman may of a man's, as may be the custom. Let the woman be obedient to the man.

11. Assume not the garb of a mendicant, nor solicit alms, nor accept gifts. Have no dread of necromancy, neither have recourse to it. Know before you confide. The meetings of the Pious are the only places of pilgrimage, but understand who are the Pious before you so salute them.

12. Let not a *Sádh* be superstitious as to days, or to lunations, or to months, or the cries or appearances of birds or animals; let him seek only the will of the Lord.

These injunctions are repeated in a variety of forms, but the purport is the same, and they comprise the essence of the *Sádh* doctrine which is evidently derived from the unitarianism of Kabir, Nanak, and similar writers, with a slight graft from the principles of Christianity. In their notions of the constitution of the universe, in the real, although temporary existence of inferior deities and their incarnations, and in the ultimate object of all devotion, liberation from life on earth, or *Mukti*, the *Sádhs* do not differ from other *Hindus*.

The *Sádhs* have no temples, but assemble at stated periods in houses, or courts adjoining set apart for this purpose. According to Mr. Fisher, their meetings are held every full moon, when men and women collect at an early hour, all bringing such food as they are able, the day is spent in miscellaneous conversation, or in the discussion of matters of common interest. In the evening, they eat and drink together, and the night is passed in the recitation of the stanzas attributed to Birbha'n, or his preceptor, and the poems of Da'du, Nanak, or Kabir.

From the term they apply to the deity, Satna'm, the *true* name, the *Sádhs* are also called *Satnámis*; but this appellation more especially indicates a different, although kindred sect.

SATNAMIS.

These profess to adore the true name alone, the one God, the cause and creator of all things, *Nirgun*, or void of sensible qualities, without beginning or end.

They borrow, however, their notions of creation from the *Vedánta* philosophy, or rather from the modified form in which it is adapted to vulgar apprehension. Worldly existence is illusion, or the work of MA'YA', the primitive character of BHAVA'NI', the wife of SIVA. They recognise accordingly the whole Hindu Pantheon—and, although they profess to worship but one God, pay reverence to what they consider manifestations of his nature visible in the *Avatárs*, particularly RA'MA and KRISHNA.

Unlike the *Sádhs* also, they use distinctive marks, and wear a double string of silk bound round the right wrist. Frontal lines are not invariably employed, but some make a perpendicular streak with ashes of a burnt offering made to HANUMAN.

Their moral code is something like that of all *Hindu* quietists, and enjoins indifference to the world, its pleasures or its pains, implicit devotion to the spiritual guide, clemency and gentleness, rigid adherence to truth, the discharge of all ordinary, social, or religious obligations, and the hope of final absorption into the one spirit which pervades all things.

There is little or no difference therefore in essentials between the *Satnámí's* and some of the *Vaishnava* unitarians, but they regard themselves as a separate body, and have their own founder JAGJI'VAN DA'S. He was a *Kshetriya* by birth, and continued in the state of *Grihastha*, or householder, through life: he was a native of *Oude*, and his *Samádh*, or shrine, is shewn at *Katwa*, a place between *Lucknow* and *Ajudhya*. He wrote several tracts, as the *Jnyán Prakás*, *Mahápralaya*, and *Prathama Grantha*: they are in *Hindi* couplets; the first is dated in Sambat 1817, or A. D. 1761, the last is in the form of a dialogue between SIVA and PA'RVATI'. The following is from the *Mahápralaya*.

"The pure man lives amidst all, but away from all: his affections are engaged by nothing: what he may know he knows, but he makes no enquiry: he neither goes nor comes, neither learns nor teaches, neither cries nor sighs, but discusses himself with himself. There is neither pleasure nor pain, neither clemency nor wrath, neither fool nor sage to him. JAGJIVANDAS asks, does any one know a man so exempt from infirmity who lives apart from mankind and indulges not in idle speech."

SIVA NARAYANAIS.

This is another sect professing the worship of one God, of whom no attributes are predicated. Their unitarianism is more unqualified than that of either of the preceding, as they offer no worship, pay no regard whatever to any of the objects of Hindu or Mohammedan veneration. They also differ from all in admitting proselytes alike from Hindus or Mohammedans, and the sect comprises even professed Christians from the lower classes of the mixed population.

Admission into the sect is not a matter of much ceremony, and a *Guru,* or spiritual guide, is not requisite; a few *Siva Nárâyanis* assemble at the requisition of a novice, place one of their text books in the midst of them, on which betel and sweetmeats have previously been arranged. After awhile these are distributed amongst the party, a few passages are read from the book, and the sect has acquired a new member.

Truth, temperance, and mercy are the cardinal virtues of this sect, as well as of the *Sâdhs;* polygamy is prohibited, and sectarial marks are not used: conformity to the external observances of the Hindu or Mohammedans, independently of religious rites, is recommended, but latitude of practice is not unfrequent; and the *Siva Nárâyanis,* of the lower orders, are occasionally addicted to strong potations.

The sect derives its appellation from that of its founder SIVANA'RA'-YAN, a *Rajput,* of the *Nerivâna* tribe, a native of *Chandâwan,* a village near *Ghazipur:* he flourished in the reign of MOHAMMED SHAH, and one of his works is dated *Sambat* 1791, or A. D. 1735. He was a voluminous writer in the inculcation of his doctrines, and eleven books, in Hindi verse, are ascribed to him. They are entitled: *Lao* or *Lava Granth,*

Santvilás, Wajan Granth, Santsundara, Guru Nyás, Sant Achári, Sant Opadesa, Sabdávali, Santparwána, Sant Mahima, Sant Ságar.

There is also a twelfth, the Seal of the whole, but it has not yet been divulged, remaining in the exclusive charge of the head of the sect. This person resides at *Balsande,* in the *Ghazipur* district, where there is a college and establishment.

The *Sivanáráyanis* are mostly *Rajputs,* and many are *Sipahis:* many of the Up-county Bearers also belong to the sect. The members are said to be numerous about *Ghazipúr,* and some are to be met with in Calcutta.

SUNYABADIS.

The last sect which it has been proposed to notice, is one of which the doctrines are atheistical. There is no novelty in this creed, as it was that of the *Chárvákas* and *Nástikas,* and is, to a great extent, that of the *Bauddhas* and *Jains;* but an attempt has been recently made to give it a more comprehensive and universal character, and to bring it within the reach of popular attraction.

A distinguished patron of the *Súnyabádis* was DA'YARA'M, the *Raja* of *Hatras,* when that fortress was destroyed by the Marquis of Hastings. Under his encouragement, a work in Hindi verse was composed by BAKHTAWAR, a religious mendicant, entitled the *Sunisár,* the essence of emptiness, the purport of which is to shew that all notions of man and God are fallacies, and that nothing, is: a few passages from this book will convey an idea of the tenets of the sect.

"Whatever I behold is Vacuity. Theism and Atheism—MAYA and BRAHM—all is false, all is error—the globe itself, and the egg of BRAHMA, the seven *Dwipas* and nine *Khandas,* heaven and earth, the sun and moon, BRAHMA, VISHNU and SIVA, KU'RMA and SESHA; the *Guru* and his pupil, the individual and the species, the temple and the God, the observance of ceremonial rites, and the muttering of prayers, all is emptiness. Speech, hearing and discussion are emptiness, and substance itself is no more."

"Let every one meditate upon himself, nor make known his self-communion to another—let him be the worshipper and the worship, nor talk of a difference between this and that—look into yourself and not into another, for in yourself that other will be found—there is no other but myself, and I talk of another from ignorance. In the same way as I see my face in a glass, I see myself in others, but it is error to think that what I see is not my face, but that of another—whatever you see is but yourself, and father and mother are nonentities; you are the infant and the old man, the wise man and the fool, the male and the female: it is you who are drowned in the stream, you who pass over, you are the killer, and the slain, the slayer and the eater, you are the king and the subject. You seize yourself and let go, you sleep, and you wake, you dance for yourself, you play and sing for yourself. You are the sensualist and the ascetic, the sick man and the strong—in short, whatever you see, that is you, as bubbles, surf, and billows are all but water."

"When we are visited in sleep by visions, we think in our sleep that those visions are realities—we wake, and find them falsehoods, and they leave not a wreck behind. One man in his sleep receives some information, and he goes and tells it to his neighbour—from such idle narrations what benefit is obtained—what will be left to us when we have been winnowing chaff."

"I meditate upon the *Suni* Doctrine alone, and know neither virtue nor vice—many have been the princes of the earth, and nothing did they bring and nothing took they away—the good name of the liberal survived him, and disrepute covered the niggard with its shadow. So let men speak good words, that none may speak ill of them afterwards. Take during the few days of your life what the world offers you. Enjoy your own share, and give some of it to others: without liberality, who shall acquire reputation? Give ever after your means, such is the established rule. To some give money, to some respect, to some kind words, and to some delight. Do good to all the world, that all the world may speak good of you. Praise the name of the liberal when you rise in the morning, and throw dust upon the name of the niggard. Evil and good are attributes of the body—you have the choice of two sweetmeats in your hands. KARNA was a giver of gold, and JANAKA as liberal as wise. SIVI, HARISCHANDRA, DADHI'CHA, and many others, have acquired by their bounty fame throughout the world."

"Many now are, many have been, and many will be—the world is never empty; like leaves upon the trees, new ones blossom as the old decay. Fix not your heart upon a withered leaf, but seek the shade of the green foliage—a horse of a thousand rupees is good for nothing when dead, but a living tattoo will carry you along the road. Have no hope in the man that is dead, trust but in him that is living. He that is dead will be alive no more: a truth that all men do not know: of all those that have died, has any business brought any one back again, or has any one brought back tidings of the rest? A rent garment cannot be spun anew, a broken pot cannot be pieced again. A living man has nothing to do with heaven and hell, but when the body has become dust, what is the difference between a Jackass and a dead Saint."

"Earth, water, fire, and wind, blended together, constitute the body—of these four elements the world is composed, and there is nothing else. This is BRAHMA', this is a pismire, all consists of these elements, and proceeds from them through separate receptacles."

"Beings are born from the womb, the egg, the germ, and vapour."

"*Hindus* and *Musselmans* are of the same nature, two leaves of one tree—these call their teachers *Muallas*, those term them *Pandits*; two pitchers of one clay: one performs *Numaz*, the other offers *Puja*: where is the difference? I know of no dissimilarity—they are both followers of the doctrine of Duality—they have the same bone, the same flesh, the same blood, and the same marrow. One cuts off the foreskin, the other puts on a sacrificial thread. Ask of them the difference, enquire the importance of these distinctions, and they will quarrel with you: dispute not, but know them to be the same—avoid all idle wrangling and strife, and adhere to the truth, the doctrine of DA'YARA'M."

"I fear not to declare the truth—I know no difference between a subject and a king—I want neither homage nor respect, and hold no communion with any but the good; what I can obtain with facility that will I desire, but a palace or a thicket are to me the same—the error of *mine* and *thine* have I cast away, and know nothing of loss or gain. When a man can meet with a preceptor to teach him these truths, he will destroy the errors of a million of births, such a teacher is now in the world, and such a one is Da'yara'm."

The survey that has thus been taken of the actual state of the Hindu religion will shew, that its internal constitution has not been exempt from those varieties, to which all human systems of belief are subject, and that it has undergone great and frequent modifications, until it presents an appearance which there is great reason to suppose is very different from that which it originally wore.

The precise character of the primitive Hindu system will only be justly appreciated, when a considerable portion of the ritual of the *Vedas* shall have been translated, but some notion of their contents and purport may be formed from Mr. Colebrooke's account of them,* as well as from his description of the religious ceremonies of the Hindus.† It is also probable that the Institutes of Menu, in a great measure, harmonise with the *Vaidik* Code.

From these sources then it would seem, that some of the original rites are still preserved in the *Homa*, or fire offerings, and in such of the *Sanskáras*, or purificatory ceremonies, as are observed at the periods of birth, tonsure, investiture, marriage and cremation. Even in these ceremonies, however, formulæ, borrowed from the *Tantras*, assume the place of the genuine texts, whilst on many occasions the observances of the *Vedas* are wholly neglected. Nor is this inconsistent with the original system, which was devised for certain recognised classes into which the Hindu community was then divided, and of which three out of four parts no longer exist—the Hindus being now distinguished into Brahmans and mixed castes alone—and the former having almost universally deviated from the duties and habits to which they were originally devoted. Neither of these classes, therefore, can with propriety make use of the *Vaidik* ritual, and their manual of devotion must be taken from some other source.

How far the preference of any individual Divinity, as an especial object of veneration, is authorised by the *Vedas*, remains yet to be determined; but there is no reason to doubt that most of the forms to which homage is now paid are of modern canonization. At any rate such is the highest antiquity of the most celebrated Teachers and Founders of

* Asiatic Researches, vol. VIII.
† Asiatic Researches, vol. VII.

the popular sects; and BA'SAVA in the *Dekhin*, VALLABHA SWA'MI' in *Hindustan*, and CHAITANYA in *Bengal*, claim no earlier a date than the eleventh and sixteenth centuries.

Consistent with the introduction of new objects of devotion, is the elevation of new races of individuals to the respect or reverence of the populace as their ministers and representatives. The Brahmans retain, it is true, a traditional sanctity; and when they cultivate pursuits suited to their character, as the Law and Literature of their sacred language, they receive occasional marks of attention, and periodical donations from the most opulent of their countrymen. But a very mistaken notion prevails generally amongst Europeans of the positions of the Brahmans in Hindu society, founded on the terms in which they are spoken of by MENU, and the application of the expression 'Priesthood,' to the Brahmanical Order, by Sir William Jones. In the strict sense of the phrase it never was applicable to the Brahmans, for although some amongst them acted in ancient times as family priests, and conducted the fixed or occasional ceremonials of household worship, yet even MENU holds the Brahman, who ministers to an idol, infamous during life, and condemned to the infernal regions after death, and the Sanscrit language abounds with synonimes for the priest of a temple, significant of his degraded condition both in this world and the next. Ministrant Priests in temples, therefore, the Brahmans, collectively speaking, never were—and although many amongst them act in that capacity, it is no more their appropriate province than any other lucrative occupation. In the present day, however, they have ceased to be in a great measure the ghostly advisers of the people, either individually or in their households. This office is now filled by various persons, who pretend to superior sanctity, as *Gosains*, *Vairágis*, and *Sanyásis*. Many of these are Brahmans, but they are not necessarily so, and it is not as Brahmans that they receive the veneration of their lay followers. They derive it as we have seen from individual repute, or more frequently from their descent from the founder of some particular division, as is the case with the *Gokulastha Gosains* and the *Goswámis* of Bengal. The Brahmans as a caste exercise little real influence on the minds of the Hindus beyond what they obtain from their numbers, affluence and rank. As a hierarchy they are null, and as a literary body they are few, and meet with but slender countenance from their countrymen or their foreign rulers. That they are still of great importance in the social system of British India, is unquestionable, but it is not as a priesthood. They bear a very large proportion to all the other tribes,—they are of more respectable birth, and in general of better education—a prescriptive reverence for the order improves these advantages, and Brahmans are accordingly numerous amongst the most affluent and distinguished members of every Hindu state. It is only, however, as far as they are identified with the *Gurus* of the popular sects, that they can be said to hold any other than secular consideration.

Aware apparently of the inequality upon which those *Gurus* contended with the long established claims of the Brahmanical tribe, the new teachers of the people took care to invest themselves with still higher pretensions. The *Achâray* or *Guru* of the three first classes, is no doubt described by MENU, as entitled to the most profound respect from his pupil during pupilage, but the *Guru* of the present day exacts implicit devotion from his disciples during life. It is unnecessary here to repeat what there has been previous occasion to notice with respect to the extravagant obedience to be paid by some sectarians to the *Guru*, whose favour is declared to be of much more importance than that of the god whom he represents.

Another peculiarity in the modern system which has been adverted to in the preceding pages, is the paramount value of *Bhakti*—faith—implicit reliance on the favour of the Deity worshipped. This is a substitute for all religious or moral acts, and an expiation for every crime. Now, in the *Vedas*, two branches are distinctly marked, the practical and speculative. The former consists of prayers and rules for oblations to any or all of the gods—but especially to INDRA and AGNI, the ruler of the firmament and of fire, for positive worldly goods, health, posterity and affluence. The latter is the investigation of matter and spirit, leading to detachment from worldly feelings and interests, and final liberation from bodily existence. The first is intended for the bulk of mankind, the second for philosophers and ascetics. There is not a word of faith, of implicit belief or passionate devotion in all this, and they seem to have been as little essential to the primitive Hindu worship as they were to the religious systems of Greece and Rome. *Bhakti* is an invention, and apparently a modern one, of the Institutors of the existing sect, intended like that of the mystical holiness of the *Guru*; to extend their own authority. It has no doubt exercised a most mischievous influence upon the moral principles of the Hindus.

Notwithstanding the provisions with which the sectarian *Gurus* fortified themselves, it is clear that they were never able to enlist the whole of Hinduism under their banners, or to suppress all doubt and disbelief. It has been shewn in the introductory pages of this essay, that great latitude of speculation has always been allowed amongst the Brahmans themselves, and it will have been seen from the notices of different sects, that scepticism is not unfrequent amongst the less privileged orders. The tendency of many widely diffused divisions is decidedly monotheistical, and we have seen that both in ancient and modern times, attempts have been made to inculcate the doctrines of utter unbelief. It is not likely that these will ever extensively spread, but there can be little doubt that with the diffusion of education, independent enquiry into the merits of the prevailing systems and their professors, will become more universal, and be better directed. The germ is native to the soil: it has been kept alive for ages under the most unfavourable circumstances, and has been apparently more vigorous than ever during the last century. It only now requires prudent and patient fostering to grow into a stately tree, and yield goodly fruit.

BISHOP'S COLLEGE PRESS.